Political Participation Capital

STUDIES IN POLITICS, SECURITY AND SOCIETY

Edited by Stanisław Sulowski
Faculty of Political Science and International Studies
University of Warsaw

VOLUME 43

PETER LANG

Jan Ryszard Garlicki

Political Participation Capital

PETER LANG

Bibliographic Information published by the Deutsche Nationalbibliothek
The Deutsche Nationalbibliothek lists this publication in
the Deutsche Nationalbibliografie; detailed bibliographic
data is available in the internet at http://dnb.d-nb.de.

Library of Congress Cataloging-in-Publication Data
A CIP catalog record for this book has been applied for
at the Library of Congress.

This publication was financially supported
by the Faculty of Political Science and International Studies University of Warsaw.

ISSN 2199-028X
ISBN 978-3-631-86682-5 (Print)
E-ISBN 978-3-631-86933-8 (E-PDF)
E-ISBN 978-3-631-86963-5 (EPUB)
DOI 10.3726/b19184

Peter Lang – Berlin · Bern · Bruxelles · New York ·
Oxford · Warszawa · Wien

This publication has been peer reviewed.

www.peterlang.com

Table of Contents

Introduction 7

Acknowledgments 15

Chapter I. Political participation: theoretical perspectives .. 17

Chapter II. Conventional forms of participation of Poles 35

Chapter III. Unconventional participation and participation on the Internet 65

Chapter IV. Social capital versus political participation capital 95

Chapter V. Political participation models' typology: a priori approach 127

Chapter VI. Political participation models' typology: a posteriori approach 153

Concluding remarks 171

Annex 1. Research methods description and research sample characteristics 179

Annex 2. Quantitative research tool 185

Annex 3. 213

Annex 4. 217

Annex 5. 219

Annex 6. 227

Annex 7. Correlations between variables (qualifications versus sociodemographic variables) 231

Annex 8. Correlations between variables (questionary variables versus variables, according to which I qualified the attitudes) 243

Bibliography 255

Index of Names 263

Introduction

Over the last two decades, scientists' reflections and studies concerning political participation became considerably fragmented. In this field, researchers tend to explore narrowly put phenomena: they are occupied with minority groups' (women, sexual minorities, immigrants) political participation, the internet's influence, disinformation, or studies on individual forms of political participation. These are very important and current issues, but it appears that we lack holistic research of the phenomenon, let alone syntheses.

Indeed, political participation involves deeper determinants. It is influenced by external economic, social, political, legal determinants, citizens' attitudes and awareness, the sense or the lack of sense of bonds, trust in the institution of the state or its lack, etc. We cannot examine political participation without referring to other relevant issues. The lack of multidimensional empirical studies and theoretical syntheses leads to a situation in which we view political participation in a largely fragmentarized way. Therefore, this book's theoretical goal is precisely to establish the context of political participation; it is to indicate which independent variables shape political participation and, on this basis, to create a model of Polish political participation. Political participation sometimes revolutionizes itself also in democratic countries, where different, fairly radical movements or parties arise. For instance, we could observe it in the past couple of years in Spain (Podemos), the USA (Tea Party, Occupy Wall Street Movement, QAnon), and the yellow vests movement in many European countries. Political scientists should conduct profound research on such phenomena and processes. What is their social and political foundation? What is their ideological nature? What will it change or what may it change in the political participation's forms and models?

In the case of Poland, the issue of whether the participation level in this political system increases or decreases, which researchers and politicians discuss, remains important. Here, it is worth mentioning at least five stereotypical opinions, which one may often hear in media:

- The citizens' knowledge concerning processes, procedures, and political institutions is superficial and stereotypical.
- Poles are politically inactive.
- The level of citizens' trust in political institutions is low.
- There is no acceptance capital regarding politicians, politics, and political parties.
- Citizens accept violence (at least verbally) in the realm of political participation.

We may take these colloquial statements as hypotheses for further research. The statements should be verified, although, in the beginning, we may take them as falsification goals.

Obviously, this is an empirical plane, but one should (or even must) accept the challenge, which involves a look at political participation in theoretical categories. How will the way in which we think about this category and analyze it change? Participation has different dimensions. Participation means something more than the political plane. For example, there is civil participation, which is mainly the domain of NGOs. There is also social activism, which is sometimes continuous and unrelated to any particular organization. Finally, there is economic activity, which is very important in the case of microenterprises and SMEs. These activities have significant effects on the economy and create jobs.

This publication aims not only to look at reality from the viewpoint of current political problems and the actual level of political participation and its determinants but also to consider to what extent does the term social capital, proposed by, among others, Pierre Bourdieu,[1] James Coleman,[2] Francis Fukuyama,[3] Nan Lin,[4] Robert Putnam,[5] is important and adequate

---

1 P. Bourdieu, "The forms of capital," in: *Handbook of Theory of Research for the Sociology of Education*, ed. J.E. Richardson (New York: Greenwood, 1986).
2 J. Coleman, "Social Capital in the Creation of Human Capital," *American Journal of Sociology* (1988), pp. 95–120.
3 F. Fukuyama, "Social Capital and the global economy," *Foreign Affairs,* 74(5), 1995, pp. 89–103.
4 N. Lin, *Social Capital* (Cambridge: Cambridge University Press, 2001).
5 R. Putnam, *Bowling Alone: The Collapse and Revival of American Community* (New York: Simon & Schuster, 2000). However, I should mention that each of the mentioned authors has and presented different vision of social capital, understood differently.

to analyze the citizens' tendencies to participate in political life or their lack of will and motivation for such a participation. The potential influence on the tendency to, e.g., conduct a discourse about politics is already a political participation's form or its introduction and foundation.[6] Therefore, I intended to introduce the category of "political participation capital," as an expansion and, at the same time, nominal accumulation of social capital research concerning political issues.

Political participation capital (PPC) may constitute an empirical indicator of the extent to which political participation (and other phenomena) will grow, and to which alienation and apolitical attitudes, which lead to anomy in society, will develop.

The research explored the issue of the existence and nature of social capital, which may be considered the basis of political participation. I conducted the study in 2017 and 2018 as a part of *Partycypacja polityczna Polaków – nowe wyzwania i formy aktywności* (Political Participation of Poles – New Challenges and Forms of Activity) research grant, financed by the National Science Center of Poland (2014/13/B/HS5/00555), awarded to the University of Warsaw team of experts under the guidance of an Author. Three methods were used during the study: first, I used the qualitative technique of Focus Group Interviews (FGI), then I used the quantitative method of narrowly understood Computer Assisted Telephone Interviewing (CATI) on a sample of 1237 respondents. Finally, the research was supported by the Individual In-Depth Interview (IDI) technique.[7]

Thus, I used a full triangulation of research methods. After I conducted focused group interviews and obtained the results, I constructed indexes to conduct research based on Computer Assisted Telephone Interviewing.

---

6 H. Blomkvist, *Social Capital, Political Partcipation, And the Quality of democracy in India*, Paper prepared for the annual meeting of the American Political Science Association (Philadelphia, 2003); M. Shahin, "The Relationship between Social Capital and Political Participation," *Mediterranean Journal of Social Sciences* 7/2016, pp. 136–142.; J. Teorell, "Linking Social Capital to Political Participation: Voluntary Associations and Networks of Recruitment in Sweden," *Scandinavian Political Studies* 26(1)/2003, pp. 49–66.

7 In Annex 1, I present the in-detail description of conducted research methods and the description of research sample in quantitative research.

It was the CATI method that allowed me to collect the data required to analyze participation capital in Polish society.

At the beginning of studies, analyses, and deliberations on political participation, which constitute this book's subject, we should organize the relevant categories of analysis and their scope. To begin with, I must state that it is not an easy task. During the stage of conceptualization and the subsequent stage of categories and research indexes' preparation, I distinguished two main levels of participation's description: forms and models. Based on these levels, I was able to create certain typologies.

Scientists who deal with political science and the sociology of politics most often use the term forms of participation. Forms of participation mean a certain arrangement of coordinated elements, a manner, a variant of conduct. It is participation that assumes a specific nature and describes a certain manner of citizens' participation in politics. We may distinguish numerous forms, but they all refer to a certain sphere of behavior, e.g., the participation in parliamentary election or demonstration, occupation of public buildings, etc.

In turn, the model political participation involves a group (or even a syndrome) of forms that share a certain common denominator. In source literature from the field of social sciences, especially political science and sociology, scholars employ the term model in a somewhat random fashion, usually without providing a definition, e.g., see, among others, Jakub Wiśniewski's *Ewolucja szwedzkiego i brytyjskiego modelu polityki społecznej w latach 1993–2003* or Phil Harkins and Phil Swift's *In Search of Leadership*. On the contrary, in economics and mathematics the term model is precisely defined, formalized, and quantifiable. Therefore, in this paper, I adopt the concept of the model as a simplified picture of a real world's part, on which I focused based on adopted premises. As a result, the model constitutes a certain hypothetical mental construct, the function of which is to allow us to notice, describe, and explain the features, relationships, and functioning of an object or social phenomenon, which constitutes a matter of concern to the researcher. My use of the term model comes close to the way it is used by researchers of organizational culture, who work at the crossroads of anthropology and management sciences.[8] Antonina

8 G. Hofstede, G.J. Hofstede, M. Minkov, *Cultures and Organizations: Software of the Mind* (McGraw Hill Professional, 2010); F. Trompenaars, C. Hampden-Turner,

Kłoskowska construes this term along similar lines and defines it as a verbal, pictorial, or any other representation of human behavior (institutions, personalities), which may serve as an example and object of reference to evaluations, and as constructions employed for practical purposes.[9]

For the purposes of this book, I suggest that by the model we should mean a relatively identical (similarity, analogy of behavior) and relatively established (as a social and cultural phenomenon) set of citizens' individual and/or collective behavior patterns in the context of political, economic, and social processes and phenomena, by which the citizens influence the political processes or at least express their positive or negative opinion.

For instance, such model, as well as all forms of electoral participation (parliamentary, presidential, and local elections, referenda), or another group of non-violent unconventional participation forms (collecting signatures for a petition, participating in a demonstration, engaging in a legally organized strike).

Political participation models, which are groups of forms, may contribute to the creation of typologies that reflect different patterns of behavior, which we may arrange and compare in different ways. Participation types or participation model types mean a study of citizens' reactions to a system, to a structure. Their reactions, evaluated by the researcher, may differ greatly. If we look at the reactions synthetically and in very general categories, we will notice that they may range from supporting the political system, through criticizing it, being ritually attached to it, to the state of apathy.

The book consists of six chapters and final remarks.

Chapter I, titled "Political participation: theoretical perspectives," concerns the description of the issue of political participation; as the very title suggests, I describe the issue in theoretical terms. First, I present different approaches to participation and studies on participation. Second, I describe the nature of different forms of citizens' participation in politics. Third, I introduce a distinction of participation into conventional and unconventional ones. Fourth, I distinguish eleven criteria of political

---

Riding the Waves of Culture. Understanding Cultural Diversity in Business (London: Nicholas Brealley Publishing, 1999).

9 A. Kłoskowska, "Modele społeczne i kultura masowa," *Przegląd Socjologiczny* 13(2)/1959, pp. 49–50.

participation characteristics. Fifth, I recognize a distinction between the lawful participation of political systems' participants and its unlawful forms. Moreover, I introduce the category of participation's legitimization (legitimization's threshold) with the reservation that such a relation may appear between citizens regardless of whether the participation is lawful or not.

Chapter II, titled "Conventional forms of participation of Poles," contains a description of empirical studies' results and concerns the forms of activity that the political system includes and accepts. Here, I present a typology of participation depending on a variety of factors: different electoral forms, political environmental and social activity, as well as direct political participation, i.e., participation in electoral campaigns, meetings with politicians, or membership in political parties. I also compare the engagement in conventional forms of participation in Poland and Germany.

In Chapter III, titled "Unconventional participation and participation on the Internet," I present the empirical research results (in this case unconventional) and in the second part – with the use of the so-called new media. I distinguish between non-violent and violent forms of unconventional participation. I present the whole issue in the context of civil disobedience. Next, I characterize the dynamically developing forms of political participation on the Internet and compared the German and Polish citizens' activity in this scope.

In Chapter IV, titled "Social capital versus political participation capital," I characterized the classical presentations of social capital and the critical approach to this category. Among other things, I distinguished: economic capital, cultural capital, and information capital. Next, I proposed the term political participation capital, as a helpful concept, when one defines whether there is a potential for political activity and participation in public life's development. During the phase of analytical works and analyses, I developed nine political participation capital indexes.

In Chapter V, titled "Political participation models' typology: a priori approach," I empirically verify Robert K. Merton's model concerning types of citizens' reactions to the social and political structure. I verify whether that typology is appropriate in the Polish context.

Chapter VI, titled "Political participation models' typology: a posteriori dimension," shows a new model of political participation types' distinction.

The typology hinges directly on empirical studies. The criterion of distinction is a set of empirical and inferential indexes, which prove useful in the characterization of citizens' reactions in the system, to what extent they are engaged, and to what extent they are willing to engage in political activity.

Acknowledgments

I wish to thank my associate from the University of Warsaw Faculty of Political Science and International Studies, Daniel Mider, Dr. hab., for the consultation of text and kind remarks. Moreover, I wish to thank Joanna Lewczuk for her help in the preparation of analyses and statistical calculations. Finally, I want to thank Izabela Lassota for her effort, as she supported me in the editing of the publication.

Chapter I. Political participation: theoretical perspectives

Citizens' participation in political life has been an important issue from as early as the times of Greek democracy and city-states, in which direct democracy dominated. The importance of political participation increased as democratic political systems developed. Political scientists and sociologists agree that citizens' political participation is an extremely important factor for the democratic system's effective functioning, or, in fact, we may even state that the existence of a developed, consolidated democracy without the actual participation of the system's participants in the public life and the procedures of representants' elections is highly improbable. Jürgen Habermas emphasizes that the rule of the people belongs to fundamental human rights.[1] Robert A. Dahl echoed Habermas' beliefs, as he stated that rule of the people constitutes a prerequisite of the recognition of a given system as democratic.[2] Giovanni Sartori, in turn, emphasizes, that the term rule of the people constitutes a peculiar incomplete statement, as one should rather speak of the rule of the people over the people due to a bottom-up way of the power's legitimization, which is an emanation of common will[3]– "*demos* precedes *cracy*."[4]

Most researchers believe that it is hard to separate studies on political participation from studies on democracy. As early as in the beginning of the 1970s, American political sociologists stated that "Where few take part in decisions there is little democracy; the more participation there is in decisions, the more democracy there is."[5] Researchers that studied citizens'

1 J. Habermas, *Between Facts and Norms: Contribution to a Discourse Theory of Law and Democracy* (Cambridge: CUP, 1996), p. 127.
2 R.A. Dahl, *O demokracji* (Kraków: Społeczny Instytut Wydawniczy "Znak", 1998), p. 45.
3 G. Sartori, *The Theory of Democracy Revisited* (Chatham: Chatham House Publishers, Inc., 1987), p. 34.
4 Sartori, *The Theory of Democracy...*, p. 34.
5 S. Verba, N. Nie, *Participation in America: Political Democracy and Social Equality* (Chicago: University of Chicago Press, 1987).

participation in politics in five Western democratic systems a couple of years later had similar comments on the issue. Max Kaase and Alan Marsh wrote: "the notion of political participation is at the center of the concept of the democratic state."[6] Samuel Huntington, one of the outstanding authors, who discussed issues concerning democratic transformations in the contemporary world, states that political participation is of a primary role in society due to its influence on the society's modernization, as well as because of that it allows for the democratic election of the country's leadership and the social acceptance of the leadership's general strategy of action.[7]

The empirical studies on the political participation issue require a precise determination of the term's connotation. The American political scientists, who were the first to introduce this term and applied it in the research, formulated multiple definitions of political participation which differed in terms of details. In textbooks, they usually present a broad and simple understanding of this term. For example, Kenneth Janda, Jeffrey M. Berry, and Jerry Goldman, in their educational work on the US system of government, titled *The Challenge of Democracy*, published several times since 1989,[8] present a general definition, which Lester W. Milbrath and Madan L. Goel formulated in 1977, according to which political participation means "those actions of private citizens by which they seek to influence or to support government and politics."[9] A German political scientist, Gerd Meyer, proposes a similarly broad definition of the term political participation, which, on the other hand, shows an important aspect of citizens' participation in politics, namely, the election of leaders. He states that political participation means: "activity by which individual or groups want to

6 M. Kaase, A. Marsh, "Political Action: A Theoretical Perspective," in: *Political Action. Mass Participation in Five Western Democracies*, eds. S. H. Barnes and M. Kaase (London: Sage Publications, 1979), p. 28.

7 S.P. Huntington, J.M. Nelson, *No Easy Choice. Political Participation in Developing Countries* (Cambridge, Massachusetts, London: Harvard University Press, 1976).

8 K. Janda, J.M. Berry, J. Goldman, *The Challenge of Democracy* (Boston: Cengage Learning, 2014), p. 226.

9 L.W. Milbrath, M.L. Goel, *Political Participation. How and Why Do People Get Involved in Politics?* (Chicago: Rand McNally College Publishing Company, 1977), p. 2.

influence the selection of rulers and representatives and/or the making and outcome of public policies."[10]

In the mid-1990s, one of the creators of the term and the concept of studying political culture, Sidney Verba, by means of, in a way, modifying the earlier presented approach, highlighted the fact that, in the contemporary political systems, political participation is not only, or rather not mainly, the authorities' choice, but the mechanisms of the system, which "afford citizens in a democracy an opportunity to communicate information to government officials about their concerns and preferences and to put pressure on them to respond."[11]

In fact, all of the definitions of the term political participation include at least four basic elements which reflect the nature of participation.

First, political participation means *activity* or *actions*, which individuals undertake. As Jan W. van Deth states in his paper: "simply watching television or claiming to be curious about politics does not constitute participation."[12] Although, on the other hand, the citizens' interest in politics makes an important basis of political activity. However, being interested in politics does not simply translate into political participation; rather, it is a form of passive participation. For one may distinguish "real," active participation from its more passive counterpart: for instance, membership in a political party limited to paying fees (or even without undertaking such an activity).[13]

Second, political participation means *citizens* or, as some authors emphasize, *ordinary citizens*. At the same time, we may notice that apart from

---

10 G. Meyer, F. Ryszka, *Political Participation and Democracy in Poland and West Germany* (Warszawa: Ośrodek Badań Społecznych, 1991), p. 11.

11 S. Verba, K.L. Scholzman, H. Brady, *Voice and Equality. Civic Voluntarism in American Politics* (Cambridge, Massachusetts, London: Harvard University Press, 1998), p. 37.

12 J.W. Van Deth, *Studying Political Participation: Towards Theory of Everything?* A paper prepared for a conference organized by European Consortium for Political Research, "Electronic Democracy: Mobilisation, Organisation and Participation via new ICTs." Grenoble, 6–11 April, 2001, p. 6.

13 J. Garlicki, *Demokracja i integracja europejska. Studium osobistych i politycznych orientacji dwóch pokoleń Polaków* (Toruń: Wydawnictwo Adam Marszałek, 2005), pp. 114–115.

citizen participation there is professional participation,[14] conducted by professional politicians and state officials.[15] Still, in the context of research, citizens' participation in politics is more important. For I mean actions, which individuals undertake as citizens: not politicians or state officials.[16] Obviously, we may distinguish citizen participation (let us call it amateur participation)[17] from professional participation, according to the professionalization criterion. Politicians also belong to this category, and political participation researchers see their civil political activity as more interesting than their professional political activity.

Third, political participation means *politics* and *government*. For the meaning of the term involves the actions undertaken in the sphere of politics. The actions are not limited to a single type of institution, but, in the broad meaning of the word, refer to the political system, whereas their goal consists in conveying an opinion, suggestion to the center of power, and achieving particular results.

Fourth, political participation means *influence*.[18] Such relationship results from what I presented in the previous item: I mean actions, which aim at shaping the desired solutions and bring results in the form of political decisions or expressing one's opposition, or showing that part of the citizens has a different view on the given issue. The expression of views may also be the essence of such actions.

This is a multidimensional approach. The approach falls into the stream of social capital and participation's research, which specialists was called *the political action approach* – as D. Mider describes it – unlike *the institutional approach*.[19] The set of participation forms is unusually broad; it involves both conventional participation and unconventional non-violent and violent types of participation.

---

14 D. Mider, *Partycypacja polityczna w Internecie. Studium politologiczne* (Warszawa: Dom Wydawniczy Elipsa, 2008).

15 See more in: H.E. Brady, *Political Participation: Measures of Social Psychological Attitudes* (San Diego: Academic Press 1999), pp. 737–738.

16 Brady, *Political Participation...*, pp. 737–738.

17 Mider, *Partycypacja polityczna...*, p. 78.

18 Brady, *Political Participation...*, pp. 737–738.

19 D. Mider, "Political Participation of Poles – Structure and Trends," *Studia Politologiczne* 31/2014, p. 89 and subsequent pages.

If we speak of the most often presented kind of distinctions of citizens' participation in politics, the American political scientists mention the typology that divides participation into *conventional participation* and *unconventional participation*.[20] The above is a conventional distinction according to the criterion of behavior compliance with customs of participation in public life, adopted in the state and society. Individuals conduct conventional participation within institutions, in the way and according to rules which exist in a given political system. Conventional political participation mainly consists in participating in elections, meetings with politicians, or participation in an electoral campaign, which supports a party or a particular candidate. Unconventional participation consists in using methods that are not widely accepted in society. Most often, they constitute a challenge to the institutional channels of views and political interests articulation. In some sense, they reject the main forms of participation, included in the system. As some American scientists believe, such methods are "personally stressful to participants and their opponents."[21] These forms involve such forms of participation as, among other things, demonstrations, strikes, blocking traffic, or occupation of buildings.

Functionalists describe the matter of relations and proportions in these relations between conventional and unconventional participation very clearly. They state that we may present the relation as a kind of dilemma between civic engagement and social confusion.[22] The greater the civic conventional participation, i.e., the greater number of citizens engage in public activities as part of an institution and official channels of influence on political decisions, the lesser the engagement in unconventional participation. The low level of citizens' engagement in different forms of conventional participation in politics (which may result from either ineffective politics that the governing center conducts, or, generally, from the lack of trust in political institutions and parties) increases the tendency to organize social protests in society, which exceed the conventional frames and often involve violence. G. B. Powell directly states that the degree to which

20 Janda, Berry, Goldman, *The Challenge of Democracy*, p. 227.
21 Janda, Berry, Goldman, *The Challenge of Democracy*, p. 227.
22 G. Bingham Powell, *Contemporary Democracies* (Massachusetts: Harvard University Press, 1982), p. 123.

a democratic system can engage its citizens in electoral activity and drag them into other channels of conventional participation indicates whether the system is effective or not. If a democratic system fails to do so, it creates favorable conditions for protests, which are both a result and a factor that escalates social and political confusion, and sometimes lead to turmoil or upheaval in society. As G. B. Powell says: "Voting and rioting levels are negatively related to each other … nations with higher voting turnout have, on average, less rioting, less turmoil of all kinds."[23]

Not only the typologies and concepts of participation characterization differ. In the literature on sociology and political science, we may encounter different participation forms juxtapositions. In 1959, Robert E. Lane listed six forms of participation. These forms included: voting in elections on different stages, organization, and participation in an electoral campaign, transferring funds for electoral campaigns, acting in organizations and political parties, communicating with politicians and government representatives, and writing letters to government representatives.[24] In Sidney Verba and Norman Nie's book, titled *Participation in America: Political Democracy and Social Equality*, we may find a presentation of ten forms of participation.[25] Jan van Deth, while he was gathering information concerning which forms of participation appeared in different kinds of papers and studies, found that there were seventy of them.[26] The most appeared in the questionary which CID – Network (Citizenship, Involvement, Democracy) prepared in 2000 for the purpose of research.[27] The number depends on the aggregation level of these forms. Sometimes, the differentiation of new forms consists in the division of categories which appeared earlier into more detailed ones. For example, we may divide the overall category "contacting the politicians and/or representatives of authorities" into

23 G. Bingham Powell, *Contemporary Democracies*, p. 132.
24 R.E. Lane *Political Life. How and Why People Get Involved in Politics* (New York: Free Press, 1969).
25 S. Verba, N. Nie, *Participation in America. Political Democracy and Social Equality* (Chicago: The University of Chicago Press, 1972).
26 Van Deth, *Studying Political Participation…*, pp. 15–16.
27 Van Deth, *Studying Political Participation…*, p. 16.

several types: contacting an MP, contacting the "City Hall" (representatives of local authorities), contacting the government administration official, etc.

The notion of political participation is very broad: Jan W. Van Deth accurately characterizes it by stating that the notion leads "towards theory of everything."[28] "Political participation is an umbrella-concept that embraces numerous and incomparable activities whose only common denominator is that they are intended to influence politics."[29] We may regard this situation as some kind of advantage as it creates grounds for analyses and interpretation.

In the scientific literature on issues concerning political participation, we may find several typologies and concepts of differentiation of citizens' participation in politics. Apart from important distinction, which specialists underlined repeatedly in literature on political science, into conventional and unconventional participation (which constitutes an alternative to institutional ways of influencing and expressing opinion), and which we should rather call a difference in terms of the level of compliance with the norms of participation in politics, adopted in the state and society. We may – or even should – identify several other important criteria that describe different forms of participation.

It appears that we may easily list at least ten of them. These criteria would involve:

- *normative* criterion, which distinguishes between legal and illegal participation;
- *social acceptance* criterion: legitimized participation (which gains public confidence in the rightness of something) versus non-legitimized one;
- *activity formalization* criterion: formalized versus non-formalized;
- *autonomy of actions* criterion:[30] division into voluntary/autonomic participation and stimulated/mobilized participation;
- *activity level* criterion: active participation versus passive participation, i.e., passive participation in some organization, party, etc.;

28 Van Deth, *Studying Political Participation...*, p. 16.
29 D. Mider, *Political Participation – Structure and Trends*, p. 90; S. Huntington, J.M. Nelson, *No Easy Choice...*, p. 14.
30 A criterion that raises doubts due to the fact that political sociologists often believed that only the voluntary participation is real.

- *openness/overtness of action* criterion: overt participation versus covert one;
- *support (affiliation) or rejection* criterion: supporting participation versus denying, avoiding participation;
- *time and engagement level* criterion: incidental, episodic participation versus constant one;
- *goals and activity motivation* criterion: instrumental participation versus expressive participation
- *means of expression* criterion: verbal and non-verbal participation;
- *social contacts and ties* criterion: participation based on social interaction versus participation which does not require social interaction.

The division into *legal* and *illegal*, and *legitimized* and *non-legitimized* political participation constitutes an important category of its analysis. It is probably worth stressing that not all forms of unconventional participation are illegal. For example, a demonstration may be organized in accordance with the law. Political participation's division into legal and illegal, on the other hand, is not identical to political participation's division into legitimized and non-legitimized. An illegal form may become a legitimized form, i.e., a form, which is gaining social acceptance or even support of large parts of society, if, according to numerous citizens, the form serves a good cause, and other forms of expressing opinion did not have any effect.

To put it simply, forms of participation that fall into the legal forms group are those, which, as the name suggests, are stipulated in the provisions of the law or at least not forbidden by the law. Among the forms of social protest, such forms of participation would include, for example, signing petitions, which I mentioned earlier, or participation in strikes, organized in a way that is stipulated in the provisions of the law. Illegal forms of participation include, for example, different kinds of violent protests, such as attacks on law enforcement. Moreover, illegal forms of participation include such forms of law-breaking actions, although non-violent, as refusing to pay taxes or other charges, stipulated by law. Forms of conventional participation, including conventional variations of protests, are legal forms. On the other hand, some unconventional forms are illegal at the same time. However, we cannot say that both of the participation forms' division criteria are identical. The concept of civil right for civil disobedience in some way justifies the violation of law by illegal social protests. However, the researchers of political systems and constitutional lawyers began formulating a set of rules, which should also regulate the use of the right for civil disobedience. For example, Ewa Łętowska, the first Polish Ombudsman (*Rzecznik Praw Obywatelskich*) in the history of the Third Polish Republic states in her book that we may speak of justified civil disobedience if we meet a set of conditions. The author believes that these conditions deal with the protesters' behavior. According to E. Łętowska, a justified and proven negative evaluation of nonconstitutional practices of the authorities or subordinate regulation which are contradictory to the constitution should form the basis of such actions.[31] Protest should be "preceded by actions, which a protester may use as part of the existing legal order" (demonstrations, activities through associations, etc.), "measures and forms of a protest should be proportionate to the goal; one should not begin with using the most serious measures,"[32] and the protesters cannot use violence. The description of rules presented above is a clear attempt of sanctioning unconventional forms of protest in particular cases. The author tries to sanction at least some of them, i.e., those, which do not involve the use of violence and are adequate to situations which citizens encounter. In this way, we approach yet another important issue, which is unconventional forms of social protests legitimization. In other words, we return to the issue of social protests acceptance; in this case, we deal with the acceptance of unconventional social protests from the point of view of procedure or level of social acceptance, which legalizes them in some sense. Citizens may accept different forms of protests while being heedless of politicians, specialists, and researchers' opinions. The level of social consent to certain kinds of unconventional participation depends on the level of how widespread is the consent to organize them in social opinion. There is no doubt that if at least half of citizens accept certain forms of protests, it means that they gain social consent. Obviously, it happens when certain conditions are met. We may describe such a level of acceptance as *legitimization's threshold of unconventional behavior*.

31 E. Łętowska, *Po co ludziom konstytucja?* (HR Helsinki Foundation for Human Rights, 1994).

32 Łętowska, *Po co ludziom konstytucja?*

Democratic systems provide and allow for certain forms of social protest. It is expressed, for example, in the adoption of the civil disobedience principle, i.e., the recognition of citizens' behavior, which involves opposing the institutions of political power, as possible, and sometimes even legitimate. However, specialists assume that such behavior must be justified by social values or the interest of social groups or the whole society. Such behavior may become regarded as permissible if the authorities' actions bring negative effects or when political authorities violate the adopted rules and socially accepted rules of conduct in their decisions. Specialists treat the scope and accepted scale of civil disobedience differently. Most political sociologists believe that, usually, in such cases, we deal with the violation of binding law. Individuals who organize and participate in acts of social protest operate under the belief that the political authorities are unjust or significantly violate the binding provisions of the law themselves. Then, the protest becomes socially and, to some extent, politically justified. As J. Rawls states: By acting in this way one addresses the sense of justice of the majority of the community.[33] Some researchers are even willing to state that civil disobedience against unjust authorities may take the form of a violent protest.[34] In any case, when we speak of different forms of social protests, we must remember that they mostly go beyond the boundaries of conventional political participation. In a study, the results of which form the main empirical basis of this book, I included a question concerning which forms of social protests do Poles accept. There are such varieties of protests, which are nominally unconventional. These protests include, for example, signing petitions, participating in legally organized demonstrations, participation in legally organized strikes, and boycotting certain products. However, all of these forms are legal in Poland. We may say that these four forms mentioned above go beyond the legitimization threshold due to the level of social acceptance. We may even risk a thesis that they began to assume a rather conventional character.

33 J. Rawls, *A Theory of Justice. Revised Edition* (Cambridge: The Belknap Press of Harvard University Press, 1999), p. 320.

34 H. Zinn, *Disobedience and Democracy: Nine Fallacies on Law and Order* (Random House Trade Paperbacks, 1968).

Bronisław Misztal, in his book *Zagadnienia społecznego uczestnictwa i współdziałania*, proposes to recognize such types of participation as, for example: *formalized* and *non-formalized*.[35] In turn, Jan Teorell, Mariano Torcal, and Jose Ramon Montero distinguish five significantly different types of political participation.[36] They state that, apart from the most obvious, institutional, i.e., formalized form of participation, which is voting in different kinds of national and regional elections (or conscious resignation from doing so), we may see that there are such distinct types of participation as activity in political parties, contacting with politicians and political organizations/institutions, or activities, which one undertakes for their benefit, organizing and participating in protests, and participation in community life as a consumer, which may become political (for example, boycotting certain products, or only buying products of particular origin). Obviously, activity in parties means a formalized participation, whereas boycotting certain products – rather informal one. Contacting politicians, on the other hand, or participation in protests, may be both formalized and informal. If a protest is led by an organization that operates legally, then we should declare it as having a formalized nature, regardless of whether the form itself is legal or illegal.

Some authors underline that we deal with political participation only when it means a voluntary activity of citizens.[37] However, this statement may be questioned in some sense. Undoubtedly, it is hard to consider participation in rallies of support, organized by the authorities in a totalitarian system, civil political participation. It is rather a result of mobilization function realization by the centers of power, whereas the participation is an effect of stronger or weaker stressed duty of some kind. However, on the scale of a certain continuum between obligatory participation, on the

35 B. Misztal, *Zagadnienia społecznego uczestnictwa i współdziałania. Analiza w świetle teorii i badań socjologicznych* (Wrocław: Wydawnictwo Polskiej Akademii Nauk, 1977), p. 208.

36 J. Teorell, M. Torcal, J.R. Montero, *Political Participation*. Second Draft of Chapter 12 of Volume B: Population Studies. European Science Foundation, Science-Network on Citizenship, Involvement and Democracy. Unpublished article; http://www.upf.edu/pdi/dcpis/mariano.torcal/en/publicaciones.htm. (Date of Access: September, 2020), p. 8.

37 Van Deth, *Studying Political Participation…*, p. 5.

one hand, and voluntary participation, on the other hand, we may find numerous varieties, or types of participation, which is not directly forced by a decision-making center, but it is also not fully spontaneous and autonomous participation. B. Misztal, who I mentioned earlier, says that apart from voluntary participation we may also observe participation *which is determined by cultural standards*, and participation, *which results from organizational or associative entanglements*.[38] The first of the types of participation that B. Misztal mentions deals with the fact that certain broadly understood models, standards of behavior may exist in different societies or even circles of one society. We may say that, to some extent, a part of society ritually got accustomed to acting in accordance with them. For example, such participation may involve participation in different kinds of national ceremonies. It is also worth adding that in some European democratic states people started to see participation in elections as a civic duty. Sometimes not participating in voting even results in punishment, e.g., in such states as Belgium or Greece. On the other hand, the second type of participation, which results from organizational or associative entanglements, consists in the manifestation of certain determinants of current activity by previously formed ties or decisions. For example, a citizen becomes a member of a party. In the parliamentary democracy system, where political pluralism and multi-party system exist, it is a purely voluntary decision. However, the resulting participation in, for example, collecting signatures for the party's candidate, or participation in a pre-election meeting organized by the party is to some extent the very consequence of organizational entanglement. Strong family or local ties, or ties in the ethnic group may also constitute a certain kind of associative entanglements of participation in politics. Should we exclude the citizens' participation in politics (which constitutes a consequence of organizational or associative entanglement or which is determined by the established standards) from the scope of activities, described by the term political participation in a democratic society? Numerous prominent authors say no. Both Samuel Huntington and, for example, Lester W. Milbrath believe that such type of participation in politics meets the criteria of political participation. It is citizens who manifest

38 Misztal, *Zagadnienia społecznego uczestnictwa i współdziałania...*, p. 208.

activity in a democratic political system, the content of that activity is politics, and the goal is to influence. To differentiate between types of participation, the first author uses the following terms: *autonomous* participation versus *mobilized* participation.[39] Apart from autonomous, independent participation, the second author distinguishes *compliant* participation, which constitutes an effect of suggestion.[40]

Lester W. Milbrath created interesting determinants which help describe political participation models. He proposes several dimensions of analysis.[41] Milbrath describes each of the dimensions by means of two opposite terms, which we may also call features. Most of the dimensions are well suited for a detailed characterization of different behavior forms in the sphere of political life. One of the first dimensions consists in dividing participation into *active* and *inactive*.[42] Admittedly, we may say that participation most often entails active behavior, but L. W. Milbrath points out that we may, for example, observe the phenomenon of conscious decline to participate in an election or resignation from a political meeting. When it is conscious, such behavior may be political participation-like, although planned passivity lies at its core. It happens that the same citizens in some situations are active, whereas in other situations they remain passive.

Mirosław Karwat, a Polish political scientist, highlights important issues related to citizens' participation in politics. He believes that we may distinguish different levels of political participation. These levels may include: generally understood participation in political relations, participation in articulation and representation of group interests, participation in public life, and participation or co-participation in the processes of social life control, conducted mainly by participation in state control processes.[43] On the empirical plane, differentiation of participation, understood as participation in public life, from participation, consisting in articulation and

39 Huntington, Nelson, *No Easy Choice...*, p. 7.
40 L.W. Milbrath, *Political Participation. How and Why Do People Get Involved in Politics?*, p. 10.
41 Milbrath, *Political Participation...*, p. 9.
42 Milbrath, *Political Participation...*, p. 9.
43 M. Karwat, *Partycypacja polityczna* (draft version of a textbook *Political participation*, unpublished), p. 28.

representation of group interests, may prove useful. The mentioned author also isolates *incidental*, *processual*, and *structural* approaches to participation.[44] Incidental participation consists in engaging in collective actions, is not permanent or continuous, but may be repetitive. We may exemplify incidental participation with participation in a legally organized demonstration or manifestation. Processual participation is causal. Individuals conduct such participation continuously and it usually involves gaining influence on political life. Structural participation means remaining in interactions that produce dependencies and create a social bond. According to the author, structural participation precisely involves the so-called *passive* and *active aspects*. In the *passive* sense, structural participation means being a part of something, e.g., declaring participation in some organization or undertaking, but without taking any real action. Structural participation may restrict itself to belonging to a group of people who are well-informed on politics. Acquiring knowledge on political events and political life mechanisms also constitutes an action, but it does not involve an important factor of influencing and does not directly lead to political results. However, the origins of citizens' knowledge on politics and how often do they acquire the said knowledge significantly affects the type and model of participation in politics. In turn, the level of engagement in the political sphere determines, as we might expect, the way and scope of using different information sources. On the other hand, the active aspect of participation consists in "contributing by one's own actions, especially the conscious and intentional ones"[45] to achieving certain goals, e.g., the election of a particular candidate or the successful performance of a candidate in an election.

Another pair that characterizes political participation forms are the terms *overt* participation versus *covert* participation. Since open (available to the public for evaluation), loud expression of support, participation in a political rally is something different from basically private matters, such as donating money for the party or discussing politics with friends.

We may also speak of participation, the nature of which ranges from *supporting* to *moving away*, *avoiding*. As I mentioned earlier, refusing to

44 Karwat, *Partycypacja polityczna...*, pp. 9–10.
45 Karwat, *Partycypacja polityczna...*, p. 13.

participate in a meeting with a politician, resigning from voting as part of a protest, or boycotting certain products constitute forms of participation that consist in moving away from something or somebody.

The important dividing criterion is *episodic* forms (or, to put it differently, *incidental*), which I signalized earlier, versus *continuous* participation. L. W. Milbrath emphasizes that activity such as voting or organizing a campaign for a candidate occurs only in peculiar periods, i.e., during or before upcoming elections. On the other hand, contacting politicians or being active in a political party is usually or may be continuous.

We should differentiate *expressive*, in some way *autotelic* participation from *instrumental* participation. The first one is based on symbols and serves the goal of expressing one's views and emotions. The second one serves the goal of achieving particular effects in the form of influencing, dealing with certain issues, or blocking some decisions, perceived by a certain social or professional group as unfavorable. This division to a greater extent relies on differences in motivations of particular behavior participants than on differences in forms.

From the times of L.W. Milbrath, scholars transformed the instrumental-expressive division into a more sophisticated concept. For example, in rational choice theory, F.J. Heunks distinguishes *instrumental*, *non-instrumental*, and *semi-instrumental* actions. The first group involves such actions, which influence reality in a tested and obvious way; an individual (or a group) gets what he/she wants, using tested modus operandi. The second group involves actions, which individuals conduct not for the benefits of exiting the system, but for psychological gratifications (emotions related to action, sense of affiliation, self-improvement, fun). In turn, semi-instrumental actions are pro bono; it is not an individual who gains, but it is a whole or a relatively big group that gains, even at the expense of the individual.

The next dimension of participation forms analysis suggests dividing them into *verbal* and *non-verbal*. In many cases, it is hard to imagine participation without communication between participants, which is most often oral or sometimes written. Not all individuals possess the skill required to exchange views freely, but not all forms of participation require it. For example, participating in a demonstration or voting in elections does not require the said skill.

The issue of social contacts and ties constitutes another criterion. We may speak of a continuum that goes from *social interaction* to participation in politics, which *does not require social interaction*. For example, writing letters or creating graffiti are not based on interaction. Interaction occurs later, given that somebody reads what the author wrote, and it usually happens without the direct participation of an individual, who was the author of a letter or graffiti. Similarly, bank transfer of funds to the bank account of the candidate's political campaign staff does not require interaction. However, there are forms of participation, which require very intensive mutual interactions. For example, conducting a campaign that consists in encouraging voters to support a particular candidate in elections via visiting the homes of the said potential voters requires much more interaction in changing conditions than, for example, voting itself or participating in meeting with the candidate.

We may broaden the criteria of typology even more. I characterized the most important divisions. However, I may mention other divisions. For example, scholars distinguish the *goal of action* criterion: in social goals versus particularistic goals. According to the *activity's addressee* criteria, we may distinguish actions against the institution of the state versus those against out-of-state institutions, concerning other entities, acting in the public sphere. Besides social interaction, *the number of participating actors* seems to be an important dimension; by the said criterion I mean individual versus collective participation. From the viewpoint of the *organizational* criterion, participation may be centralized, and in the era of the growth of the Internet and the influence of social media, participation may be decentralized (scattered, network-based).

In the research conducted for this study, I used a total of sixty-six forms of participation. They were divided into four groups. The first group is conventional participation. The second group is unconventional non-violent participation (these are various forms of political protests). The third group is participation in politics involving violence. Moreover, the division is relative as non-violent unconventional actions, such as legal demonstrations, may turn into clashes with law enforcement. And finally, political participation using the power of the Internet constitutes the fourth group.

In the case of the first group of conventional forms, I asked directly whether and how often Poles participate in activities of this nature. For the second group, I examined both participation and acceptance of such participation forms by other citizens. For unconventional participation involving violence, I measured only the level and conditions of possible acceptance. In the last group covering online political participation, I asked questions concerning both activity and acceptance.

It is worth emphasizing that the issue concerning the acceptance of various social protest forms is an issue that is relevant from the point of view of at least two aspects (in two dimensions). First, there is the tendency of citizens to consent to or at least tolerate different behavior of other citizen groups that goes beyond the routine forms of political action sanctioned by law and consistent with the principles of social action in democratic systems. Second, the acceptance reaction may constitute an indicator of possible own behavior if the authorities break certain rules in the opinion of citizens. In this sense, the extent of consent to certain unconventional forms of participation may become a determinant of potential, acceptable behavior in crises.

In the research conducted by a team from the Faculty of Journalism and Political Science at the University of Warsaw (now Faculty of Political Science and International Studies) as part of the National Science Center of Poland grant 4884 *Partycypacja polityczna Polaków – nowe wyzwania i formy aktywności* (Political Participation of Poles – New Challenges and Forms of Activity), I identified four groups of participation forms: conventional, unconventional, non-violent, violent, and online. Then, I distinguished six research categories of political participation in more detail:

- participation in conventional forms,
- participation in unconventional, non-violent forms,
- the level of unconventional non-violent political participation acceptance,
- the level of unconventional violent political participation acceptance,[46]
- political participation on the Internet,
- the level of aggressive forms of action acceptance on the Internet.

46 In this case, I did not ask questions concerning participation in violent actions.

An important issue is what forms of political participation become the Polish citizens' main standard of behavior. Is it mainly electoral participation, which occurs every few years with elections held at various levels? Or is it a set of other forms of participation, which are also unconventional? And even more important is the question of whether there is political participation capital in Polish society, which can constitute a good basis for the growth of participation and the development of its forms at different levels, including political activity on the Internet?

Chapter II. Conventional forms of participation of Poles

As I have already stated, political participation has different dimensions and takes different forms. In empirical research, on the one hand, it is worth distinguishing conventional and non-conventional participation, and, on the other hand, exploring the developing forms of participation on the Internet. Such a trend in analysis developed under the research on political participation and is called the *Political Action Approach*.[1] Another important division includes applied forms of participation, i.e. these in which citizens participate, and the question of the acceptance level for other forms of participation that they are willing to consider valid.

From sixty-six forms of participation that the aforementioned study asked about, for further analysis, I selected forty-nine forms that are, as the study shows, apparently crucial in the group of more frequently applied ones and well characterize Poles' political activity profiles.

We may say that conventional participation in fact is foreseen or projected in every political system. Especially democratic systems concentrate on this aspect; however authoritarian or totalitarian systems also want to show that their citizens participate in systemic events (e.g. rallies, marches, demonstrations, and elections, regardless to what extent they are "set up"), although it was already stated that it is stimulated or mobilized participation. There are fifteen forms selected from the first category, i.e. conventional political participation, that I examined and analyzed:

1. Discussing politics.
2. Persuading someone to vote for a specific candidate or cause (political agitation).
3. Expressing beliefs through campaign and political buttons, stickers, or preaching political slogans (symbolic political actions).
4. Voting in parliamentary or/and presidential elections.
5. Voting in local elections.
6. Voting in referendums.

1 Brady, *Political Participation...*, pp. 742–796.

7. Participating in public consultations.
8. Participating in political meetings or/and rallies.
9. Communicating with politicians to "get something done."
10. Organizing financial support for a candidate, organization, or cause.
11. Acting to solve problems of local communities (village/town/commune/powiat/region).
12. Participation in the organization of an electoral campaign.
13. Being a member of or forming a political party, social movement, or other political organization, or acting in it now or in the past.
14. Being a candidate for a political office (in local governments or parliament) now or in the past.
15. Holding an elective political office or held one in the past, e.g. councilor, village administrator, commune administrator.

As we discover, Poles most often declare participation in nationwide elections. Participation in the elections of local authorities takes second place. This means that, above all, Poles tend to participate in forms of civic participation that we may call conventional. According to the study, more than seventy percent of the surveyed citizens participate in nationwide elections (cf. Mider 2014). Noteworthy, these declarations exceed the actual level of participation in the elections but this is due to at least two reasons. First, as the results of many years of research in Poland (but not only) show, declarations usually exceed the actual scale of participation in elections. Second, we may divide the citizens participating in elections into at least two groups: those who participate systematically and those who, depending on different conditions and reasons, would or would not go to the election. In other words, the group of citizens who do not participate in elections at all is not as numerous as the data about the turnout in subsequent elections would indicate. I present the detailed data in Table 2.1.

The intensity of Poles' electoral participation was alarming. About half or less of the eligible participated in parliamentary elections, and the voter turnout was systematically decreasing throughout the twenty years of the Third Polish Republic's existence. After this period, it started to grow. There was a parliamentary election in 2007, followed by elections in 2018, 2019, and 2020 (respectively: local government election, the European Parliament election, the Sejm election, and the presidential election). All of these elections took place in the circumstances of a negative strong political polarization that suggested a significant political conflict.

Table 2.1. Conventional forms of participation of Poles and the scope of their occurrence in politics

Please consider and answer whether you:	Name in the language of the researcher / label	Often	Rarely / occasionally	Never
Voting in parliamentary or/ and presidential elections	Elections and referendums	74.1	8.5	17.4
Voting in local elections		65.2	16.1	18.7
Voting in referendums		53.2	14.0	32.8
Discussing politics	Political discussions	39.2	49.5	11.3
Participating in public consultations	Public consultations	11.7	24.9	63.4
Persuading someone to vote for a specific candidate or cause	Political agitation	10.8	24.6	64.6
Acting to solve problems of local communities (village/ town/commune/powiat/ region)	Local activism	10.3	25.7	64.0
Participating in political meetings or/and rallies	Public gatherings	3.1	18.4	78.5
Expressing beliefs through campaign and political buttons, stickers, or preaching political slogans	Symbolic political actions	3.0	11.1	85.9
Holding an elective political office or held one in the past, e.g. councilor, village administrator, commune administrator)	Acting as a politician in office	3.0	2.1	94.9
Were a candidate for a political position (in local governments, regional council, or parliament)	Use of the passive suffrage	2.7	4.7	92.6
Being a member of or forming a political party, social movement, or other political organization, or acting in it now or in the past	Party and organizational activity	2.3	6.3	91.4

(*continued*)

Table 2.1. Continued

Please consider and answer whether you:	Name in the language of the researcher / label	Often	Rarely / occasionally	Never
Participation in the organization of an electoral campaign	Supporting political campaigns	2.2	5.4	92.4
Communicating with politicians to "get something done"	Lobbying	1.9	12.1	86.0
Organizing financial support for a candidate, organization, or cause	Donations	1.0	5.9	93.1

Source: *Partycypacja polityczna Polaków – nowe wyzwania i formy aktywności* study, 2017, NCN grant 4884, N=1237.

Three forms of conventional participation received over fifty percent of indications. In addition to those specified above, i.e. participation in nationwide and local elections, conventional forms of participation also include participation in referendums. The declarations again exceeded the actual average turnout in referendums organized in Poland since the system transition – usually, less than a quarter of the eligible voters constituted the entire turnout, except for the two-day (7–8 June 2003) referendum on Poland's accession to the European Union, where the share of voters constituted 55.21 percent.[2]

The fourth form of conventional participation in terms of participation rate was discussing politics. According to the declarations, nearly forty percent of Poles discuss politics. Moreover, a group of nearly half the adult Polish population does it occasionally. Thus, in total, more than eighty-eight percent of Polish citizens has the habit of discussing politics, although only a part of them practices such discussions regularly. Respondents less frequently declared such forms of participation as participating in public

2 In this referendum, 77.33 percent of participating Poles voted for accession.

consultations, persuading someone to vote for a specific candidate – i.e. private political agitation – and activity for solving local communities' problems (in a commune, town, or powiat). Every tenth participant of the study declared taking up such an activity.

About three percent of citizens often participate in activities such as public gatherings, holding an office – mainly in local government, or expressing their beliefs through wearing political buttons or stickers, or preaching political slogans. According to the respondents' declarations, more than ten percent of the surveyed participate in public gatherings and political activities. 2.3 percent of Poles were active members of a political party, social movement, or other political organization. Few groups (one to 2.7 percent of respondents) declared that they often participated or participate in such activities as running for an office in local government, city council, regional council, etc., organizing an election campaign, communicating with politicians to solve certain problems or achieve something, or providing financial support to a candidate or organization. Donations to parties or election campaigns are not particularly popular in Poland. This is the least mentioned category among the other fifteen forms of political participation.

Survey participants most often chose the "never" category regarding such forms as acting as a politician in office and providing financial support for a candidate or organization. This was the declaration of nearly ninety-five percent of the respondents. Poles also usually do not exercise passive suffrage, participate in political party activities, organizational activities, or support political campaigns.

It is worthwhile to compare this study's results with data from the surveys conducted by other research centers. As the analysis shows, many Poles engage in various social activities; however, only a part of them is active directly in the sphere of politics. Since 1998, Public Opinion Research Center (CBOS Foundation) conducts such surveys, i.e. studies of Poles' civic activity.

Table 2.2. The activity of Poles in civic organizations

There are various opportunities for social action in Poland. Do you spend your free time working for an organization, association, movement, club, or foundation? The question concerns specifically your participation in this organization's/these organizations' work and not only whether you belong to it/them	I 2002	I 2004	I 2006	I 2008	I 2010	I 2012	I 2016	II 2018
Charity organizations acting for children in need	1.0	2.4	3.5	2.4	5.1	5.6	10.0	11.0
Organizations acting for education, e.g. parents' committee, parents' council, school or university foundation, Civic Educational Association (Społeczne Towarzystwo Oświatowe)	3.2	4.2	4.8	4.8	8.0	6.9	10.9	10.3
Charity organizations acting for people in need, i.e. elderly, poor, homeless, sick, disabled, victims of natural disasters or wars, etc.	1.3	2.4	2.1	2.4	4.0	4.8	8.6	9.6
Religious or church organizations or movements, parish communities	2.0	3.9	3.4	2.8	4.5	5.4	6.9	7.9
Sports organizations (unions, clubs, associations)	2.7	4.8	3.5	2.8	5.8	4.0	7.5	7.1
Associations or unions of allotment owners, breeders, fishermen, or hunters	1.8	2.9	2.5	1.6	3.3	4.0	5.0	6.1
Volunteer fire brigade, mountain volunteer rescue service, etc.	3.0	2.2	3.4	1.4	2.7	3.2	4.7	5.3
Youth organizations, e.g. Scouts, youth clubs, student unions, and associations	2.1	2.3	2.3	1.8	3.2	2.7	6.1	5.2

Table 2.2. Continued

There are various opportunities for social action in Poland. Do you spend your free time working for an organization, association, movement, club, or foundation? The question concerns specifically your participation in this organization's/these organizations' work and not only whether you belong to it/them	I 2002	I 2004	I 2006	I 2008	I 2010	I 2012	I 2016	II 2018
Mutual aid organizations, e.g. associations of people with disabilities, single fathers, alcoholics anonymous, unemployed people	0.4	1.0	1.3	0.8	2.5	1.6	2.7	4.1
Artistic organizations or associations, e.g. choir, orchestra, dance, or theater ensemble	0.9	1.9	1.6	0.8	2.6	2.9	4.4	4.0
Animal protection associations	0.7	0.8	1.6	0.3	2.3	1.5	4.2	4.0
Organizations of pensioners, senior citizens clubs	1.2	1.8	1.8	1.2	1.8	2.6	3.0	3.7
District or neighborhood self-governments, e.g. residents' councils, house committees	0.3	1.0	1.2	0.9	1.6	2.3	3.0	3.6
Organizations supporting health care facilities	0.6	0.8	1.5	0.9	1.7	1.2	2.0	3.4
Women's organizations, e.g. farmer's wives' association	0.8	1.2	0.8	1.0	0.8	1.0	2.6	3.3
Committees striving to get a specific issue done (e.g. parking lot), protest groups	0.3	0.4	1.0	0.4	1.3	1.7	3.3	3.2
Environmental organizations	0.3	1.2	1.8	0.9	1.5	1.6	3.2	3.1
Labor unions	3.3	3.8	3.9	3.2	2.1	2.8	4.3	2.9
Associations of enthusiasts of a city or region that e.g. protect historical monuments or develop the regional culture	0.4	0.6	0.8	1.0	1.9	0.9	2.7	2.9

(continued)

Table 2.2. Continued

There are various opportunities for social action in Poland. Do you spend your free time working for an organization, association, movement, club, or foundation? The question concerns specifically your participation in this organization's/these organizations' work and not only whether you belong to it/them	I 2002	I 2004	I 2006	I 2008	I 2010	I 2012	I 2016	II 2018
Professional associations and self-governments	0.5	0.9	0.5	0.5	1.0	1.6	2.9	2.7
Tourist organizations and associations	0.6	1.3	0.9	1.1	1.7	1.0	2.3	2.3
Scientific societies	0.8	1.4	1.2	0.5	2.3	1.4	2.7	2.2
Commune self-governments	0.2	1.1	0.9	0.8	1.1	1.4	2.7	1.9
Workers' self-governments (workers' councils)	0.2	0.8	1.1	0.4	0.6	1.2	2.1	1.8
Associations and clubs of collectors and hobbyists	0.7	1.2	0.7	1.0	1.5	0.7	2.0	1.8
Societies of friendship with other countries or nations	0.1	0.7	0.6	0.4	1.1	1.1	1.2	1.3
Voivodeship and powiat self-governments	0.1	0.5	0.2	0.7	0.7	0.5	1.5	1.1
Organizations of veterans and war victims	0.9	1.4	1.2	1.0	0.6	1.2	0.9	1.0
Political parties or associations	0.6	0.7	0.7	0.4	0.7	1.1	1.1	0.9
Other organizations, associations, movements, clubs, or foundations	0.2	0.3	0.9	1.7	1.4	1.7	3.5	1.5

Source: *Activity of Poles in civic organizations* study, CBOS statement from the study "Current Problems and Events," Warsaw, February 2018, N=1527, implementation method: CAPI.

It is visible that the respondents' activity increased only slightly between 2016 and 2018 but the upward trend continued. However, this activity is mainly not political participation but participation in non-governmental organizations (NGOs) from the so-called third sector. In the period between 2012 and 2016, this increase was even greater. Currently, the majority of those who participate in associations and charity organizations chose organizations acting for children, people with disabilities, or education. According to the respondents' answers, 10–11 percent of them participate in such organizations. If we compare these data with the year 2002, it turns out that the activity of Poles increased by several times. In the case of *Charity organizations acting for children in need*, the participation increased eleven times in sixteen years. Of course, in most cases, we probably do not deal with continuous involvement but only episodic one that is associated with some action. For example, the Great Orchestra of Christmas Charity (WOŚP) collects money for hospital equipment (also for sick children) once a year, but then tens of thousands or even hundreds of thousands of volunteers, organizations, and companies engage in this operation. Another example is the Noble Gift (Szlachetna Paczka) action, which starts before Christmas to supply poor families and the elderly with various necessary things. Again, this NGO acts continuously but many citizens participate in it only in this period. Political parties or voivodeship and powiat self-governments situate in the end with a small number of indications, although the study showed an increase in this form of participation in general. On the other hand, the study also showed a decrease in participation in labor unions.

Therefore, we should revise the thesis that the "democratic community" is only a myth. Jan Błuszkowski and Daniel Mider stressed that contemporary political culture generates rather particularistic, egoistic, and individualistic attitudes and the mechanical conformism caused by democracy destroys interpersonal bonds also at the level of acting for the common good.[3] Błuszkowski and Mider repeated the hypotheses of Ferdinand Tönnies[4] and Émile Durkheim,[5] who alarmed about leading societies to the state of moral death due to the "loss of community." These concepts were also repeated later with relentless force. Benjamin R. Barber wrote about civic schizophrenia: "we know that certain things are bad for the community, but good

3 D. Mider, J. Błuszkowski, *Demokracja późnej nowoczesności* (Warszawa: Dom Wydawniczy Elipsa, 2012), 26–27.

4 F. Tönnies, *Community and Society* (Mineola, New York: Dover Publications, 2002).

5 É. Durkheim, *The Division of Labor in Society* (New York: Free Press, 1999).

for us, yet we put the individual interest before the common interest."[6] Michel J. Crozier, Samuel P. Huntington, and Jōji Watanuki[7] point to the problem of loosening interpersonal bonds due to increased vertical and horizontal mobility of individuals and social groups. Richard Stivers[8] expressed similar concerns by introducing the notion of culture of cynicism. On the other hand, Stefan Nowak used the notion of sociological vacuum meaning the disappearance or failure of social organizations on an above-family level.[9] In contrast, currently, we may notice a fragmentary increase in integration and engagement in different forms of social activity in Poland.

It is worth analyzing what changes within political participation of the Polish society occurred in the twentieth-first century so far. This enables us to compare the 2017 research results with the data obtained with the application of similar indicators in 2002. The same two forms of political participation are most popular among Poles throughout fifteen years. Those are: voting in nationwide (parliamentary or presidential) elections and participation in local elections. However, both these forms received a higher percentage of indications. In 2017, the number of citizens who declared frequent participation in nationwide elections was higher than fifteen years ago by 6.3 percent. According to the recipients' declarations, participation in local and self-government elections increased even more. The number of people, who participate in them frequently (this does not mean always) increased by nearly eleven percent. This is probably due to the change within the electoral system and the introduction of direct election for the offices of commune administrators and mayors, and the growing sense among citizens of having influence over matters concerning their closest environment or local community. Participation in referendums was in third place. Noteworthy, this category was absent in the 2002 research. Therefore, the comparison is not possible. I present the detailed result of the comparative analysis in Table 2.3.

6 B. R. Barber, *Consumed: How Markets Corrupt Children, Infantilize Aduldts, and Swallow Citizens Whole* (New York, London: W.W. Norton &. Co., 2008), p. 158.
7 M.J. Crozier, S.P. Huntington, J. Watanuki, *The Crisis of Democracy. Report on the Governability of Democracies to the Trilateral Commission* (New York: New York University Press, 1975).
8 R. Stivers, *The Culture of Cynicism* (Oxford: Blackwell, 1994).
9 S. Nowak, "System wartości społeczeństwa polskiego," *Studia Socjologiczne*, No. 4/1979, pp. 155–173.

Table 2.3. Forms of political participation of Poles and the scope of their occurrence (comparison 2002–2017)

Forms of participationa	Scope of participation (in %)	
	Often (data from 2002) N=1206	Often (data from 2017) N=1237
Voting in parliamentary or/and presidential elections	67.8	74.1
Voting in local elections	54.3	65.2
Voting in referendums	*	53.2
Political discussions	27.4	39.2
Participating in public consultations	*	11.7
Persuading someone to vote for a specific candidate or cause	4.3	10.8
Acting to solve problems of local communities (village/town/commune/powiat/region)	3.6	10.3
Participating in political meetings or/and rallies	2.2	3.1
Holding an elective political office or held one in the past, e.g. councilor, village administrator, commune administrator)	*	3.1
Expressing beliefs through campaign and political buttons, stickers, or preaching political slogans	*	3.0
Being a candidate for a political office (in local governments or parliament)	*	2.7
Being a member of or forming a political party, social movement, or other political organization, or acting in it now or in the past	*	2.4
Collecting signatures for petitions	2.5	2.3
Participation in the organization of an electoral campaign	1.0	2.2
Communicating with politicians to "get something done"	2.1	1.9
Organizing financial support for a candidate, organization, or cause	*	1.0

*no data available for 2002.
Sources: J. Garlicki, *Demokracja i integracja europejska* (Toruń: Wydawnictwo Adam Marszałek, 2005), N=1206; study *Partycypacja polityczna Polaków – nowe wyzwania i formy aktywności* (2017), NCN grant 4884, N=1237.

As the studies show, in general, Poles became more politically active during this fifteen-year period. Poles much more often discuss politics, persuade others to vote for a specific candidate, party, or cause. Concerning these two activities, there is a visible increase of 2.5 times (from the declared 4.3 percent to 10.8). Relatively rarely mentioned in 2002, participation in actions for the local environment almost tripled. As the respondents stated, in 2017, such activities reached the level of over ten percent. On the other hand, the scale of lobbying or the number of people collecting signatures for petitions did not increase.

It is worthwhile to thoroughly analyze the different kinds of declarations concerning engagement in politics and forms of participation corresponding to them presented above. The main purpose of this analysis should be an attempt to systematize these forms and extract specific models of Poles' political participation. The similarity of the participation forms and their characteristics were the basis for the models' development. In the analysis, I considered different kinds of participation described in the introduction to this chapter. The next phase was making a diagnosis about the degree of certain models' prevalence.

As the research showed, the most spread forms of participation include voting in nationwide elections and voting local elections. Possibly, we could combine these two forms into a single model. It is the model of *civic participation*, which we may call not only *conventional*[10] but also *elective*.

Applying the typology of participation proposed by B. Misztal,[11] we may classify this model into the group of formalized ones. In fact, the model in question is an activity implemented within the official operating structures of the state which is foreseen or even "planned" as one of the basic forms of civic participation in social life. Additionally, electoral participation occurs in circumstances that are strictly determined by proper legal regulations. To some extent, it is a participation model determined by the standards of democratic political culture. As I already mentioned, nearly three-quarters of Poles declare frequent participation in nationwide elections, and two-thirds of them declare participation in local elections. The arithmetic mean for this model would be over sixty-four percent. Noteworthy, a group constituting more than sixty percent claims that they often participate in at least one of these forms.

---

10 Janda, Berry, Goldman, *The Challenge of Democracy*, p. 227.

11 Misztal, *Zagadnienia społecznego uczestnictwa i współdziałania...*, p. 208.

Table 2.4. Models of conventional political participation of Poles (data from 2017) – minimum and maximum percentages of indications for the model and arithmetic mean

Group – the model of participation	Forms of participation in the model	Minimum percentage of indications	Maximum percentage of indications	Arithmetic mean	Percentage of people participating in at least one form from the group
Conventional civic participation – electoral participation	Voting in parliamentary or/and presidential elections		74.1	64.2	
	Voting in local elections				
	Voting in referendums	53.2			
Environmental and social engagement	Discussing politics		39.2	17.7	
	Persuading someone to vote for a specific candidate or cause				
	Expressing beliefs through campaign and political buttons, stickers, or preaching political slogans	3.0			
Contacting politicians – citizen interest in the reception of politics	Communicating with politicians to “get something done”	1.9		5.6	
	Participating in political meetings or/and rallies				
	Participating in public consultations		11.7		

(*continued*)

Table 2.4. Continued

Group – the model of participation	Forms of participation in the model	Minimum percentage of indications	Maximum percentage of indications	Arithmetic mean	Percentage of people participating in at least one form from the group
	Being a member of or forming a political party, social movement, or other political organization, or acting in it now or in the past				
Direct political involvement	Acting to solve problems of local communities (village/town/commune/powiat/region)	1.0	10.3	3.6	
	Participation in the organization of an electoral campaign				
	Being a candidate for a political office (in local governments or parliament)				
	Holding an elective political office or held one in the past, e.g. councilor, village administrator, commune administrator)				
	Organizing financial support for a candidate, organization, or cause				

Source: *Partycypacja polityczna Polaków – nowe wyzwania i formy aktywności* study, 2017, NCN grant 4884, N=1237.

Another relatively widespread model – although it clearly gives way to the first one – is an *environmental and social engagement of a political nature*. This model consists of three participation forms, i.e. discussing politics, persuading someone to vote for a specific candidate or a cause, and expressing beliefs through political buttons, stickers, or preaching political slogans. Which one is more common? In terms of participation form, it is discussing politics with friends. Almost forty percent of Poles usually do so. This would lead us to the conclusion that the second most common model of participation in terms of popularity in Poland is environmental and social engagement. However, the second participation form of this model, namely persuading someone to vote, is spread in a narrower range. One in ten citizens often behaves in such a way. Only a small percentage of people expresses their views through political buttons or stickers. The arithmetic mean for this model would be 17.7 percent.

The environmental and social engagement participation model consists in conducting informal activity[12] among friends, colleagues, neighbors, or immediate and distant family. It is voluntary participation. To some extent, it is incidental. Nevertheless, such participation helps to transmit and spread views on institutions and political events. It may contain elements of pressure inclining to specific behaviors in politics. This is the case with persuading someone to vote for a specific candidate or party. It may, but does not have to, link with direct activity in political life. This kind of participation may accompany political activity, however, there is no reason to claim such participation implies it. Of course, it is an informal kind of participation. We cannot underestimate this sphere of participation. First, precisely because it is quite widespread. Second, because transmitted views and behavioral patterns may shape activity in different spheres of conventional participation, e.g. elections.

As mentioned above, the third most widespread model of participation is *citizen interest in the reception of politics*, which consists in communicating with politicians to "get something done," participating in political meetings or/and rallies, and public consultations.

12 Misztal, *Zagadnienia społecznego uczestnictwa i współdziałania…*, p. 208.

According to the survey, more than one in ten citizens participates or wants to participate in public consultations on various solutions that are proposed by state or local authorities. It is the most often mentioned category in this model. Communicating with politicians to "get something done" is the rarest in this group. Less than two percent of political system participators admit performing such actions.

The arithmetic mean for such forms of participation, i.e. citizen interest in the reception of politics, is 5.6 percent. Engagement in searching and acquiring pieces of information on political topics in the form of meetings with politicians or authority representatives does not mean a literal political activity.

We may describe the fourth most widespread model of conventional participation as *direct political engagement*. We should include the following forms of participation into this group: acting to solve problems of local communities (town/commune/powiat/region), participating in the organization of an election campaign, running for a political office (in local governments, regional council, or parliament), holding an elective political office (e.g. councilor, village administrator, commune administrator), and providing financial support for a candidate, organization, or cause.

This is certainly the character of active participation in an electoral campaign conducted by staffs acting within political parties or established coalitions, or committees established on the occasion of elections. Work aimed at solving local problems is also usually conducted within a political party or other political groups. Local organizations or social movements with varying degrees of formalization also may initiate this kind of activity. Sometimes grassroots activity leads to the creation of a movement, association, or another organization. It does not matter whether it is a formalized structure that motivates citizens to undertake particular activities in a district or municipality or whether it is – initially – spontaneous activity of residents that ultimately leads to the emergence of more formalized structures. All this justifies the thesis that direct political engagement is formalized in most cases. As American political scientists describe it, it is also conventional participation. To describe it in more detail, we may say that it is voluntary participation. However, when applying this notion introduced by Bronisław Misztal, we must state that sometimes it may result from *organizational or associative entanglements.*[13] Membership in a political party or affiliation with some organization may be an example of such entanglements determining a specific type of participation. However, we must also notice that the scope and character of the mentioned entanglements may be different. The very membership in organizations that are or become political does not entail the same requirements or obligations toward all its members. It depends on the function that the citizen performs in a given organization – sometimes members take a less formal role and sometimes it is assigned to them. It would be trivial to claim that all members of a party or other organization are equally or at least comparably active. Apart from common experience, we may find the confirmation of this fact even in a cursory analysis of the described study's results and comparison of some data. As I stated earlier, 2.4 percent of all citizens declares that they participate in the activities of a party, political group, or nationwide organization. However, in none of the listed forms constituting the direct political engagement model of participation – apart from growing engagement in activity for local communities (village/town/commune/powiat/region), in which one in ten citizens participates – does the average of participation level exceed 3.6 percent of the citizens. Of the six forms constituting this participation model, Poles most often choose activities for solving problems in their commune or district. After all, not only members of political parties and organizations may be active in terms of direct political engagement. The fewest people engage in providing financial support for a candidate, organization, or cause. According to the survey, every hundredth citizen does so. The arithmetic mean calculated for the constituent forms of this model is 3.6 percentage points.

If we want to characterize this model of political participation according to levels and scopes of engagement, we may define it as fitting within participation in articulation and representation of groups interests. By taking a relatively permanent character, such a type of engagement may become processual participation – i.e. one that leads to the realization of certain

---

13 Misztal, *Zagadnienia społecznego uczestnictwa i współdziałania…*, p. 208.

objectives – and causes changes at least on a microscale. The expression “by my own actions I mark … my place” reflects the sense of this type of engagement.

A detailed analysis of social determinants for taking up activity and, especially, of the above-average level of engagement in some models of participation leads to some interesting conclusions. Similar environments, groups, and social circles tend to engage in most forms of participation constituting the described models. In practically every participation model, people, who declared their strong interest in politics earlier, exceed the average level of engagement. Also, members of parties and other nationwide organizations are more active in all models of participation, which should not be surprising. In a sense, this type of participation results from associative entanglements, i.e. party affiliation. I present the detailed analysis of social and demographic determinants of conventional participation in Table 2.5.

Table 2.5. Conventional forms of participation of Poles and sociodemographic characteristics

Sociodemographic variables		Conventional forms of political participation often used by respondents							
		Voting in parliamentary or/and presidential elections	Voting in local elections	Voting in referendums	Discussing politics	Participating in public consultations	Persuading someone to vote for a specific candidate or cause	Acting to solve problems of local communities (village/town/ commune/ powiat/region)	Participating in political meetings or/ and rallies
Level of education (recoded question)	primary	73.3	60.0	40.0	30.0	3.3	6.7	6.7	0.0
	vocational	81.2	78.8	62.4	36.5	12.9	8.2	10.6	2.4
	secondary	88.9	82.8	64.0	46.4	15.3	14.6	10.7	5.4
	higher	91.6	85.0	75.8	43.6	12.8	10.6	13.2	4.8
Year of birth (recoded question)	18–34	82.6	73.3	62.1	32.9	10.6	13.7	7.5	3.7
	35–64	88.4	82.8	66.6	42.8	15.3	9.7	12.8	5.0
	65+	94.3	91.0	74.6	57.4	12.3	14.8	13.1	4.1
Hometown population size (recoded question)	village	86.5	83.0	61.4	39.0	15.7	14.3	16.1	3.6
	city	88.9	81.3	70.3	45.5	12.1	10.3	8.7	5.0
Sex	male	89.0	82.5	70.4	49.5	14.8	15.5	14.1	5.5
	female	87.2	81.4	63.8	37.2	12.2	8.3	9.0	3.5

(*continued*)

Table 2.5. Continued

Sociodemographic variables		Conventional forms of political participation often used by respondents							
		Voting in parliamentary or/and presidential elections	Voting in local elections	Voting in referendums	Discussing politics	Participating in public consultations	Persuading someone to vote for a specific candidate or cause	Acting to solve problems of local communities (village/town/commune/powiat/region)	Participating in political meetings or/and rallies
Hometown population size	village or smaller settlement	88.1	83.1	61.3	38.1	17.5	13.8	18.1	1.9
	village at a city's edge	82.5	82.5	61.9	41.3	11.1	15.9	11.1	7.9
	town with fewer than 20,000 inhabitants	88.9	82.7	70.4	45.7	11.1	8.6	11.1	3.7
	town with 20,000 to 100,000 inhabitants	84.0	74.5	60.6	40.4	6.4	5.3	7.4	2.1
	city with 100,000 to 200,000 inhabitants	88.4	76.7	67.4	46.5	11.6	18.6	7.0	0.0
	city with over 200,000 inhabitants	92.0	85.8	76.5	48.1	16.0	11.7	8.6	8.6

Sociodemographic variables		Conventional forms of political participation often used by respondents							
		Voting in parliamentary or/and presidential elections	Voting in local elections	Voting in referendums	Discussing politics	Participating in public consultations	Persuading someone to vote for a specific candidate or cause	Acting to solve problems of local communities (village/town/ commune/ powiat/region)	Participating in political meetings or/ and rallies
Voivodeship	Lower Silesian	86.8	84.2	60.5	42.1	21.1	7.9	13.2	2.6
	Kuyavian-Pomeranian	95.5	95.5	72.7	63.6	13.6	13.6	18.2	4.5
	Lublin	76.5	76.5	47.1	23.5	0.0	17.6	5.9	5.9
	Lubusz	88.2	70.6	64.7	35.3	5.9	5.9	11.8	0.0
	Łódź	89.2	86.3	68.6	38.2	11.8	7.8	8.8	7.8
	Lesser Poland	88.9	86.7	68.9	37.8	13.3	13.3	4.4	4.4
	Mazovian	85.4	77.7	64.6	46.2	12.3	10.0	9.2	4.6
	Opole	100.0	85.7	85.7	28.6	28.6	28.6	14.3	0.0
	Subcarpathian	95.2	81.0	85.7	47.6	23.8	14.3	4.8	9.5
	Podlaskie	78.9	84.2	57.9	57.9	15.8	15.8	26.3	0.0
	Pomeranian	85.7	76.2	71.4	52.4	23.8	14.3	9.5	9.5
	Silesian	85.5	80.3	67.1	42.1	9.2	10.5	7.9	5.3
	Świętokrzyskie	92.3	76.9	69.2	53.8	15.4	15.4	15.4	0.0
	Warmian-Masurian	96.8	90.3	77.4	54.8	22.6	16.1	25.8	0.0
	Greater Poland	90.3	74.2	54.8	32.3	9.7	19.4	9.7	0.0
	West Pomeranian	92.3	84.6	76.9	30.8	7.7	15.4	46.2	0.0

(*continued*)

Table 2.5. Continued

Sociodemographic variables		Conventional forms of political participation often used by respondents							
		Voting in parliamentary or/and presidential elections	Voting in local elections	Voting in referendums	Discussing politics	Participating in public consultations	Persuading someone to vote for a specific candidate or cause	Acting to solve problems of local communities (village/town/ commune/ powiat/region)	Participating in political meetings or/ and rallies
Occupation	management staff	92.4	88.6	79.7	46.8	17.7	17.7	12.7	8.9
	creative professions and specialists with higher education	92.9	82.9	75.7	34.3	8.6	8.6	11.4	5.7
	average staff, trade and service workers	88.0	79.2	64.8	38.4	13.6	11.2	11.2	1.6
	workers	86.4	80.2	58.0	35.8	16.0	8.6	12.3	3.7
	non-working	75.0	66.7	52.4	39.3	10.7	9.5	10.7	4.8
	pensioners	92.0	89.6	71.2	54.6	13.5	13.5	11.0	4.3

Source: *Partycypacja polityczna Polaków – nowe wyzwania i formy aktywności* study, 2017, NCN grant 4884, N=1237.

It is evident that political participation increases with the level of education. Higher or secondary education determines the greater activity of citizens. This happens in almost all of its forms. Moreover, better-educated citizens participate more often in public consultations concerning various significant issues and legislation; this form engages four times more Poles with higher education than people with primary education. Two times more representatives of people with higher education act to solve the problems of local communities. They also tend to participate in political meetings and rallies more often in comparison to all lower education groups.

Conventional participation is rather the domain of middle-aged and older people. Sex differentiates the level of political participation to a little extent. The only difference is that men discuss politics definitely more often.

In terms of how the size of the residence place influences political participation, we can observe the so-called *curvilinear dependence*. In most cases, the most active are, on the one hand, inhabitants of the countryside (perhaps except participation in meetings with politicians), and of large cities, on the other.

It is evident that such factors as material, social, and professional status and using contemporary means of communication strongly influence the level of political participation. Noteworthy, this diversity does not consist in choosing different participation forms and shaping different models; it displays in more often and more common engagement in all or almost all participation models. The scale of participation in different models increases for such groups of citizens as managers, people of high-skill occupations, e.g. lawyers, academics, business owners, wealthy or middle-class people, and people holding higher positions in the company hierarchy. Pensioners declare a high level of political participation – probably due to their status.

Correlation analyses conducted with the use of sophisticated methods and statistical measures also show that in the case of conventional participation, the relationship between participation and the education level of the respondents is particularly strong. The higher the level of education, the greater the tendency to participate, e.g. in referendums ($R=0.213$, $p \leq 0.05$).[14] In this case, we can conclude that the probability of determining

14 See: Annex 7.

particular behavior is high and statistically significant. The obtained result means that the category of education explains about five percent of variance variability in the category of self-government elections. It is a noticeable, although not dominant feature of the model explaining this phenomenon. Noteworthy, holding a political elective office (e.g. councilor, commune administrator, village administrator) is strongly correlated with the size of residence place. In small and medium-sized settlements such declarations are much more common.

In characterizing the four distinguished models of participation, it is worth referring to crucial criteria describing different forms of participation that create these models. Let us recall that there were eleven criteria distinguished. For further analysis, I created two four-point parallel but opposing scales. I formed the scales with the principle of semantic differentiation, where there are opposite terms on both sides, e.g. participation: *formalized* vs. *informal*. On each side of the differential corresponding to the criterion type, the scale has four points indicating the character of participation within a given model: 1 – the smallest degree, 2 – small degree, 3 – average degree, 4 – large degree. The "0" category in the middle of two opposite scales means that it is difficult to clearly define the character of a given participation model. Sometimes, the participation character goes one way and another time – just the opposite. I present the detailed way of qualifying each of the models in the chart.

Chart 2.1. Characteristics of conventional participation — a semantic differential.

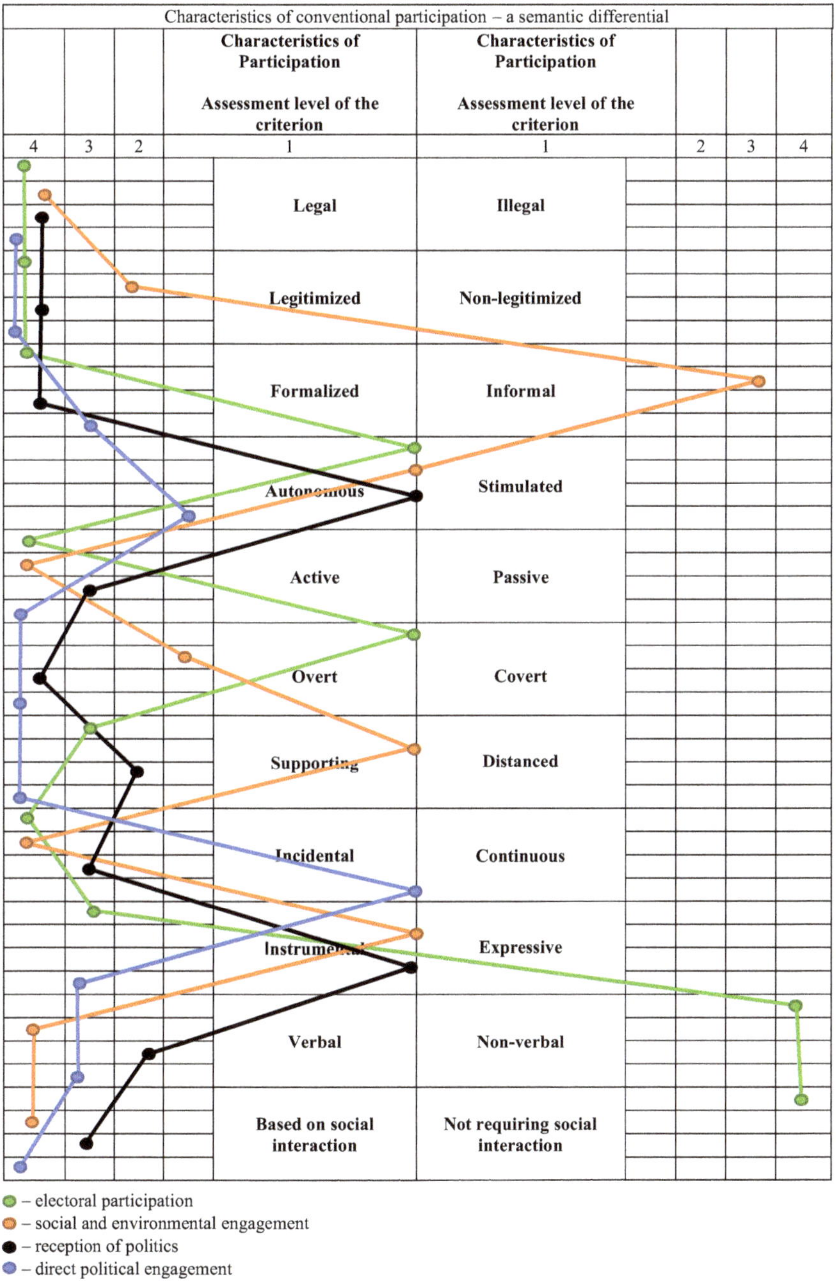

It is not difficult to imagine that most forms of conventional participation involved in the four main models are legal activities and, to a great extent, legitimized participation (electoral participation, reception of politics, direct political engagement); however, it is also legitimized participation in a slightly smaller plane (social and environmental engagement). Besides the latter, we deal with formalized participation. Also, in most situations – which is quite normal in this case – conventional participation forms include active actions and more often incidental ones but based on social interaction.

Nevertheless, there are at least two criteria where the assessment is not so simple. First, the question of to what extent conventional participation is, in general, autonomous or stimulated. There is no straightforward answer in this respect. Both electoral participation and reception of politics may be and is stimulated to some extent. Even social and environmental engagement may be mobilized by certain associative entanglements.

Second, to what extent participation is instrumental or expressive. It would seem that this is an entirely instrumental model, i.e. oriented toward performing tasks and realization of specific objectives. This is generally the case with electoral participation. However, in this situation, we can also notice some symbolic gestures. For example, refusing to participate, boycotting, revealing who did one vote for, etc. In the case of reception of politics, i.e. contacting representatives of authorities, and especially in the case of environmental and social engagement, instrumental and expressive goals clearly intersect.

It is not easy to compare the political participation of citizens of such neighboring countries as Poland and Germany basing on the results of the available studies. This difficulty results, among other things, from different research methods applied on both sides of the border and different political cultures prevailing in both countries. However, the empirical data – in the cases where some indicators are comparable – let us conclude that there are certain similarities but also differences in terms of political participation. Noteworthy, in the studies conducted in Poland, the number of participation forms is greater than the number of categories applied in Germany. In addition, there are differences in response patterns. In Poland, every participation form included the following options for the respondents: I participate "often," "rarely/occasionally," "never." In contrast, the German study included two possible answers: "I participate" or "I do not participate." To compare the indicators from both countries, in the case of the research conducted in Poland, we must combine the "often" category with the "occasionally" category. I present the detailed data in Table 2.6.

Table 2.6. Conventional participation in Poland and Germany

Please consider and provide an answer about:	Name in the language of the researcher / label	Poland			Germany	
		Often	Rarely / occasionally	Never	Participated	Did not participate
Voting in parliamentary or/ and presidential elections	Elections and referendums	74.1	8.5	17.4	*	*
Voting in local elections		65.2	16.1	18.7	86.3	13.7
Voting in referendums		53.2	14.0	32.8	*	*
Discussing politics	Political discussions	39.2	49.5	11.3	*	*
Participating in public consultations	Public consultations	11.7	24.9	63.4	*	*
Persuading someone to vote for a specific candidate or cause	Political agitation	10.8	24.6	64.6	*	*
Acting to solve problems of local communities (village/ town/commune/powiat/ region)	Local activism	10.3	25.7	64.0	*	*
Participating in political meetings or/and rallies	Public gatherings	3.1	18.4	78.5	6.6	93.4
Expressing beliefs through campaign and political buttons, stickers, or preaching political slogans	Symbolic political actions	3.0	11.1	85.9	7.6*	92.4*
Holding an elective political office or held one in the past, e.g. councilor, village administrator, commune administrator)	Acting as a politician in office	3.0	2.1	94.9	*	*

(*continued*)

Table 2.6. Continued

Please consider and provide an answer about:	Name in the language of the researcher / label	Poland			Germany	
		Often	Rarely / occasionally	Never	Participated	Did not participate
Were a candidate for a political position (in local governments, regional council, or parliament)	Use of the passive suffrage	2.7	4.7	92.6	*	*
Being a member of or forming a political party, social movement, or other political organization, or acting in it now or in the past	Party and organizational activity	2.3	6.3	91.4	3.5	96.5
Participation in the organization of an electoral campaign	Supporting political campaigns	2.2	5.4	92.4	3.4	96.6
Communicating with politicians to "get something done"	Lobbying	1.9	12.1	86.0	*	*
Organizing financial support for a candidate, organization, or cause	Donations	1.0	5.9	93.1	5.3	94.7

Sources: *Partycypacja polityczna Polaków – nowe wyzwania i formy aktywności* study, 2017, NCN grant 4884, N=1237; Leibniz Institut für Sozialwissenschaften (2017), N=2112 (implementation method: CAPI).

Both Poles and Germans are most often active in the conventional form of electoral participation. In the Polish study, the questions concerned participation in different types of elections: parliamentary, local, etc. In Germany, the question concerned elections in general. We may suppose that the question meant parliamentary elections (especially that the study was conducted in the year of the Bundestag election). As I mentioned, when comparing the Polish data, we must consider the "often" and "occasionally" categories together. Such an analysis indicates that 82.6 percent of Poles declares frequent or occasional participation in this type of elections. In comparison, in Germany, it is 86.3 percent of citizens. Therefore, the results are similar. Four percentage points more Germans say that they participated or participate in parliamentary elections. Once again, it is worth emphasizing that it is the declared level. This does not mean that people describing their activity in such a way do it regularly.

Next, let us discuss the political participation form called *participating in political meetings or/and rallies*. As the study shows, Poles participate in meetings and rallies three times more often than Germans. In fact, in all cases – besides parliamentary elections – where comparable indicators are available, it turns out that the Polish citizens are more active than the German citizens – at least according to their declaration. Two times more Poles express their beliefs through political buttons, stickers, or preaching political slogans. Participation in political organizations, parties, or groups also is more common in Poland. Moreover, participating in organizing and conducting an election campaign is twice as common in Poland.

To sum up this cycle of analyses on the forms and models of conventional political participation, we must refer to what we hypothesized. The research results allow us to conclude that Poles use various conventional forms of participation in politics. Contrary to popular belief, one can even say that the level of political participation in Poland does not fundamentally differ from what we may observe in the democratic states of Western Europe. Political participation in Poland is similar to the one in Western Europe in terms of its models and the level of activity. The comparison – as far as it is possible in the light of the available data – of political participation level in Poland and Germany may even lead us to the thesis that Poland has a higher level of such participation. However, this similarity to the models functioning in Western democracies may be in fact quite superficial in some respects if we analyze participatory phenomena more thoroughly. The conventional civic model of electoral participation prevails. It is one of the basic models of civic participation in politics; however, it is not particularly complex or sophisticated. Such participation is episodic and to some extent stimulated within the political system. Additionally, the actual turnout in parliamentary and local elections (we do not consider presidential ones) is lower than the declarations show. Therefore, the declaration of frequent participation implies a certain variability. Some citizens participate in one election and then "take a break." Such a situation deepens the already episodic character of this participation model. On the other hand, Poles are relatively active in environmental and social forms of participation. They discuss politics or persuade friends to certain political behaviors more often than the citizens of other countries. It seems that Poles engage a little less in acting to solve the problems of their local community than their Western neighbors; however, this engagement clearly and systematically grows. The model of direct participation in politics, i.e. active, continuous, and aimed at supporting and achieving goals, is not widely spread in Poland. On the other hand, the participatory model consisting in contacting politicians and authority representatives is not so popular but clearly becomes more common due to political conflicts in Poland. Noteworthy, the study in question allowed for capturing the difference between frequent and rare participation in a given form. In many cases, occasional participation occurs in Poland more often than regular or continuous participation. Moreover, one may also encounter passiveness or the symptoms of political apathy. Noteworthy, political participation in Poland becomes strongly conditioned by social, material, and professional status. Social groups that are better-educated, wealthier, and have good jobs participate in politics through all available conventional forms more often and more systematically.

Chapter III. Unconventional participation and participation on the Internet

Social protests and the tendency of the citizens who do not participate in them to tolerate, assent, and sometimes even support different forms of such protests are an inherent and significant aspect of political participation. Participation in politics is not limited only to the expression of support or engagement in public life in its everyday manifestations or scope defined by political institutions. Citizens often use various means for expressing their disapproval or organizing and participating in different forms of protest. Expressing discontent or demands through protest became an immanent feature of contemporary democracies – already in the 1970s, Amitai Etzioni introduced the notion of demonstration democracy,[1] and more than a decade later, Harry Pross wrote about the society of protest (*Protestgesellschaft*).[2] For half a century, numerous scholars and analysts prophesized the twilight of the classical ways of political participation in favor of those related to protest.[3] Simultaneously, we observe a significant increase in the number and intensity of protests around the world in recent years (Global Protest Tracker).

The current development of new electronic media also creates new possibilities for political participation. The study considered many of their forms. The further analysis includes ten forms of non-violent political participation, ten forms of violent unconventional participation, and fourteen selected ways of political activity on the Internet.

3.1. Unconventional forms of participation in politics – applied and accepted in Polish society

Democratic systems anticipate and allow certain forms of social protest. This is the case with **civil disobedience**, i.e. recognizing the actions of

---

1 A. Etzioni, *Demonstration Democracy* (New York: Gordon and Breach, 1977).

2 H. Pross, *Protestgesellschaft* (Munchen: Artemis and Winkler, 1992).

3 R. Inglehart, *The Silent Revolution. Changing Values and Political Styles among Western Publics* (Princeton: Princeton University Press, 1977).

citizens who oppose political authority institutions as possible and sometimes even legitimate.[4] However, it is accepted that such behavior must be justified by social values or interests of social groups or the whole society. Civil disobedience may be considered acceptable if the actions of authorities bring negative consequences or when some political authority violates the adopted rules and accepted conduct norms with its decisions. On the other hand, the scope and acceptable scale of civil disobedience is treated differently. Most political sociologists believe that such cases involve a violation of the binding law. People who organize and participate in acts of social protest believe that political authority is not just or that it violates the binding law in a significant way. Then, a protest becomes socially and – to some extent – politically justified. As J. Rawls stated, "when acting in such a way ... one addresses the sense of justice of the majority of the community..."[5] Some scholars even argue that civil disobedience toward unjust authority may even take the form of a violent protest.[6] In any case, when speaking about various forms of social protest, we must remember that they overstep the limits of conventional political participation to a large extent.

The previous chapter presents different forms and models of conventional participation; however, proportions will be reversed when characterizing various types of social protests. Of course, there are forms of protest that could belong to the conventional category, such as mentioned earlier participation in legally organized demonstrations and protest marches or collecting signatures for petitions. However, most forms of protest are unconventional, e.g. participation in the so-called wild strikes organized contrary to the binding law. All protests that use violence or anticipate it are also unconventional forms of political participation. American political and social scientists believe that such forms of protest include behaviors that deviate from common and accepted customs present in politics and public life. They define unconventional political participation as those behaviors of

---

4 W. E. Scheuerman, "Recent Theories of Civil Disobedience: An Anti-Legal Turn?", in: *Political* Philosophy, 23/4 (2015), pp. 427–449.

5 J. Rawls, *Theory of Justice: Original Edition* (London: The Belknap Press of Harvard University Press, 1971), p. 364.

6 H. Zinn, *Disobedience and Democracy: Nine Fallacies on Law and Order* (Random House Trade Paperbacks, 1968).

citizens that "challenges or defies government channels or the dominant culture (and thus is personally stressful to participants and their opponents)."[7]

Noteworthy, the issue concerning different forms of social protest presented in the subsection title is a significant matter in at least two aspects. First, the very tendency of the citizens to allow for or at least tolerate different behaviors of other groups that go beyond routine forms of political actions that are sanctioned by the law and consistent with the rules of social action in democratic systems. Second, acceptance reaction may be the indicator of possible own behavior in the case when the authorities in the opinion of citizens break certain rules. In this sense, the scope of consent for certain unconventional forms of participation may become a determinant for potential own acceptable behaviors in crises.

Functionalists very clearly described the question of the relationship and proportion between conventional and unconventional participation. They claim that this relationship is a kind of dilemma between civic engagement and social turmoil.[8] The more conventional civic participation, i.e., the more citizens will engage in public activities within institutions and official channels of influence on political decisions, the fewer people engage in unconventional participation. The citizens' low engagement in various forms of conventional political participation – which may result from an ineffective policy pursued by the decision-making body or a lack of trust toward political institutions and parties in general – expands the social tendency to organize protests that go beyond the conventional framework and often involve violence. G. B. Powell even argues that the extent to which the democratic system can engage citizens in electoral activity and other channels of conventional participation proves its effectiveness. If the system does not operate in such a way, it creates a convenient field for protests; protests are both a result and a factor increasing social and political unrest and sometimes lead to the state of turmoil or boiling point in politics. As G. B. Powell claims, "voting and rioting levels are negatively related to each other ... These nations with higher voting turnout have, on average, less rioting, less turmoil of all kinds."[9] Protesters

7 K. Janda, J. M. Berry, and J. Goldman, *The Challenge of Democracy*, p. 227.
8 G. Bingham Powell, *Contemporary Democracies*, p. 132.
9 Bingham Powell, *Contemporary Democracies*, p. 132.

should not use violence. The above description of the rules is a clear attempt to legitimize unconventional forms of protest in certain cases. Or at least some of them, i.e. those that do not involve violence and are appropriate to the situation approached by the citizens. Therefore, we come to another crucial issue, i.e. the **legitimization** of unconventional forms of social protest. In other words, we return to the problem of accepting social protests; in this case, those that are unconventional from the point of view of mode or the level of social acceptance that would, in a sense, legalize them. Citizens may accept different forms of protest without considering the opinions of politicians, experts, or scholars. The level of consent to organize certain varieties of unconventional participation determines the emergence of such social consent to these forms. There is no doubt that if at least half of the country's citizens accept certain forms of protest, they gain social approval. Of course, if they fulfill certain conditions. As mentioned above, we may define such a level of acceptance as the **threshold of the legitimization of unconventional behavior**.

The study, the results of which are the main empirical basis of this book, contains two sets of questions concerning forms of non-violent unconventional participation that Poles engage in, forms of such social protests that they accept, and forms of non-violent unconventional participation that they are willing to accept.

The first set of questions contains ten forms of non-violent unconventional participation:

- Signing petitions /Petition campaign I/,
- Collecting signatures for petitions /Petition campaign II/,
- Participation in organization of legal political demonstrations or marches /demonstrations, marches, pickets/,
- Participation in or organization of political demonstrations and illegal marches,
- Participation in a legal strike,
- Participation in an illegal strike,
- Ridiculing and joking about politicians and politics in public space / political practical jokes, Cacareco votes/,
- Participating in or organizing a boycott,
- Violating laws consciously in the act of protest (civil disobedience),
- Creating alternative political institutions or being a member of such an institution.

Participants of the survey answered whether and how often they participated in such forms of protest. Next, participants specified whether they uncritically accept, conditionally accept, or do not accept under any conditions such forms of participation.

Three kinds of protests received the highest number of indications. These include: signing petitions, ridiculing and joking about politicians and politics in public space, and participating in legal strikes. Noteworthy, declarations of frequent performance of such forms of protest reach the highest rate of fourteen to fifteen percent. It is a quite high percentage. According to declarations, a much smaller group of 3.1 percent often participates in legal strikes. It is thought-provoking that 2.5 percent of the surveyed participate in legal demonstrations. Apparently, the situation in this regard changes due to the aggravation of political conflicts in Poland after 2017.[10] I present the detailed data in Table 3.1.

Six forms of unconventional political participation received the highest level of acceptance. Uncritical acceptance and conditional acceptance apply to: signing petitions and legal strikes – more than eighty percent of indications, legal demonstrations – eighty percent, organizing actions and collecting signatures for petitions – nearly eighty percent, creating alternative political institutions and/or supporting them – sixty percent, and finally, ridiculing politicians – fifty-seven percent. Noteworthy, in all the cases the majority of citizens accept these forms under certain conditions or in certain situations. All these forms are legal and allowed for in Polish law.

We may conclude that the six mentioned forms **exceed the threshold of legitimization** due to the level of social acceptance. In fact, these are behaviors that to some extent take conventional nature.

---

10 The dispute over the judiciary system in Poland and its independence, the so-called Independence Marches, legalized but often ending in clashes with the police due to the aggressive behavior of some radical participants, the protests concerning the attempts to narrow the already restrictive (in comparison to other European countries) abortion law at the end of 2020, and also less spectacular, and therefore less discussed by the media, protests of entrepreneurs.

Table 3.1. Unconventional forms of non-violent political participation performed and accepted by Poles

Please consider and answer whether you:	Name in the language of the researcher / label	Often	Uncritically accept	Accept under certain conditions or in certain situations	Do not accept under any conditions
Sign petitions	*Petition campaign I*	15.4	24.9	56.2	18.8
Ridicule and joke about politicians and politics in public space	"Orange" participation (*political practical jokes, Cacareco votes*)	14.3	20.5	36.7	42.9
Participate in legal strikes	Strikes	3.1	38.0	43.3	18.7
Participate in wild (illegal) strikes		0.2	6.4	35.0	58.6
Participate in or organize legal political demonstrations, marches	Demonstrations, marches, pickets	2.5	33.7	46.3	20.1
Participate in or organize illegal political demonstrations, marches		0.4	8.3	33.8	57.9
Collect signatures for petitions	*Petition campaign II*	2.3	27.6	51.1	21.3
Create alternative political institutions or support existing ones	Duplicating existing political institutions	1.9	18.5	44.5	37.1
Violate the law in protests (civil disobedience)	Civil disobedience	0.9	3.6	31.8	64.6

Table 3.1. Continued

Please consider and answer whether you:	Name in the language of the researcher / label	Often	Uncritically accept	Accept under certain conditions or in certain situations	Do not accept under any conditions
Participate in or organize boycotts	Boycotts	0.6	7.9	34.0	58.1

Source: *Partycypacja polityczna Polaków – nowe wyzwania i formy aktywności* study, 2017, NCN grant 4884, N=1237.

Besides the threshold of legitimization, we may also develop another indicator of social acceptance level. In the empirical sense, a percentage of indications exceeding thirty percent but not exceeding fifty percent may constitute such a level. Then the possible support does not have the approval of half of the citizens, but a significant part of them is ready to allow for such behavior. We may specify this as the **category of actions acceptable in a wider social scope**, providing that some certain conditions or circumstances justify the use of such methods. In other words, we may call this level of acceptance the **threshold of social acceptance.**

From the list of ten forms of social protest used in the study, there were four forms of action (as shown in the table) that ranged from more than thirty percent to less than fifty. Thus, all forms reached the level of social acceptability; however, these are, in principle, non-violent forms.

A comparison of 2002 and 2017 data on the acceptance of non-violent unconventional forms of political participation (Table 3.2.) may be thought-provoking.

Table 3.2. Non-violent unconventional forms of political participation performed and accepted by Poles – a comparison of results from 2002 and 2017

Please consider and answer whether you:	Name in the language of the researcher / label	Acceptance level (data from 2002)	Acceptance level (data from 2017)
Sign petitions	*Petition campaign I*	86.7	88.2
Ridicule and joke about politicians and politics in public space	"Orange" participation (*political practical jokes, Cacareco votes*)	*	61.0
Participate in legal strikes	Strikes	77.3	86.6
Participate in wild (illegal) strikes		23.3	44.4
Participate in or organize legal political demonstrations, marches	Demonstrations, marches, pickets	80.3	83.7
Participate in or organize illegal political demonstrations, marches		36.1	46.4
Collect signatures for petitions	*Petition campaign II*	*	84.9
Create alternative political institutions or support existing ones	Duplicating existing political institutions	*	68.5
Violate the law in protests (civil disobedience)	Civil disobedience	18.2	38.5
Participate in or organize boycotts	Boycotts	54.5	46.4

* no data for 2002.
Source: *Partycypacja polityczna Polaków – nowe wyzwania i formy aktywności* study, 2017, NCN grant 4884, N=1237.

Such a form of participation as signing petitions is on a similar level. Both in 2002 and 2017, groups of citizens numbering well above eighty percent were willing to accept such an activity.

In the 2002 study, there was no such category as "ridiculing and joking about politicians in public space;" currently, this rate exceeds sixty percent. This phenomenon occurred at least due to two reasons. First, the prestige of being a politician has decreased. Second, the political dispute among opposite political sides and the supporters of the main parties has intensified. Those are also almost certain reasons for the greater acceptance of most forms of non-violent participation such as legal and wild strikes, demonstrations, marches, pickets, attempts to duplicate the existing political institutions, or civic disobedience. In some cases (e.g. acceptance of illegal strikes) the increase of the acceptance level is almost double. Only in the case of boycotts, the acceptance decreased by eight percent.

In general, the comparison of these studies' results indicates that the acceptance for applying non-violent unconventional forms of protest in Poland has increased. Also, the potential tendency of the citizens to participate in such forms of protest is greater.

In the case of non-violent unconventional forms of participation, which gained a high level of acceptance (above eighty percent of the surveyed uncritically or conditionally accepts them), the analysis of correlations with demographic characteristics does not provide information about the existence of significant dependencies on the sociodemographic characteristics of the respondents. People with a higher social status, i.e. citizens with higher education, specialists, people of creative professions – in other words, the middle class – are a little more inclined to consider such forms as signing petitions or participating in legal demonstrations as acceptable. Inhabitants of big cities and the villages on the outskirts of cities are willing to accept legally conveyed strikes. Men accept ridiculing and joking about politicians and politics in public space three times more often than women.

The second set of questions concerned the level of violent unconventional forms acceptance. Noteworthy, there are different definitions of violence. As D. Mider notices in his book *Polacy wobec przemocy politycznej*, this notion "considered a pathology in the moral, social, and legal sense, until recently was taboo and was placed on the outskirts of scientific reflection."[11] The research project in question used "observational" ("...every use of physical force or threat to use it – potential use")[12] and "dualistic" (indicating that physical or mental harm may be the result) definitions as the set point.

Max Kaase and Alan Marsh were one of the first ones to perform an empirical, quantitative study on the phenomenon of political violence. Kaase and Marsh created a classification of violent participation forms as part of the project *Political Action Study* (*Political Action Survey*). Kaase and Marsh's work was a comparative study conducted between 1973 and 1981 in seven Western European countries. Among various policy-influencing actions, Kaase and Marsh indicated a group of "elite-challenging" people.[13] It is difficult to directly ask questions about the frequency of taking unconventional actions due to the belief that they can meet with potential reluctance on the part of the surveyed before admitting such an activity.

The presented study conducted in Poland in 2017 and 2018 raised the question about the acceptance level of violent unconventional forms of participation. Among other things, the study asked for nine such forms:

- Taking a hunger strike;
- Self-harm, suicide (e.g. self-immolation);
- Insulting (shouting, writing signs insulting dignity);
- Threatening with violence;
- Occupation of office;
- Blocking communication paths (passive);
- Destruction of public property of little value by a mob or organized group (e.g. garbage bins, road signs, or plaques);
- Destruction of public property of big value by a mob or organized group (e.g. vandalizing or robbing the offices of authorities, setting officials' cars on fire);
- Fighting with officers (police, army) in a mob or organized group.

11 D. Mider, *Polacy wobec przemocy politycznej: studium typów postaw i ocen moralnych* (Warszawa: Dom Wydawniczy Elipsa, 2017), pp. 19–20.
12 D. Mider, *Polacy wobec przemocy politycznej*, p. 33.
13 S. Barnes, M. Kasse, *Political Action: Mass Participation in Five Western Democracies* (London: Sage Publications, 1979).

To assess the level of individual forms of violent political participation, three categories of answers were used: "I uncritically accept," "I accept under certain conditions or in certain situations," and "I do not accept under any conditions."

I present the detailed data in Table 3.3.

Four forms of this type of protest received more than four percent of indications in the category "I uncritically accept." Those are: taking a hunger strike, occupying an office or other object, destroying own property (eg. burning one's own house), and blocking communication paths. We may describe the support for the other forms as scant. It oscillates around one percent except for self-destructive forms such as self-harm or suicide (e.g. self-immolation) which are uncritically accepted by a group of 1.6 percent.

Table 3.3. Violent unconventional forms of political participation accepted by Poles

From a moral point of view, according to your sense of right and wrong, do you or do you not accept the following ways of influencing politics?	Name in the language of the researcher / label	Uncritically accept	Accept under certain conditions or in certain situations	Do not accept under any conditions
Taking a hunger strike	Self-destructive violence	10.7	37.1	52.2
Occupation of office	Riots	6.7	39.3	54.0
Destruction of own property (e.g. burning one's own house)	Self-destructive violence	4.6	5.1	90.3
Blocking communication paths (passive)	Riots	4.2	32.7	63.1
Self-harm, suicide (e.g. self-immolation)	Self-destructive violence	1.6	3.4	95.0

(*continued*)

Table 3.3. Continued

From a moral point of view, according to your sense of right and wrong, do you or do you not accept the following ways of influencing politics?	Name in the language of the researcher / label	Uncritically accept	Accept under certain conditions or in certain situations	Do not accept under any conditions
Fighting with officers (police, army) in a mob or organized group	Riots	0.9	17.1	82.0
Intimidation with violence	Verbal and para-verbal violence (threats and intimidation)	0.8	5.1	94.1
Insulting (shouting, writing, insulting, depriving of dignity)	Verbal violence (threats and intimidation)	0.7	11.4	87.9
Destructing public property of little value by a mob or organized group (e.g. garbage bins, road signs, or plaques)	Riots	0.4	3.5	96.1
Destruction of public property of big value by a mob or organized group (e.g. vandalizing or robbing the offices of authorities, setting officials' cars on fire)	Riots	0.3	0.4	99.3

Source: *Partycypacja polityczna Polaków – nowe wyzwania i formy aktywności* study, 2017, NCN grant 4884, N=1237.

It is worth combining the categories "I uncritically accept" and "I accept under certain conditions or in certain situations," as was the case with other forms of participation. Then, it becomes obvious that the three violent forms of political participation get the greatest acceptance or even approval of the study participants. For example, taking a hunger strike. After combining the two categories of responses, it is clear that 47.8 percent of the respondents accept this form. Another form with the highest level of acceptance is the occupation of authorities' offices and facilities. Forty-six percent of the surveyed accept such a form of political participation. The third form with the highest rate of acceptance is blocking communication paths. 36.9 percent of the study participants are willing to accept this form uncritically or (mostly) under certain conditions.

The above data show that the level of acceptance for violent unconventional activities is quite high in Poland. On the other hand, the most accepted forms of violent participation are not the most radical ones in the set. None of the most accepted forms of political participation exceeds the threshold of legitimization, but they are above the threshold of social acceptance.

Moreover, it is worthwhile to analyze the declarations on forms of participation and see how are they similar. In relation to Table 3.3, it will be a comparison and vertical analysis. As we see, a group of different forms of self-destruction gained most indications (among other things, hunger strike, destruction of own property, self-immolation, etc.). 16.9 percent of the citizens are willing to accept it uncritically.

The second category is the acceptance of various forms of riots, e.g. occupying offices or blocking roads. In total, more than twelve percent of Poles are willing to accept such forms.

It is worth comparing whether and how the acceptance of violent unconventional political participation has changed over the past fifteen years. Data for comparative analysis are provided in Table 3.4.

Table 3.4. Violent unconventional forms of political participation accepted by Poles (comparison)

From a moral point of view, according to your sense of right and wrong, do you or do you not accept the following ways of influencing politics?	Name in the language of the researcher / label	I uncritically accept (data from 2002)	I uncritically accept (data from 2017)
Taking a hunger strike	Self-destructive violence	*	10.7
Occupation of office	Riots	20.1	6.7
Destruction of own property (e.g. burning one's own house)	Self-destructive violence	*	4.6
Blocking communication paths (passive)	Riots	14.5	4.2
Self-harm, suicide (e.g. self-immolation)	Self-destructive violence	*	1.6
Fighting with officers (police, army) in a mob or organized group	Riots	20.1	0.9
Intimidation with violence	Verbal and para-verbal violence (threats and intimidation)	*	0.8
Insulting (shouting, writing signs insulting dignity)	Verbal violence (threats and intimidation)	7.0	0.7
Destructing public property of little value by a mob or organized group (e.g. garbage bins, road signs, or plaques)	Riots	2.4	0.4
Destruction of public property of big value by a mob or organized group (e.g. vandalizing or robbing the offices of authorities, setting officials' cars on fire)	Riots	4.1	0.3

*no data available for 2002.
Source: *Partycypacja polityczna Polaków – nowe wyzwania i formy aktywności* study, 2017, NCN grant 4884, N=1237.

The comparative analysis of the 2002 and 2017 studies shows that in the category of uncritical acceptance, the acceptance of violent unconventional forms of participation has clearly decreased for virtually all forms.

It is worth looking at these results in holistic categories – what do we observe from synthetic analyzes that consider various indicators – and, at the same time, their overall dimension.

Potentially greatest public support is for forms of unconventional protest which we may describe as legal and which, although unconventional, may be considered non-controversial in the public reception. The arithmetic mean for the acceptance of such protest forms exceeds eighty-five percent and the percentage of people accepting at least one of them is more than ninety percent. The surveyed most strongly accept the form of signing petitions. I present the detailed data in Table 3.5.

Table 3.5. The scope of Poles' acceptance for social protest forms (data from 2017)

The group of protest forms – the model of unconventional participation	Forms of group protest	Minimum percentage of indications	Maximum percentage of indications	Arithmetic mean	Percentage of people accepting at least one form in the group
Legal, non-controversial	Signing petitions		88.2	86.2	96.5
	Participating in or organizing legal political demonstrations, marches	83.7			
	Participating in legal strikes				
Legal, controversial	Organizing or participating in boycotts	46.4	46.4	46.4	46.4
Unconventional, illegal, and non-violent	Participating in or organizing illegal political demonstrations, marches		46.4	45.4	57.4
	Participating in wild (illegal) strikes	44.4			
	Refusing to pay taxes or other compulsory charges*	-	-		
	Writing inscriptions on the walls*	-	-		
Unconventional, illegal, and violent	Occupation of office		49.9	28.0	61.4
	Blocking communication paths (passive)				
	Fighting with officers (police, army) in a mob or organized group				
	Destructing public property of little value by a mob or organized group (e.g. garbage bins, road signs, or plaques)	3.5			

Source: *Partycypacja polityczna Polaków – nowe wyzwania i formy aktywności* study, 2017, NCN grant 4884, N=1237.

The broad category of boycott is a form of unconventional legal political participation, although it may be considered a controversial one. It does not exceed fifty percent in terms of the acceptance threshold. Therefore, we may not claim that it reaches or exceeds the legitimization threshold; however, it definitely exceeds the social acceptance threshold.

The third model of unconventional political participation is non-violent illegal participation; among other things, it includes such forms as participation in, and even more so organization of illegal demonstrations, or participation in wild strikes, etc. The acceptance of such participation forms usually exceeds forty percent of the surveyed population. The arithmetic mean constituted over forty-five percent.

The fourth model is unconventional illegal participation. The last group of protest forms is a model that we must define as unconventional and illegal, and, at the same time, involving or causing violence. Those are, e.g., such forms of participation as the occupation of offices or blocking communication paths. The arithmetic mean for acceptance of such forms of activity is twenty-eight percent. The most accepted form is the occupation of offices. 61.4 percent of the respondents are ready to support at least one of the listed forms of unconventional, illegal, and violent participation.

In characterizing the four distinguished models of participation, it is worth referring to crucial criteria describing different forms of participation that create these models. Let us recall, that there were eleven criteria distinguished. For further analysis (as was the case with conventional participation), I created two four-point parallel but opposing scales. I formed the scales with the principle of semantic differentiation, where there are opposite terms on both sides, e.g. participation: legitimized vs. non-legitimized. On each side of the differential corresponding to the type of criterion – in accordance with what was the case with conventional participation – the scale had four points specifying the nature of participation within the given model. I present the detailed way of qualifying each of the models in the chart.

Chart 3.1. Characteristics of non-violent unconventional participation – a semantic differential

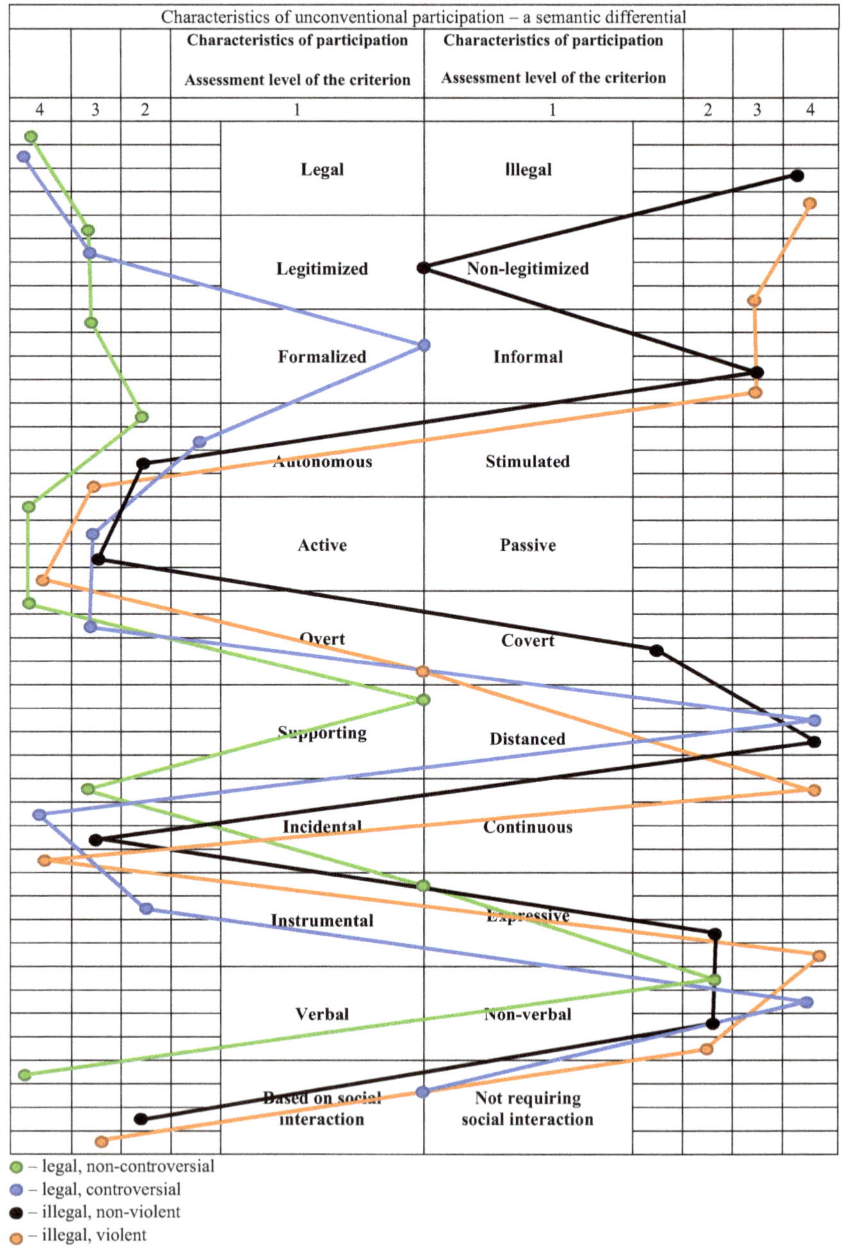

Obviously, the characteristics of unconventional participation and the semantic differential developed on its basis differs from the one developed for models and forms of conventional participation. First, when describing different varieties of unconventional participation, we must remember about a much greater variety of forms and their description. The qualification categories of particular models are highly diversified. In fact, the differences apply to all models of participation: unconventional, legal non-controversial, legal controversial, non-violent illegal, or violent illegal.

It is relatively easy to describe the latter one. It is surely illegal, rather non-legitimized (although a small group is willing to accept it), informal, expressive, rather than instrumental (because it rather does not have a positive effect on its organizers, contrary to their expectations), distanced from the system, and usually non-verbal kind of participation.

On the other hand, unconventional, legal, and non-controversial participation may be the opposite of this. It is – as the name implies – legal. Research shows that it is socially legitimized. It is autonomous, active, and overt. This kind of participation is also rather instrumental, i.e. oriented toward practical effects, although it is also non-verbal to a great extent.

In general, we may state that in Poland, the potential tendency to accept any unconventional forms of protest is relatively big. If we put together both models of unconventional protest, i.e., non-violent and violent, it will turn out that more than ninety percent of citizens are willing to accept at least one form of protest from such a broad group. Noteworthy, usually, non-violent unconventional forms may get the most social acceptance and justification. Regarding these forms and this model of protest, the acceptance of them in Poland increased in recent years. On the other hand, the tendency to accept violent political participation clearly decreases.

The analysis of the social determinants of social protest forms acceptance leads to conclusions different from those previously discovered in the area of conventional participation. While people with a strong interest in politics displayed a tendency to be more active in most conventional forms of political participation, in the case of accepting different activities related to social protest, which we may describe as unconventional participation, people with less interest in politics exceed the average level. In the case of unconventional, illegal, and violent protests, the greatest support was among people completely uninterested in politics. Moreover, individual in-depth interviews conducted in 2018 after quantitative studies as part of the research triangulation also confirm this. The interviews served to complement the obtained results and helped to learn the way of thinking of the surveyed citizens. Assuming that at least some of the people who declare their acceptance for certain forms of protest are ready to participate in them, we may suppose that people who are not interested in politics are more likely than others to support or participate in the most radical forms of protest in a situation threatening their interests. This would be an empirical confirmation of G. B. Powell's theory suggesting that the more conventional participation – e.g., electoral – and interest in politics, the less the tendency to participate in riots and other kinds of social unrest.[14]

In general, we may assume that the Poles display a rather high tendency to accept different forms of social protest. Not only conventional forms of protest may anticipate high social legitimization. Non-controversial and unconventional forms obtain a very high level of acceptance oscillating around seventy percent. The citizens also may understand non-violent and unconventional forms of social protest. Those forms reach the threshold of social acceptance as long as they occur due to issues that are significant to the community. In terms of possible acceptance, the most radical forms of unconventional, illegal, and violent protests obtained the lowest rates. However, in this case, almost half of the respondents are willing to accept one of such forms (occupation of public buildings) under certain conditions.

3.2. Political participation on the Internet

The role of the Internet in political communication dynamically increased in the second decade of the twentieth-first century; also, new mechanisms of participation emerged. From the perspective of political participation and communication on the Internet, the technical possibilities are now enormous and will become even greater. New forms, tools, and instruments for communication in new media emerge.

For example, from an information recipient, a citizen may become its sender. Some kind of "social memory"[15] has formed – it is difficult to hide

14 G. Bingham Powell, *Contemporary Democracies*.

15 J. Garlicki, "Kultura polityczna polskich internautów," *Studia politologiczne*, 21 (2011), p. 302.

information. Noteworthy, social media became the new source of political participation and they develop dynamically. D. Mider describes this phenomenon in detail.[16] Such processes also occurred in Poland. Internet access in Poland in 2017 was on the level of seventy-six percent,[17] i.e., seventy-six percent of households could use it.

Therefore, there emerged a study aiming to explore the development of online forms of political participation.

The study described the citizens' online political participation with the following fourteen forms:

1. Do you seek political content on the Internet (if necessary, explain that you mean communication channels such as information websites, citizen journalism websites, social networks, encyclopedia websites, social content aggregators, traditional websites, blogs, microblogs, discussion forums, chats/IRC, discussion groups, USENET)?
2. Do you perform actions such as liking/disliking/subscribing/giving pluses or minuses (if necessary, explain that you mean symbolic expression of acceptance or lack of acceptance for posted content with likes/dislikes/subs/pluses/minuses, etc.)?
3. Do you share information, links, memes, articles, commentaries, presentations, and other content on social media?
4. Do you comment on the content found on the Internet?
5. Do you participate in discussions (forums, discussion groups, chats, e-mails)?
6. Do you collectively comment or ridicule other users, politics, or politicians?
7. Do you persuade others to act on or off the Internet?
8. Do you donate to political movements, parties, and ventures via the Internet?
9. Do you create memes?
10. Do you create videos or recordings?
11. Do you write a blog, microblog, social media account, website, YouTube channel, discussion forum, or group?
12. Do you write and publish articles?

16 D. Mider, *Partycypacja polityczna w Internecie.*
17 https://datacommons.org/place/country/POL?topic=Economics

13. Do you participate in virtual sit-ins?
14. Do you participate in theft and the disclosure of data or acts of content destroying?

As the study shows, there are four types of most widespread and frequently performed political activity. These are: browsing the Internet for political content, expressing approval or disapproval toward posted content or posts (with likes/dislikes), commenting on the content found on the Internet, and sharing commentaries, presentations, links, memes, and other content in social media. All these forms received over five percent of indications. The simplest form, i.e. browsing the Internet for political content received the most indications. Over a quarter of the surveyed use this form of online participation. Browsing the Internet for political content consists in viewing information websites, citizen journalism websites, social networks, encyclopedia websites, social content aggregators, traditional websites, blogs, microblogs, discussion forums, and chats. I present the detailed data in Table 3.6.

Table 3.6. Forms of political participation on the Internet

Please consider and answer:	Name in the language of the researcher / label	Often	Rarely	Never
Do you seek political content on the Internet (if necessary, explain that you mean communication channels such as information websites, citizen journalism websites, social networks, encyclopedia websites, social content aggregators, traditional websites, blogs, microblogs, discussion forums, chats/IRC, discussion groups, USENET)?	Interest in politics on the Internet	25.8	33.4	40.8
Do you perform actions such as liking/disliking/subscribing/giving pluses or minuses (if necessary, explain that you mean symbolic expression of acceptance or lack of acceptance for posted content with likes/dislikes/subs/pluses/minuses, etc.)?	Commenting on politics on the Internet	8.2	17.9	73.9

Table 3.6. Continued

Please consider and answer:	Name in the language of the researcher / label	Often	Rarely	Never
Do you comment on the content found on the Internet?	Commenting on politics on the Internet	6.8	18.9	74.3
Do you share information, links, memes, articles, commentaries, presentations, and other content on social media?	Interest in politics on the Internet	5.4	16.9	77.7
Do you participate in discussions (forums, discussion groups, chats, e-mails)?	Interest in politics on the Internet	4.1	11.5	84.4
Do you collectively comment or ridicule other users, politics, or politicians?	Commenting on politics on the Internet	2.0	8.4	89.6
Do you participate in virtual sit-ins?	Spreading information on the Internet	1.4	4.4	94.2
Do you write a blog, microblog, social media account, website, YouTube channel, discussion forum, or group?	Spreading information on the Internet	0.8	2.1	97.1
Do you persuade others to act on or off the Internet?	Interest in politics on the Internet	0.7	6.0	93.3
Do you donate to political movements, parties, and ventures via the Internet?	Spreading information on the Internet	0.6	3.6	95.8
Do you write and publish articles?	Spreading information on the Internet	0.5	2.5	97.0
Do you create memes?		0.4	1.5	98.1
Do you create videos or recordings?	Spreading information on the Internet	0.3	2.3	97.4
Do you participate in theft and the disclosure of data or acts of content destroying?	Spreading information on the Internet	0.1	0.4	99.5

Source: *Partycypacja polityczna Polaków – nowe wyzwania i formy aktywności* study, 2017, NCN grant 4884, N=1237.

If we were to merge the "often" and "rarely" categories in our analysis, these online participation forms would receive from twenty percent in the case of sharing links and sending memes to nearly sixty percent in the case of browsing the Internet for political content.

As in the previous chapter, it is worthwhile to compare the data concerning online participation in Poland and Germany. We also must revise two remarks. First, the questionnaires of the Polish study were broader than those applied in Germany. Therefore, we may not compare all the forms. Second, German citizens were asked whether at all they participated in such forms or not. Poles were also asked about the frequency of their participation. In other words, whether they are active often or rather occasionally. Thus, for comparison, we must merge the data from Poland into one category, i.e. "I participate." I present the detailed data in Table 3.7.

Table 3.7. Forms of participation on the Internet. Poland vs Germany

Please consider and answer:	Name in the language of the researcher / label	Poland			Germany	
		Often	Rarely / occasionally	Never	Participated	Did not participate
Do you seek political content on the Internet (if necessary, explain that you mean communication channels such as information websites, citizen journalism websites, social networks, encyclopedia websites, social content aggregators, traditional websites, blogs, microblogs, discussion forums, chats/IRS, discussion groups, USENET)?	Interest in politics on the Internet	25.8	33.4	40.8	*	*
Do you perform actions such as liking/disliking/subscribing/giving pluses or minuses (if necessary, explain that you mean symbolic expression of acceptance or lack of acceptance for posted content with likes/dislikes/subs/pluses/minuses, etc.)?	Commenting on politics on the Internet	8.2	17.9	73.9	17.0	83.0
Do you comment on the content found on the Internet?	Commenting on politics on the Internet	6.8	18.9	74.3	6.2	93.8
Do you share information, links, memes, articles, commentaries, presentations, and other content on social media?	Interest in politics on the Internet	5.4	16.9	77.7	14.2	85.8

(*continued*)

Table 3.7. Continued

Please consider and answer:	Name in the language of the researcher / label	Poland			Germany	
		Often	Rarely / occasionally	Never	Participated	Did not participate
Do you participate in discussions (forums, discussion groups, chats, e-mails)?	Interest in politics on the Internet	4.1	11.5	84.4	4.2	95.8
Do you collectively comment or ridicule other users, politics, or politicians?	Commenting on politics on the Internet	2.0	8.4	89.6	*	*
Do you participate in virtual sit-ins?	Spreading information on the Internet	1.4	4.4	94.2	24.7**	75.3**
Do you write a blog, microblog, social media account, website, YouTube channel, discussion forum, or group?	Spreading information on the Internet	0.8	2.1	97.1	0.9	99.1
Do you persuade others to act on or off the Internet?	Interest in politics on the Internet	0.7	6.0	93.3	*	*
Do you donate to political movements, parties, and ventures via the Internet?	Spreading information on the Internet	0.6	3.6	95.8	*	*

Please consider and answer:	Name in the language of the researcher / label	Poland			Germany	
		Often	Rarely / occasionally	Never	Participated	Did not participate
Do you write and publish articles?	Spreading information on the Internet	0.5	2.5	97.0	2.2	97.8
Do you create memes?		0.4	1.5	98.1	*	*
Do you create videos or recordings?	Spreading information on the Internet	0.3	2.3	97.4	*	*
Do you participate in theft and the disclosure of data or acts of content destroying?	Spreading information on the Internet	0.1	0.4	99.5	*	*

** in the study conducted for Germany it is only a form of offline participation / no data on online participation
Sources: *Partycypacja polityczna Polaków – nowe wyzwania i formy aktywności* study, 2017, NCN grant 4884, N=1237; Leibniz Institut für Sozialwissenschaften (2017), N=2112 (study conducted on 25/09/2017–30/11/2017).

It is clear that the Poles are more active than the Germans. An especially significant difference occurs in commenting on the content found online. Almost seven percent of Poles do so.

In total, more than a quarter participate in politics in such a way. On the other hand, in Germany, 6.2 percent of the recipients declare participation in this form. The second form in which the Poles excel Germans – by almost four times – is participating in forum, group, or chat discussions (15.6 and 4.2 percent). Moreover, Poles also eagerly share memes, articles, commentaries, presentations, links, and other content on their social media. Almost twenty percent of the surveyed declare such an activity. Poles run microblogs and publish articles more often than the Germans (currently, this trend moves toward posting vlogs via YouTube).

The question of how will the development of electronic media, called until recently new, change political participation and whether politicians and regular Internet users keep up with these changes is disputable.[18] In terms of predicting the future of political participation on the Internet, even Internet users do not comply. Many approaches emerged in the discussion on this subject; however, the conviction about growing possibilities and a cautious prediction on the possibility of using them, and the perception of different barriers gained the greatest support. Such conclusions come to mind after analyzing focus group interviews that preceded the quantitative study. It seems that the development of the Internet's role in politics will proceed, at least for now, according to the scenario called technorealism.[19] This means that people who are active in various areas of social life, including politics, and who use the Internet will have greater and better opportunities to obtain and create information on political topics.[20] The possibilities of the Internet will not tempt people who are inactive and uninterested in politics to become interested in and participate in it. Besides, still, some part of the citizens do not use the Internet. We may call them a digital marginalization group. It is possible that the scenario

18 B. Dobek-Ostrowska, J. Garlicki, *Political Communication in the Era of New Technologies*, (Warszawa: Peter Lang, 2013), pp. 11–27.

19 Wilhelm, 2000, pp. 14–24.

20 J. Garlicki, "Dynamika kultury politycznej i partycypacji politycznej internautów w Polsce," *Studia Politologiczne*, 26 (2012), pp. 38–19.

of technological disorientation will fulfill because the phenomenon of fake news generates serious political threats. This phenomenon is significant because there are numerous top-bottom and institutionalized attempts to prevent fake news from spreading; people speak of global “information disorder.”[21] As the research shows, political parties and governments spent over half a billion dollars for disinformation campaigns in the past decade; moreover, manipulating information in social media became a professional and well-financed sector.[22]

Poles are not apolitical. After the period of revival and growth of interest in politics at the beginning of the transition process, there was a time when Poles lost their interest. However, now we may observe another growth in terms of interest in politics. This is partially due to rough political disputes. In general, citizens use such sources of political information as the national media. The role of media in Poland has recently significantly increased. This applies especially to electronic media, particularly television. The Internet and social media become more and more popular.

Poles engage in actions aimed at influencing political decisions.

The acceptance of civil disobedience reaches a quite high level in Poland. However, in comparison with the attitudes at the beginning of the century, the level of acceptance decreased. Poles are willing to allow for various social protests of unconventional participation character. Some forms of protest become socially legitimized. Also, we may notice a trend (particularly visible among the young and middle-aged generations) in the Polish society to perceive politics in pragmatical and rational categories; in other words, in the category of the effect reached ad hoc. This is a phenomenon that not only normalizes civil disobedience but also – potentially – violent political actions.[23] As shown, when more than half of the citizens accept

---

21 C. Wardle, H. Derakshan, *Information Disorder Toward an interdisciplinary framework for research and policymaking*, Council of Europe report DGI, 2017. Downloaded from: https://rm.coe.int/information-disorder-toward-an-interdisciplinary-framework-for-researc/168076277 (access: August 2020).

22 L. M. Neudert, *Future Elections May Be Swayed by Intelligent, Weaponized Chatbots*. MIT Technology Review, August 22, 2018. https://www.technologyreview.com/s/611832/future-electionsmay-be-swayed-by-intelligent-weaponized-chatbots/ (access: August 2020).

23 D. Mider, *Polacy wobec przemocy politycznej*, pp. 236–240.

certain protests, we may state that those actions exceed the threshold of legitimization for unconventional behaviors. In Poland, six forms of unconventional participation exceeded this level; these are: signing petitions, legal demonstrations, legal strikes, collecting signatures for petitions, creating alternative political institutions and/or supporting them, and ridiculing politicians in public space. In fact, we may observe a phenomenon of blurring the boundaries between conventional and unconventional participation types. The least citizens are willing to accept violent protests. An assumption made twenty years ago about the trend to reject traditional participation forms such as elections and focus on other ways of influencing politics that are more adjusted to the needs of popular culture such as voluntary associations of the third sector or participation in protests comes true.[24]

24 J. W. Van Deth, *Studying Political Participation.*

Chapter IV. Social capital versus political participation capital

The "social capital" term has become popular in the social sciences. Scientists believe that Pierre Bourdieu[1] created a systematic description of this category in the 1970s. Bourdieu believed that if social capital exists in society, then social capital depends on the existence of a network of ties, social bonds, and individuals' mutual trust. Such relationships encourage social entities' mobilization and enable social groups – and possibly the whole social community – to achieve greater effectiveness. According to Bourdieu, social capital means one of the elements of a triad of some sort that also includes economic capital and cultural capital. In a way, the capitals are interconnected.

Such scientists as James Coleman,[2] Francis Fukuyama, and Robert D. Putman[3] approached the issue of social capital, its existence or nonexistence, and possibly its nature and level. In R. Putnam's view, social capital means a certain set of norms, mutual trust, and loyalty in a social group.

We can ask at least two questions based on the scientific debate on social capital. First, whether the social capital's existence means a value per se or whether social capital is of broader significance for the creation of networks of links in society. In the latter case, the networks of links encourage society's integration and the creation of new, shared values. Second, will social capital always remain a positive phenomenon, or will one be able to use social capital in various ways not always compatible with the interests of the broader community?

Apart from these issues, we should consider whether the only types of capital include those that P. Bourdieu mentioned as a kind of social capital's correlates. Namely, Bourdieu mentioned **economic capital** and **cultural**

---

1 P. Bourdieu, "Outline of a Theory of Practice," *Cambridge Studies in Social and Cultural Anthropology* (1977), No. 16.

2 J. Coleman "Social Capital in the Creation of Human Capital," *American Journal of Sociology* (1988), pp. 95–120.

3 R. Putnam, *Bowling Alone: The Collapse and Revival of American Community* (New York: 2001).

capital, as well as **human capital**, which forms the economic and cultural capitals' basis. Human capital involves such phenomena as motivations, creative attitudes, talents, communication skills, knowledge, education, abilities.[4]

I should underline that the concept of social capital became an ambiguous and sometimes misleading conceptual category. Nowadays, specialists criticize the concept of social capital due to the concept's excessive capacity and fuzziness.[5] Claude Fischer, among others, believes that the "social capital" term is unnecessary, as simpler terms exist and function. The terms include membership, sociability, and trust, and can satisfy the requirements of any researcher.[6] Until specialists identify the social capital's empirical indexes, we should treat the term only as a useful and impressive metaphor, though not very contributive. Moreover, the metaphor tempts us to interpret social phenomena, provided that, at the same time, our interpretation would involve broad consideration of non-economic categories. I should remark that such indexes must mostly refer to material truth, as social capital's subjectivistic research tools led to the negation of this concept. Moreover, the tools made specialists characterize the concept as "fundamentally flawed."[7]

The question of to what extent does "social capital" mean "capital" remains the subject of criticism and investigation since specialists do not know whether "social capital" has the same basic definitional features as "capital." From the primary, economic point of view, "social capital" should possess the definitional features:

---

4 P. Bourdieu, "The forms of capital," in: *Handbook of Theory of Research for the Sociology of Education*, ed. J.E. Richardson (New York, 1986).

5 T.G. Poder, "What is Really Social Capital? A Critical Review," *The American Sociologist* (2011), No. 42(4), pp. 341–367. See more in: B. Fine, "They F**k You Up Those Social Capitalists," *Antipode* (2002), No. 34(4), pp. 796–799.

6 C.S. Fischer, "Bowling Alone: What's the Score?," *Social Networks* (2005), No. 27(2), pp. 155–167.

7 B. Fine, "They F**k You Up Those Social Capitalists," *Antipode* (2002), No. 34(4), pp. 796–799; P. Haynes, *Before Going Any Further With Social Capital: Eight Key Criticisms to Address* (2009) (Feb. 2020) https://core.ac.uk/download/pdf/36025661.pdf.

a. transferability (fluidity), which means that we can transfer social capital's property from one person or group to another.
b. deliberate and calculated sacrifice of the present for future benefit.[8]

The above accusations formulated by Kenneth Arrow seem at least partially misguided. Social capital and other forms of capital are subject to limited ceding. Moreover, individuals build social capital and other forms of capital consciously.

In 2018, Mathew O. Jackson, in work titled *A Typology of Social Capital and Associated Network Measures*, distinguished seven different types/variations of social capital.[9] One may wonder whether we can characterize all these categories of trust as well distinguished and whether the categories actually exist, but the proposal remains intellectually interesting. The categories include:

- information capital,
- brokerage capital,
- coordination and leadership capital,
- bridging capital,
- favor capital,
- reputation capital,
- community capital.[10]

As I generally describe the above categories, I must state that **information capital** means the possibility to acquire socially and politically important information, and the ability to spread it thanks to, for example, social media.

Brokerage capital means the possibility of participation in the interaction process with other individuals or subjects, and the possibility of help in possible transactions that are not the only commercial in nature. One may characterize the above as, in a way, a market glance on some aspects of capital, which forms in society.

---

8 K. J. Arrow, "Observations on social capital," in: *Social Capital: A multifaceted perspective*, eds. P. Dasgupta & I. Serageldin (Washington, 1999), pp. 3–6.
9 M. O. Jackson, *A Typology of Social Capital and Associated Network Measures* (SSRN, 2019) https://papers.ssrn.com/sol3/papers.cfm?abstract_id=3073496
10 Jackson, "A Typology of Social Capital," p. 5.

According to M. O. Jackson, **coordination and leadership capital** means the ability to mutually cooperate and influence individuals who have difficulties in interaction. One acts this way to overcome barriers in social contacts/relationships.

Bridging capital means the creation and existence of groups, which create a "link" of some kind. The groups' aims involve the spread of information, the establishment of bonds, and the reduction of aversions and superstitions.[11] These characteristics make bridging capital somewhat similar to brokerage capital. Bridging capital can play an important role, especially in societies that are pluralistic in terms of culture and nationality.

Favor capital means the ability to exchange various benefits without risk. The benefits are not only material in nature. Moreover, the capital involves the creation of social interaction ties and actions based on mutual trust in communication.

Reputation capital means an important aspect of social capital's variety. Reputation capital deals with people, companies, and organizations. Moreover, reputation capital deals with the question of whether citizens, consumers, and clients assume that the entity they deal with shows reliability; when they deal with a company, we deal with a question of whether the company provides services or goods of satisfactory quality.

Community capital means the ability to cooperate and sustain cooperation, especially when one handles common public goods. Moreover, community capital means cooperation in the creation of associations and NGOs, as well as activities in local communities.

We can characterize the above aspects or dimensions of social capital as vital. But how do these aspects relate to political capital? How do the above aspects or dimensions relate to political participation capital in particular? On the one hand, political participation capital results from the processes of social capital's creation to some extent. On the other hand,

---

11 Undoubtedly, this is a developed R. Putnam's idea. Putnam in his later works introduced a distinction between bonding social capital and bridging social capital. Bonding social capital means the bond of given community's members, while bridging social capital refers to individuals who belong to different communities.

political participation capital determines the engagement of citizens and social groups in public activities and directly influences political activity.

Basically, we can define political participation capital as a part or even a variety of social capital. Political participation capital involves such phenomena as interest in politics, willingness to acquire knowledge, creation of political bonds based on common views, political trust, and social trust in the political system's institutions. These factors will foster citizens' participation in politics if they exist. Political engagement will be based on the belief that one can make a difference. Moreover, political engagement should shape the political subjectivity of individuals, groups, organizations, and the whole society. During the process of creation of participatory capital's concept, I was inspired by Lawrence R. Jacobs, Fay Lomax Cook, and Michael X. Delli Carpini's political capital and public deliberation factors.[12] These factors determine electoral participation, civic participation, and elite contacting.[13] Moreover, we can find a detailed description of the relationships between social capital, civic engagement, participation, and trust in a book titled *Social Capital. An International Research Program*.[14] The book presents a multifaceted approach and fits the social, political, and participatory capital research trends. As I mentioned earlier, specialists described the trend as **political action approach**, in contrast to the **institutional approach**. Moreover, D. Mider described the differences between the two approaches too.[15]

Obviously, participatory capital will not always turn into reality as a rise in citizens' participation in politics and public affairs. The above phenomenon highly depends on external factors concerning citizens' stances in the form of the political system's shape, political game's rules, and political institutions' activity. The party system's nature is also important. The inclination to civic participation is, to a great extent, subject to factors that

12 L. R. Jacobs, F. L. Cook, M. X. Delli Carpini, *Talking together. Public Deliberation and Political Participation in America* (Chicago, 2009), pp. 116–117.

13 Jacobs, Cook, Delli Carpini, "Talking Together," p. 116.

14 N. Lin, B. H. Erickson, *Social Capital. An International Research Program* (Oxford, 2010), pp. 185–331.

15 D. Mider, "Political Participation of Poles – Structure and Trends," *Studia Politologiczne* (2014), No. 31, p. 89 and subsequent pages.

depend on the party system. The factors include such notions as the level of trust in the parties, whether the parties are exclusive or inclusive, the parties' programs, as well as the parties' competences in political communication. Importantly, the general political culture in society influences the political participation capital's creation. The general political culture issue deals with questions of how common participant political culture is,[16] whether political culture's components are mostly eufunctional or whether they are dysfunctional in relation to the political system.[17]

Political participation capital means a phenomenon that is subject to changes, which makes it similar to every other phenomenon in society. The research can show a certain characteristic, namely the participatory capital's nature, which exists in a particular period. Still, we must remember that in the long run, one must apply the approach that considers this social phenomenon's dynamics. I should add that one should not presume that the result will always be positive, similarly to a situation in which one characterizes the general social capital. Probably we could say that social capital can transform into a kind of an "anti-capital." The anti-capital can take the form of, for example, different informal political agreements, as well as political participation, thanks to which the elites or pressure groups can pursue their narrowly defined particularistic interests.

Specialists increasingly often use the "anti-capital" term in the source literature, which includes, for example, J. Tittenbrun's *Anti-capital: Human, Social, and Cultural. The Mesmerising Misnomers*,[18] as well as A. Becla and S. Czaja's work.[19] I mentioned the term, among other things, because of its rising popularity. The use of the "anti-capital" term suggests that a phenomenon possesses features that are opposite to capital's features. That

---

16 G. A. Almond, G. B. Powell, *Comparative Politics: A Development Approach* (Boston, 1966), pp. 53–54.

17 J. Garlicki, A. Noga-Bogomilski, *Kultura polityczna w społeczeństwie demokratycznym* (Warszawa, 2004), pp. 70–71.

18 J. Tittenbrun, *Anti-capital: Human, Social, and Cultural. The Mesmerising Misnomers* (London, 2016).

19 A. Becla, S. Czaja, "Kapitał i 'antykapitał' społeczny jako czynniki wpływające na rozwój cywilizacyjny – próba identyfikacji teoretyczno-empirycznej na przykładzie Dolnego Śląska," in: M. Adamczyk, A. Chmiel, *Społeczności lokalne. Przestrzeń dla współpracy i rozwoju* (Wrocław, 2019), pp. 23–37.

issue would require regulation in a separate work. Indeed, we can distinguish eufunctional and dysfunctional capital for broader social wholes. Eufunctional capital would involve actions undertaken for the benefit of the society, whereas dysfunctional capital would involve particularistic actions undertaken for the benefit of one's group. Finally, it would be worthwhile to refer to the way in which individuals realize the capital, i.e., by what means do individuals implement the capital, realize the capital, and how does the capital manifest itself. Namely, three ways exist. First, I mean the persuasive way, which involves the ability of a group to lobby something or conduct a social campaign that changes the social awareness. Second, I mean the coercive way, which involves protests. Finally, I mean the violent way, which involves the activity of terrorist or national liberation groups.

The prominent American sociologist Robert King Merton claimed that no good theory exists without good empiricism[20] and vice versa. At the same time, given the criticism of the notion of "capital" in relation to society and relations within it as a subjective approach, I decided to conduct in-depth field study. The study was, to some extent, speculative. I empirically explored the issue of capital's existence and nature, which can become a basis for political participation. I conducted the study in 2017 and 2018 as part of *Partycypacja polityczna Polaków – nowe wyzwania I formy aktywności* (Political Participation of Poles – New Challenges and Forms of Activity) research grant, financed by the National Science Center of Poland (2014/13/B/HS5/00555). The Center assigned the funds to the Warsaw University team, which I led. I used three methods during the study: first, I used the qualitative technique of Focus Group Interviews (FGI), then I used the quantitative method of narrowly understood Computer Assisted Telephone Interviewing (CATI). Finally, I conducted research supported by the Individual In-Depth Interview (IDI) technique. Therefore, I used a full triangulation of research methods. After I conducted focused group interviews, I constructed indexes to conduct research based on Computer Assisted Telephone Interviewing. Moreover, I created the indexes based on

20 R. K. Merton, *Social Theory and Social Structure* (New York: The Free Press, 1968), pp. 140–142.

the results obtained.[21] The CATI method let me collect the data required to analyze participatory capital in Polish society.

In the study, I used nine political participation capital indexes.[22] Together they should answer the important question of whether citizens in Poland show a tendency and willingness to participate in political and public life. I explored each index (dimension) by means of one or several questions.

The developed indexes include:

The interest in politics

At the declaratory level, the basis for this dimension of political participation capital definition involved the question of whether the participants are interested in political issues and important events in the country's life.

The used response variants were supposed to reflect four different levels of interest. The levels of interests involved the "I am not interested in political matters at all" category, two intermediate categories, and the stance characterized by "I try to know as much as possible not only about current events but also about the mechanisms of political life" expression. You can find the full content of questions and categories of responses in the Annex 5.

The attitude to democracy as a system of government and the attitude to democracy's real functioning in Poland

I used two questions to explore this index. The first question dealt with respondents' attitudes to the democratic political system, whether they believe that democracy has an advantage over all other forms of government or the other way round. The second question dealt with the issue of evaluation of democracy's functioning in Poland. Moreover, the second question measured to what extent the citizens were satisfied or dissatisfied

---

21 I conducted the study using Computer Aided Telephone Interviewing (CATI) as part of *Partycypacja polityczna Polaków – nowe wyzwania i formy aktywności* research grant funded by the National Science Center of Poland (2014/13/B/HS5/00555). I conducted the study in 2017. The sample consisted of 1200 people. I realized the partition/questions module of political participation capital on a subsample of 603 respondents. I used Random Digital Dialing (RDD).

22 Jacobs, Cook, Delli Carpini, "Talking Together," pp. 172–176.

with the real use of democratic values in the political system's practical operation. In other words, I tried to verify and compare two sides of the attitude to democracy. The first side involves the axiological level concerning the acceptance of values of a democratic system and democratic governing. The second side involves the perception of the real functioning of the political system, which is democratic by right and by name.

Political trust

Variables that verified how much did the respondents trust politicians or the broader political elite involved two questions. The first question dealt with the issue of whether and to what extent one can be convinced that rulers fulfill their duties. The second question involved the evaluations of the ruling elite's engagement in the realization of general social interests or the realization of some group's interests or particularistic interests. In the case of particularistic interests, I mean the narrow sense of the word "particularistic." Moreover, the second question concentrated on the issue of whether those in power in Poland are involved in important matters/interests to achieve something solely for themselves, or whether they try to act for the benefit of all people.

The feeling of being able to influence decisions

This index is also of high importance. It involves the issue of citizens' subjectivity and the issue of how the citizens perceive their role and whether they feel that they can influence political decisions. That issue deals with at least two levels: nationwide and local. I divided the questions that verify the stance and opinions concerning what we can scientifically call subjectivity into two categories. The first category included questions that assessed one's own influence on the country's matters, whereas the second category included questions that assessed one's own influence on the city's or commune's matters.

Social trust in multifaceted and general approach

While the political trust index relates to citizens'/electors' views on elites and their activities, this index focuses on other aspects of trust. The other aspects of trust include, among other things, views on politicians compared to fellow citizens, as well as the evaluation of interpersonal contacts with other persons, whom the participants of the study meet or can meet. I used a set of four questions to create that index. The first question dealt with the issue of whom Poles trust more: politicians or ordinary citizens. The second question referred to the issue of other people actions' perception, i.e., the question dealt with the issue of whether most of the people in Poland would try to use others for their own purposes if they would be able to do so, or whether they would try to act right. The third variable within the scope of social trust index dealt with the issue of whether people more often try to help others, or whether they take care of themselves. The fourth, final variable verified the dilemma of whether one can trust most Poles, or whether one should be cautious in contacts with the majority of Poles.

Political knowledge

We can characterize the political knowledge index as important, yet always threatened by the fact that questions used may not reflect the nature of citizens' political knowledge and, first of all, the level of citizens' political knowledge. To verify the basic knowledge level concerning issues related to politics, I created a set of six questions concerning such issues as:

- Which opposition party has the most MPs in the Sejm (lower house of Polish parliament)?
- What type of majority is required to change the Constitution of Poland?
- Which party's politicians most often refer to Christian values in their statements?
- What is the position of Mateusz Morawiecki in the Polish government?
- Who decides whether laws passed by the Sejm are in accordance with the Constitution of Poland?

Political tolerance

The political tolerance index reflected the Polish citizens' attitudes to otherness and minority groups. The index consisted of two questions. The first question dealt with the Polish citizens' attitudes to refugees, whereas the second question dealt with their attitudes to the tolerance of political extremist groups' public speeches.

Direct engagement in politics

I used the "Direct engagement in politics" index to define the percentage of Poles that are members of political parties, political groups, social movements that engage in political activity. On the other hand, I used the index to define whether citizens who participate in NGOs or labor unions defend the interests of certain groups and thus become involved in political activities.

Intergenerational capital

The last variables used to diagnose the scale and nature of political capital involve two questions. The first variable dealt with the issue of whether the respondents were persuaded by their families to have a certain worldview during the process of socialization. The second variable was to show whether the current generation of youth is more or less involved in politics than the older generations.

I divided the responses provided in the scope of all the mentioned indexes into two types. First, I distinguished negative reactions concerning the creation of political capital, which I qualified as "0." Second, I distinguished positive reactions that support the creation of political capital, which I qualified as "1."

*

The average of all indexes should determine the rating of political participation capital

In the context of the first index concerning **interest in politics**, one could choose one of four versions of the cognitive attitude to politics (Table 4.1).

Table 4.1. Index 1 – Interest in politics

Political Participation Capital Index	Variable's scope	Values in percent (%)	Dichotomous index	Index value in percent (%)
Interest in politics	I am not interested in political matters at all	4.2	0	31.3
	Political matters interest me as long as my living conditions depend on political decisions	27.1		
	One must be fundamentally aware of what is happening in politics	34.0	1	68.7
	I try to know as much as possible not only about current events but also about the mechanisms of political life	34.7		

Source: *Partycypacja polityczna Polaków – nowe wyzwania i formy aktywności* study, 2017, NCN grant 4884, N=603.

I included categories of answers such as "I am not interested in political matters at all" and "Political matters interest me as long as my living conditions depend on political decisions" into the negative reactions, which do not offer greater opportunities to create political participation capital. I have marked two categories of reactions with an index score of "1," i.e., positive in terms of the political participation capital creation's possibility. The positive reactions included such responses as "One must be fundamentally aware of what is happening in politics" and "I try to know as much as possible not only about current events but also about the mechanisms of political life." These are types of functional attitudes to the process of political capital's creation.

Based on the study, I can state that, contrary to appearances, the index concerning the interest in politics indicates that political participation capital exists in this scope. More than two-thirds of citizens declare that they are at least relatively interested in political affairs, whereas one-third of citizens are definitely interested in political affairs.

The second political participation capital's index, on the one hand, is a matter of **attitude to democracy as a system of government**, whereas, on the other hand, the index is a matter of **real functioning of such a system** in Poland. The above means different levels. We can characterize the first one as axiological, as it deals with the sphere of values and their acceptance on a democratic dimension. The second one, which we can characterize as realistic, deals with the evaluation of the way and quality of democratic values' realization in the political system's practical functioning. The participants' reactions differed (Table 4.2).

Table 4.2. Index 2 – The attitude to democracy

Political Participation Capital Index	Variable's scope	Values in percent (%)	Dichotomous index	Index value in percent (%)
Evaluation of democracy as a system: "Democracy has an advantage over all other forms of government.	I do not agree that democracy has an advantage over all other forms of government	19.4	0	24.5
	I agree that democracy has an advantage over all other forms of government	59.7	1	75.5
	It is difficult to say whether democracy has an advantage over all other forms of government	20.9	.	.
Evaluation of democracy's functioning in Poland	Dissatisfied with the functioning of democracy in Poland	48.8	0	58.9
	Satisfied with the functioning of democracy in Poland	34.5	1	41.1
	It is difficult to say	16.7	.	.

Source: *Partycypacja polityczna Polaków – nowe wyzwania i formy aktywności* study, 2017, NCN grant 4884, N=603.

We should categorize the statement, located on the index's first level, which claims that "democracy has an advantage over all other forms of government," as a factor that contributes to political participation capital's creation. The above is the opinion of nearly sixty percent of citizens. When we subtract the undecided respondents, we can observe that the above opinion represents three-quarters of people who decided on their stance regarding democratic values. As we can see, most Poles are convinced that the democratic political system is good or even the best form of government.

Opinions differ concerning the way and quality of realization of democratic values in the Polish political system. Half the citizens are not satisfied with the functioning of democracy in Poland. If we do not take the undecided into account, almost sixty percent are not satisfied at this second level of the attitude to democracy. At the second level, we cannot observe the symptoms of the attitudes that contribute to participatory capital's creation. Still, a critical approach to the functioning of the democratic system may be a foresight for actions that are supposed to change the situation.

The results of research that the CBOS Foundation conducted since 1992 provide concurrent data, although not identical. On the one hand, when it comes to the democratic system's assessment, which involves the question of "whether ... democracy has an advantage over all other forms of government," around sixty to seventy percent of respondents still give a positive answer.[23] On the other hand, when we consider the assessment of ideas and democracy rules' implementation in Poland, then we can almost always observe that the dissatisfied outnumber the satisfied. Exceptions include November 2007, August 2011, March, and June 2014. In 2018, these ratings were almost equal to a slight advantage of the satisfied, but the number of satisfied respondents did not exceed 50 percent.

23 *Opinie o demokracji*, research statement, CBOS, June 2018.

Table 4.3. Democracy functioning's evaluation in Poland

Evaluation of democracy's functioning in Poland	Respondents' indications by studies' dates																			
	2007			2008	2009	2010	2011		2013	2014		2015		2016			2017			2018
	IV	V	XI	VII	I	III	VIII	XI	VII	III	VI	IV	XI	I	IV	VI	I	VII	VIII	V
	in percent (%)																			
Satisfied	31	32	46	43	42	43	45	47	35	49	50	47	43	39	45	39	39	45	40	48
Unsatisfied	59	54	42	47	49	50	41	47	58	41	39	44	49	50	49	53	52	45	52	43
It is hard to tell	10	14	12	10	9	7	14	6	7	10	11	9	8	11	6	8	9	10	8	9

Source: *Opinie o demokracji* (Opinions on Democracy), research statement, CBOS, June 2018.

The third index deals with a very important and sensitive **subject of trust** or the lack of trust in political relations. As I explored this issue, I used two variables. The first variable involved opinions concerning whether politicians do what they are supposed to do as part of their duties and competencies. The second variable involved opinions concerning the interests that political elites pursue.

Table 4.4. Index 3 – Political trust

Political Participation Capital Index	Variable's scope	Values in percent (%)	Dichotomous index	Index value in percent (%)
Is it possible to be convinced in Poland that rulers fulfill their duties?	Never	18.1	0	77.1
	Sometimes	59.1		
	Most of the time	14.1	1	22.9
	Always	8.7		
Are the rulers in Poland engaged in important matters/ interests to achieve something solely for themselves, or do they try to act in the interest of the general public?	They are primarily engaged in doing business for their own benefit	28.0	0	69.5
	They pursue the interests of small, selected social groups	41.5		
	Act for the benefit of general social interests	30.5	1	30.5

Source: *Partycypacja polityczna Polaków – nowe wyzwania i formy aktywności* study, 2017, NCN grant 4884, N=603.

The first variable of the index concerning trust cannot form a basis for the political participation capital's creation. Most citizens believe that rulers only sometimes fulfill their duties or even never do so. In total, more than three-quarters of the survey participants share these two categories of reactions. People that are convinced that politicians often fulfill their duties amount to fourteen percent, whereas those who believe that politicians always fulfill their duties amount to less than ten percent. As we can observe from the study, trust in rulers as individuals who fulfill their duties correctly reaches a very low level.

The analysis of citizens' opinions analysis concerning the rulers' engagement in the realization of different social groups' interests does not provide positive impulses in the context of the creation of political participation capital's bases. Moreover, the above interests involved general social interests.

The fourth political participation capital index deals with a very important issue of **political subjectivity**'s sense among the citizens. In a way, the sense comes down to the assessment of the ability to **influence.** First, I mean the ability to influence the **country's affairs**. Second, I mean the ability to influence the **affairs of a city or commune** in which the respondents live.

Table 4.5. Index 4 – The feeling of being able to influence decisions

Political Participation Capital Index	Variable's scope	Values in percent (%)	Dichotomous index	Index value in percent (%)
People such as you have an influence on the country's affairs	No	56.7	0	60.4
	Yes	37.2	1	39.6
	It is hard to tell	6.2	.	.
People such as you have an influence on the affairs of their city, commune	No	27.9	0	29.8
	Yes	65.6	1	70.2
	It is hard to tell	6.6	.	.

Source: *Partycypacja polityczna Polaków – nowe wyzwania i formy aktywności* study, 2017, NCN grant 4884, N=603.

A small number of citizens believe that they can influence the country's affairs. In this regard, the "0" political participation capital index dominates. Over sixty percent of participants state that they do not feel that they can influence the national politics' course of action.

The situation concerning the sense of being able to influence local society's affairs manifests itself differently. In this regard, we can observe that most respondents believe that one can feel like a subject in the context of his or her city's or commune's affairs. As many as seventy percent of those respondents claim to be able to influence affairs in their local environment.

The results of research conducted by CBOS provide similar data. In the context of national affairs, the opinion characterized by the words "we have no influence" prevails. In March 2018 study, fifty-seven percent of respondents stated that they do not have an influence on the country's affairs, whereas thirty-eight percent stated that they do. The above thirty-eight percent is still a lot in comparison to the research conducted in previous periods.[24] However, the sense of subjectivity in the sphere of local affairs clearly increases. According to CBOS research, in 1992, seventy-nine percent of citizens believed that they have no influence, and only sixteen percent believed that they have influence. As the years passed, the trend changed. Since 2014, the number of people who believe that they have influence increases, whereases the number of people who believe that they do not have influence decreases. In 2018, fifty-nine percent of respondents believed that they have an influence on the country's affairs.

24 *Poczucie wpływu obywateli na sprawy publiczne*, research statement, CBOS, March 2018.

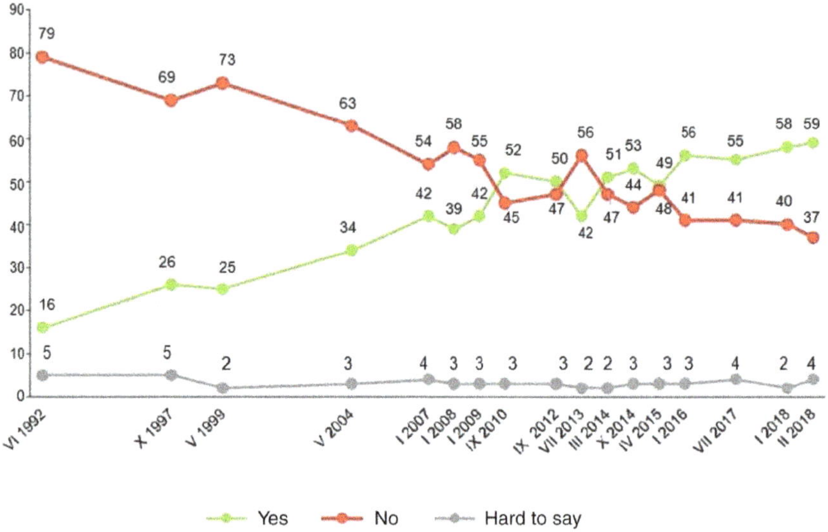

Chart 4.1. Citizens' sense of influence on the affairs of their city or commune
Source: *Poczucie wpływu obywateli na sprawy publiczne* (Subjective Influence on Public Affairs), research statement, CBOS, March 2018.

The other aspect of trust in the political elite involves **social trust in a multifaceted and general approach,** i.e., citizens' opinions concerning not only relationships with politicians. Even though the opinions concerning relationships with politicians mean an important aspect, we should also consider the other citizens' perceptions concerning whether and to what extent one can trust politicians.

In this regard, I used a set of indexes, which do not provide a conclusive answer. One should analyze the issue in detail. One can find the results of the study in the table beneath.

Table 4.6. Index 5 – Social trust

Political Participation Capital Index	Variable's scope	Values in percent (%)	Dichotomous index	Index value in percent (%)
Do you think that most Poles rather trust politicians or ordinary citizens?	The majority does not trust either one or the other	53.3	0	53.3
	The majority rather trusts politicians	16.9	1	46.7
	The majority trusts both	29.8		
Will most people in Poland try to use you for their own purposes if they can, or will they try to act right (fair)?	They will try to use me for their own purposes	42.6	0	42.6
	They will try to act fair	57.4	1	57.4
Do people more often try to help others, or do they care only about themselves?	People only care about themselves	56.2	0	56.2
	People try to help others	43.8	1	43.8
In the opinion of the majority of people in Poland, can you trust others, or should you be cautious as you contact them?	One should be cautious in contacts with others	82.0	0	82.0
	Most people can be trusted	18.0	1	18.0

(*continued*)

Table 4.6. Continued

Political Participation Capital Index	Variable's scope	Values in percent (%)	Dichotomous index	Index value in percent (%)
Small groups with strong ties arise in Poland. For whose benefit do they work?	For the benefit of their own narrowly defined (particularistic) interests	44.2	0	44.2
	For the benefit of the broader community's interests (local, professional)	13.9	1	55.8
	They work for the benefit of both their own interests and those of the wider community	41.9		

Source: *Partycypacja polityczna Polaków – nowe wyzwania i formy aktywności* study, 2017, NCN grant 4884, N=603.

Most citizens, i.e., more than a half, declares that in general, they do not trust either politicians or ordinary citizens. Less than thirty percent of citizens trust both groups. The citizens who trust politicians form the smallest group. In this regard, we cannot observe factors that contribute to political participation capital's creation.

We can characterize the next reactions as incoherent and hard to interpret. The research participants were clearly divided when they had to formulate their opinions concerning the "Will most people in Poland try to use you for their own purposes if they can, or will they try to act right (fair)?" question. Over forty percent of respondents decided that they can be used by others, whereas 57.4 percent thought that fellow citizens "will try to act fair." The above means a phenomenon, which may not be that strong, but still gives hope for the political participation capital's creation. Then I asked the respondents whether "people more often try to help others, or do they care only about themselves?" More than half of the respondents answered that people care only about themselves. Less than forty-four percent of people believed that people try to help others. The findings taken from this data indicate that divisions exist, which does not serve the political participation capital's creation well.

The next aspect of the social trust level evaluation means the interpersonal contacts' evaluation. More than eighty percent of research participants state that one should be cautious as he or she contacts the others. In the context of group relationships, the respondents believe that local elite groups pursue their own interests as well as the broader community's interests. The broader community's interests involve the professional groups' interests as well as those of local associations. Moreover, in the respondents' opinion, the local elite groups' actions even strengthen the ties between the local population.

The unambiguous analysis of general social trust indexes is difficult. There is no simple answer to the question of whether social life's phenomenon exists in Poland or not. On the one hand, the slight majority of Poles neither trust politicians nor fellow citizens. According to the results of the study, the slight majority of respondents believe that people "will try to act right," but still, there is a group equal in numbers, which states that the citizens of Poland care only about themselves and do not try to help others at all. I find it hard to synthesize these indexes, but it seems that in the context of social trust, the Polish society is not a model of civic trust. One can state that different limitations of awareness and behavior are present. In conclusion, the general public confidence index does not present itself as a factor that contributes to the political participation capital's creation.

An important dimension of political participation capital involves the cognitive aspect, i.e., **political knowledge**.

Table 4.7. Index 6 – Political knowledge

Political Participation Capital Index	Variable's scope	Values in percent (%)	Dichotomous index	Index value in percent (%)
Which opposition party has the most MPs in the Sejm (lower house of Polish parliament)?	PO	67.0	1	67.2
	I do not know	26.0	0	32.8
	PiS	6.1		
	Other responses	0.8		
What type of majority is required to change the Constitution of Poland?	Two thirds	26.1	1	25.0
	Less than two thirds	8.7	0	75.0
	More than two thirds	17.3		
	I do not know, other wrong responses	48.9		
Which party's politicians most often refer to Christian values in their statements?	PiS	81.9	1	81.9
	I do not know, other wrong responses	18.1	0	18.1
What is the position of Mateusz Morawiecki in the Polish government?[a]	Minister of Finance	14.3	1	28.6
	Minister of Economy	7.5		
	Deputy Prime Minister, Minister of Finance	6.8		
	I do not know, other wrong responses	71.4	0	71.4
Who decides whether laws passed by the Sejm are in accordance with the Constitution of Poland?	Constitutional Tribunal	48.6	1	48.6
	I do not know, other wrong responses	51.4	0	51.4

Table 4.7. Continued

Political Participation Capital Index	Variable's scope	Values in percent (%)	Dichotomous index	Index value in percent (%)
In the context of parliamentary elections to the Sejm, which voting system is used in Poland: majoritarian or proportional?	Proportional	30.8	1	30.8
	Majoritarian	51.7	0	69.2
	I do not know, other wrong responses	17.5		

Source: *Partycypacja polityczna Polaków – nowe wyzwania i formy aktywności* study, 2017, NCN grant 4884, N=603.

a In 2017, when I conducted the study, Mateusz Morawiecki was not a Prime Minister yet.

A political scientist would perceive indicator questions as easy. However, indicator questions proved difficult for the research participants. The majority responded correctly to two of six questions, which we can characterize as the easiest ones. The first easiest question dealt with the situation in the Sejm in 2017 and said: "Which opposition party has the most MPs in the Sejm (lower house of Polish parliament)?" Two-thirds of respondents mentioned the PO (Civic Platform), whereas one-third of respondents stated that they do not know, and some chose the PiS (Law and Justice). The second question, which most respondents answered correctly, said: "Which party's politicians most often refer to Christian values in their statements?" In contrast, when it comes to fundamental issues concerning the Polish political system, wrong answers prevailed. I mean the questions concerning the type of majority required to change the Constitution of Poland, whether parliamentary elections to the Polish Sejm are majoritarian or proportional, as well as the question of who decides whether laws passed by the Sejm are in accordance with the Constitution of Poland. Three-quarters of those surveyed were unable to provide adequate figures regarding the definition of the so-called supermajority. Moreover, the citizens involved in the 2017 survey did not know the position held by the later Prime Minister Mateusz Morawiecki.

In conclusion, Poles' knowledge concerning politics and the political system cannot be considered as high, contrary to research participants' earlier declarations of interest in politics. The cognitive dimension does not give any grounds to claim that political participation capital's foundations exist.

The subsequent seventh political participation capital's index deals with the issue of the existence or nonexistence of **political tolerance to otherness.** Such tolerance means a sensitive issue in many countries, including the Polish society. Therefore, I selected the indicator questions in such a way that I would obtain knowledge on the issue without causing too much irritation.

Table 4.8. Index 7 – Political tolerance

Political Participation Capital Index	Variable's scope	Values in percent (%)	Dichotomous index	Index value in percent (%)
Poland should not accept refugees from Africa and Arab countries	I agree with the statement	61.7	0	61.7
	I do not agree with the statement	38.3	1	38.3
Anarchists and nationalists should be forbidden from speaking out and demonstrating their views even if they are not breaking the law	I agree with the statement	38.7	0	38.7
	I do not agree with the statement	61.3	1	61.3

Source: *Partycypacja polityczna Polaków – nowe wyzwania i formy aktywności* study, 2017, NCN grant 4884, N=603.

Two questions dealt with the current issues, on which the Polish public opinion concentrated, and which were a topic of discussion. The research participants' answers do not allow us to unambiguously decide whether Poles are tolerant to others, including minorities, or not. Interestingly, most respondents do not want Poland to accept refugees. A comparable group of respondents claimed that there is no reason to "forbid anarchists and nationalists speak out and demonstrate their views if they do not violate the law." In other words, public opinion believes that legal demonstrations of nationalists and anarchists should remain allowed. The results of the study show that the tendencies regarding the tolerance of otherness are polarized. The above facts do not encourage us to formulate a thesis that tolerance in Poland can become the political participation capital's basis.

The eight political participation capital's index involves **direct political engagement**. In other words, direct political engagement means membership and activity in parties, factions, political movements, or NGOs, which enter the political realm.

Table 4.9. Index 8 – Direct engagement in politics

Political Participation Capital Index	Variable's scope	Values in percent (%)	Dichotomous index	Index value in percent (%)
Are you a member of a party, political faction, or a social movement, which takes a stance on political matters?	No	96.0	0	96,0
	Yes	4.0	1	4.0
Do you act in an NGO, association, or a labor union, which defends group or environmental interests, and by those means enters the political sphere?	No	91.7	0	91.7
	Yes	8.3	1	8.3

Source: *Partycypacja polityczna Polaków – nowe wyzwania i formy aktywności* study, 2017, NCN grant 4884, N=603.

In this regard, it would be hard to expect that most citizens participate in political activities. Nevertheless, the percentage of positive declarations is very low. One could expect that Poles would more often choose to participate in NGOs and other associations than, for example, choose to become members of a political party. Namely, I mean the activity "in

NGO, association, or a labor union, which defends group or environmental interests, and by those means enters the political sphere." Less than ten percent of Poles declare that they participate in such activities. I cannot state that the above level can contribute to the political participation capital's creation.

The last index means the phenomenon, which the specialists called the **intergenerational capital.** They meant the issue concerning whether members of a family convey political values to the younger generation and how much is the younger generation engaged in politics in comparison to their parents or their senior relatives.

Table 4.10. Index 9 – Intergenerational capital

Political Participation Capital Value	Variable's scope	Values in percent (%)	Dichotomous index	Index value in percent (%)
Has your family given you an attachment to certain values and/or political orientations (e.g., liberal, nationalist, or left-wing)?	No	30.0	0	30.0
	The family persuaded me to choose a specific political option	4.4	1	70.0
	My family gave me some universal values	65.6		
Do you think that the current generation of 18–20-year-olds is more involved in political affairs or less involved than previous generations?	They are less involved	69.8	0	69.8
	I do not see any differences in the involvement	13.7	1	30.2
	They are more involved	16.5		

Source: *Partycypacja polityczna Polaków – nowe wyzwania i formy aktywności* study, 2017, NCN grant 4884, N=603.

In this case, the indexes' components are ambiguous as well. Most respondents answered "yes" when they were asked whether their families have given them an attachment to certain values and/or political orientations, such as liberal, nationalist, and left-wing. The respondents most often stated that their families gave them some universal values. Undoubtedly, the above means a factor that can contribute to the political participation capital's building. On the other hand, most respondents stated that the youngest voters are less active in the political sphere than older generations.

The summary of the results of the empirical research on political participation capital consisted of three stages of analyses and phases of conclusions' formulation.

The first stage involved the research results' aggregation for all indexes and averages' calculation. Based on averages, I created statistics, such as standard deviation and variance. At this stage, I calculated the averages for each subindex, i.e., variables. Next, I calculated averages for the given category's aggregate index, which could involve one variable, like the first "interest in politics" index or the ninth "intergenerational capital" index.[25] The aggregate index could also involve multiple variables. For example, at the common knowledge testing level, I used six variables to explore the "political knowledge" index. I presented the detailed first-stage analysis results in Annex 1. The data once again shows that political participation capital means a multifaceted phenomenon, whereas empirical research results do not provide unambiguous answers. There are indexes, which lead to a conclusion that grounds for political participation capital's creation exist. Such grounds involve, for example, declarations concerning interest in politics or multigenerational capital's existence in terms of civic attitudes' formation. On the other hand, part of the indexes proves something totally different. I mean, for example, the third index. The indications' average amounts to 0.267, i.e., only a quarter of citizens trust the political elite.

We can characterize the standard deviation's level in all categories as high, which means that the participants' opinions differ greatly. One can even state that in many respects, their opinions are polarized.

---

25 In the case of the "intergenerational capital" category, at the further stage of the analysis I did not use the question concerning the evaluation of political involvement of the youngest generation, as it does not have much influence on the evaluation of political participation capital of the whole Polish society.

The second stage involves the political participation capital index's formulation based on aggregated synthetic indexes (Annex 4).

The synthetic indexes values' construction relies on arithmetic means calculated individually for each index. In a situation in which an index includes one component, I calculated only the index's high-intensity value. I assumed that the index is equal to the percentage of research participants' responses, which equaled one dichotomous index's component. In the case of indexes created out of a greater number of components, I calculated the high intensity based on the average of each variable component of each index.

The synthetic indexes' analysis lets us state that the political participation capital's evaluation in Polish society does not provide unambiguous findings. Only three indexes calculated based on averages exceed half of the potential indications. First, I mean the declared interest in politics. Second, I mean the feeling of being able to influence decisions formed mainly because of the belief that there is a rise in subjectivity in the local society, such as city, village, commune, and other forms of self-governance. Finally, I mean the intergenerational capital, which involves the passage of some ideological values to the next generations. Two indexes oscillate around half, i.e., their values equal to a bit less than fifty percent or a bit more. The indexes deal with the respondents' relation to democracy: on the one hand, they believe that democracy "has an advantage over all other forms of government," whereas, on the other hand, the respondents are dissatisfied with the functioning of democracy in Poland. In the aggregated sense, such dualism in evaluation, i.e., ideal versus the political systems' action practice, manifests itself in the index's ambivalent value. The second index deals with the issue of political tolerance. Once again, the index approaches the indications' half on the continuum of values between "0" and "1." Still, we should note that, on the one hand, the index features tolerance to, for example, nationalists, whereas, on the other hand, the index features the unwillingness to accept refugees. Therefore, we deal with a peculiar and selective nature of tolerance.

According to the empirical exploration's results, in the case of four out of nine political participation capital's synthetic indexes, we can observe the prevalence of opinions which hardly serve the political participation's formation. The indexes include political trust (index's value: 26.7), social trust in multifaceted and general approach (44.3), political knowledge (47.0), and direct political engagement (6.2), which involves membership in parties, political factions, organizations.

The third stage of analysis, which determined the political participation's capital level and nature, involved the global index's calculation. The global index means the synthetic indexes' aggregate category. In other words, the global index means the summary of the research and partial analyses concerning this kind of capital. Moreover, this analysis included the exploration of dependencies between the globally understood political participation capital's level and sociodemographic variables, as well as between the above level, and orientations, and political views (Annex 5).

As we recapitulate the results of the study and presented indexes' values, we should state that the "global" cumulative mean equals 44.4. Therefore, we cannot state that political participation capital does not exist in Poland. The capital is in the intermediate stage, slightly below fifty if we put it on a "zero-to-hundred" scale. On the one hand, I should state that the level is not high, whereas, on the other hand, I presented evidence that indexes, which can strengthen the capital, exist. By the evidence, I mean the following indexes' indications: declared interest in politics, intergenerational capital, belief in the democratic system's value, and subjectivity, expressed in the belief of having influence in the local society.

The analysis lets us state that many sociodemographic variables do not generate more significant differences in political participation capital. For example, the differences that originate from the research participants' sex, age, location of residence, or their attitudes to religion do not determine the diversification when one shows a willingness to participate. The averages oscillate around the global value, which equals forty percent. For example, the following variables cause differences: education, political views, party preferences, a professional status, an interest in politics. I observed the averages above fifty percent, which identify a higher-than-average political participation capital's level. The above was the case with respondents with higher education; people who characterize their views as center-left, center-right, and right-wing; citizens who in 2015 voted for the "Nowoczesna"

(Modern) or the "Partia Razem" (Together).[26] Moreover, the above group includes companies' directors and presidents, artists, employed in creative occupations, and the middle class in general. Finally, the above group includes respondents who declared that "one must be fundamentally aware of what is happening in politics." On the opposite side, we can observe groups in which the political participation capital's average amounts to about ten percentage points less than the global average. The groups include people who declare themselves as far-right and far-left. As we can observe, they think of other forms of participation than conventional participation. Finally, there are people from the poorest groups, qualified workers, to some extent, the unemployed, and citizens who declared that politics does not interest them at all. The above means social groups which can become victims of political apathy, although we cannot exclude a possibility in which political apathy already affected some of them.

Based on the analysis, we can characterize the Polish participatory capital's nature as stratified to some extent. Citizens who are better educated, active, and work in senior professional positions are more likely to engage in politics and participate in different forms of politics.

In conclusion, I should state that it would be cognitively interesting to use the created political participation capital indexes to conduct international empirical research. Obviously, specialists would have to modify some elements to consider the characteristics of different political systems and each society's different political culture. The above would allow specialists to conduct comparative analyses and, as a result, define the similarities and differences. Moreover, the above would allow specialists to describe the expected dynamics of the capital and the political participation itself.

26 In 2015, both political parties were a new addition to the Polish multi-party system. The "Nowoczesna" means a liberal party, which presents a program targeted at the upper middle class. In 2015, the "Nowoczesna" succeeded in elections and entered the Sejm. In turn, the "Partia Razem" means a new left-wing party, which emphasizes social matters.

Chapter V. Political participation models' typology: a priori approach

Political participation means a multifaceted phenomenon.[1] Both the habits of individual citizens and the habits of social groups vary greatly in terms of their participation in different forms of activity and the level of engagement. The participation's nature ranges from highly active, aware, and organized participation to political apathy and the lack of even the slightest signs of willingness and readiness to participate in any forms of activity in the political realm.

The structure of typologies that researchers create strictly depends on the research questions they formulate. In this case, the a priori approach obliged me to choose the most universal, important, understandable, recognized, and, at the same time, empirically verifiable approach from the source literature. I chose Robert King Merton's classical typology of deviance. By "classical," I mean the typology's universality in changing sociopolitical conditions.[2] Typological notions that I used mean a useful and sometimes even integral heuristic and analytical tool, as they originate from George Jellinek and Max Weber's German methodological culture. Scientists often use the notions in social sciences, humanities, as well as in natural sciences. The tools' function involves ordering and systematization of phenomena. Moreover, the tools' usefulness manifests itself in the formulation and verification of hypotheses and formulation of opinions on cause and effect

1 J.M. Nelson, S.P. Huntington, *Political Participation in Developing Countries* (Cambridge: Harvard University Press, 1976), p. 14 and subsequent pages.; J.W. van Deth, "Studying Political Participation: Towards Theory of Everything?," *Joint Sessions of Workshops of the European Consortium for Political Research Workshop "Electronic Democracy: Mobilisation, Organisation and Participation via new ICTs"* Grenoble, April 6–11, 2011 (Jun. 2020) https://ecpr.eu/Filestore/PaperProposal/c8b57aab-51d9-4aca-b65d-4510ccfc19a3.pdf.

2 R.K. Merton, "Social Structure and Anomie," *American Sociological Review*, Vol. 3, No. 5, 1938, pp. 672–682.

relationships. Finally, the tools can successfully serve the function of a prognostic instrument.[3]

The Mertonian typology refers to citizens and social groups' reactions to the social and political structure. In other words, the typology refers to the whole of political participation. Merton stated that we could distinguish two groups of crucial elements, which define the system participants' modes of behaviors and can determine the participation's nature. As R. K. Merton writes: "The first [group] consists of culturally defined goals, purposes and interests."[4] Merton adds: "The second phase of the social structure defines, regulates, and controls the acceptable modes of achieving these goals."[5] Norms, which regulate social modes of behavior and moral imperatives, do not have to and often do not coincide with sociotechnical norms of achieving goals nor with the effectiveness dimension. Let us continue with Emil Durkheim's approach and his "social anomie" concept. R.K. Merton distinguished five types of subject's reactions to social and/or political structure. In the process, he followed the issue of convergence or divergence between, on the one hand, the socially accepted goals and intentions, and, on the other hand, methods, ways, and means of their effective accomplishment.[6] Let us note, in passing, that both variants of the structure – i.e., social and political – are tightly interconnected, especially in the modern world.

---

3 A.M. Rose, "A Deductive Ideal-Type Method," *The American Journal of Sociology*, 1950, Vol. 56, No. 1, 9, 1950, p. 35.

4 R.K. Merton, "Social Structure and Anomie," *American Sociological Review*, Vol. 3, No. 5, 1938, p. 672.

5 Merton, "Social Structure," p. 672.

6 However, we should underline that the deviant behaviors' categories can manifest themselves in a broader spectrum. The more unstable the social and political order are, the stronger and clearer the categories manifest themselves. According to Talcott Parsons, eight types of ideal deviant situations exist: dominance (over people), compulsive enforcement (in terms of norms), aggressiveness (toward others), incorrigibility (ostentatious violation of norms), submission (to others), perfectionism (Merton's ritualism), compulsive independence (from others), evasion (of a situation that forces compliance with norms). I tried to consider these situations as I moved between different types of stances. Cf. T. Parsons, *The Social System* (Glencoe: Free Press, 1951), p. 290.

The five types of reactions to the structure that I mentioned include:

- Conformity;
- Ritualism;
- Innovation;
- Retreatism;
- Rebellion.[7]

When we characterize the above stances, we must refer to already known categories of reactions, created by R. K. Merton: first, the attitude to goals of society's functioning; second, the acceptation or the lack of acceptation of means used to achieve goals which the society accepted as important and right.

Types of reactions to the structure influence the citizens' willingness to participate in politics and the way in which participatory capital's creation conducts. Moreover, the types of reactions to the structure may make the citizens reject thoughts concerning involvement in public affairs and discourage them from such involvement.

R. K. Merton called the first type of citizens' reactions to structure *conformity*. According to Merton, the nature of the *conformity* term does not involve evaluation. Moreover, the nature of the *conformity* term does not involve negative connotations. *Conformity* means a descriptive category that relates to the normal attitudes of the system's participants to the system's conditions. By system's participants, I mean individuals that accept both the goals as well as means and ways to achieve the goals. In societies that differ in terms of system and structure, people may, to a different extent, understand and accept goals and values that dominate because of social acceptance and values which the society embraces.[8] First, I mean socio-centric societies in which the community matters. Moreover, what matters in such societies involves the ability to work for the community's benefit and satisfy the needs of different social groups in a balanced way. Second, I mean altruistic societies, in which the majority defends and supports the weakest social groups, provides them with opportunities to reduce economic differences and differences in social status. Third, I mean

---

7 Merton, "Social Structure," p. 676.
8 This is my own interpretation of R. K. Merton's concept.

egocentric societies, in which it is a common belief that an entity is superior to the community, and citizens prefer to pursue their careers and achieve their goals. Fourth, I mean non-tuistic societies in which it is also a common belief that an entity is superior to the community and, at the same time, such society's members believe that personal success generates collective good. Finally, I mean nationalist societies in which people characterize their nation's benefit as the most important. Moreover, nationalist communities tend to subordinate many aspects of social and political life to the national community. At the same time, nationalist societies ignore their members' individual needs as well as the needs of ethnic and national minorities.

However, *conformists* agree with whatever goals the community accepts, and we can characterize their stance as eufunctionalist to the system, as well as to the social and political structure. When we speak of means to achieve individual and collective goals, *conformists* accept and apply measures provided by the system. *Conformists* participate in conventional forms of involvement to a greater or lesser extent.

R. K. Merton called the next type of system participants' reaction *ritualism*. On the one hand, *ritualism* deals with the attitude to social and political structures, which involves the lack of goals' acceptance or a situation in which one treats goals as unimportant. On the other hand, the attitude involves conventional acceptance of means and modes of behavior that the community perceives as valuable and widely accepted. *Ritualists* may not accept or recognize authorities as legitimate, but they may still participate in state ceremonies. Moreover, they may criticize the introduced legal regulations, but they may still obey them without question. For example, *ritualists* may not believe in God, but they may still participate in religious rituals.

Innovation means another type of reaction. On the one hand, such an attitude to structure involves the acceptance of goals, whereas, on the other hand, *innovation* involves disbelief in applied and popularized means used to achieve these goals. We can distinguish two types of *innovation*.[9] To put

9 This is also my own interpretation that goes beyond the R. K. Merton's statements.

it simply, we can speak of the *negative innovation* and the *positive innovation*, which exist on the opposite ends of the social modes of behavior scale.

The goals may involve the personal career, professional success, the achievement of high social status in economic and/or occupational prestige categories. One may achieve these goals in different ways. The ways related to *negative innovation* involve almost criminal or, in fact, criminal actions. Such actions include, for example, involvement in illegal activities, participation in different forms of organized crime, or the use of performance-increasing substances in sports. In the case of *positive innovation*, such ways may involve inventive activity and the creation of new solutions. In other words, I mean a situation in which one enters the field, which specialists call the "blue ocean," i.e., a "pioneer" innovative activity. As part of that innovative activity, people or companies creatively implement new solutions and engage in actions that nobody engaged in earlier.

Retreatism means a type of reaction to structure, which typifies the individuals and groups that neither accept goals, nor values, which dominate in a political system, nor the social structure related to that political system. The representatives of *retreatism* mean individuals in a situation of apathy. They engage neither in social nor political activity. The above means a situation known from authoritarian and totalitarian systems. To a considerable extent, such an attitude also exists in democratic countries. The reasons for such a situation may differ and involve such phenomena as concentration on a political career and economic aspects, or even a situation in which some people characterize the current authorities as illegitimate. Moreover, such people believe that the authorities do not create opportunities to participate in political processes and influence decisions. The bases of such attitudes involve the lack of conviction in that the system is based on values which those groups interiorized. The above means a situation in which one somewhat "emigrates internally" and limits his or her activities to the family and friends sphere. According to E. Durkheim and R. K. Merton's concept, the above means the clearest manifestation of social anomie.

Rebellion means a category of reaction to structure that differs from other categories. *Rebellion* involves both rejection of goals and rejection of measures and methods required to achieve them. We can characterize the goals as recognized and dominant in society's structure. However, in contrast to the *retreatism* type of structure, *rebellion* proposes distinct goals, values, and distinct measures to implement ways of new goals' achievement, which differ from the commonly accepted ways. The above, as the name suggests, means rebellious attitudes. We can even characterize the attitudes as revolutionary, which does not mean that one can always effectively accomplish the planned goals.

I empirically verified the above models of reactions to social and political structures, which include political participation models. To conduct the research, I chose a set of ten questions, which I later modified. I implemented the changes in several stages. In general, the changes involved the reduction in the questions' content, as their goal was to characterize individual types of reactions, and the questions were not always able to accurately describe a given category of attitudes.

I a priori chose the following sets of questions to characterize the models of participation and types of reaction:

- Conventional political participation (involvement level) (questionnaire questions 1–16),[10]
- Unconventional political participation (involvement level) (Q. 17–26),
- Non-violent unconventional political participation (acceptance level) (variant II from Q. 17–26),
- Violent unconventional political participation (acceptance level) (Q. 27–52),
- Opinions on democracy as a governance system (Q. 6),
- Evaluation of Polish democracy's functioning (Q. 7),
- Evaluation of whether political elites (rulers) fulfill their duties (Q. 8),
- Evaluation of whether Polish rulers try to act in the interest of all people (Q. 9),
- Evaluation of citizens' influence on the country's affairs (Q. 10),
- Evaluation of one's influence on his or her city or commune's matters (Q. 11).

Next, I chose values for each variable or a group of variables, which should properly characterize the model, according to its description. Moreover, I chose the relevant variables, which I gradually reduced, so that I could move from the analytical level to the synthetic generalizations. The synthetic

10 You can find a full set of questions from the questionnaire in Annex 1.

generalizations correspond to the model of participation and reactions to structure in a most accurate way. In total, I made four classifications.

Classification 1

Conformists (should present the following features):

- *High* level of conventional political participation (Q. 1–16) – based on "median" type values,
- *Low* acceptance of unconventional political participation (Q. 17–52),
- *The belief* that democracy has an advantage over all other forms of government (Q. 6),
- *Satisfaction* with the Polish democracy's functioning (Q. 7),
- *Sense of influence* on the country's affairs (Q. 10),
- *The belief* that rulers almost always fulfill their duties (Q. 8),
- *The belief* that rulers act for the benefit of general social interest (Q. 9).

Ritualists

- *High* level of conventional political participation (Q. 1–16),
- *Low* acceptance of unconventional political participation (Q. 17–52),
- *The belief* that democracy has an advantage over all other forms of government (Q. 6),
- *Lack of decision* concerning whether one can be satisfied with the Polish democracy's functioning (Q. 7),
- *Lack of sense of influence* on the country's affairs (Q. 10),
- *Lack of sense of influence* on their city or commune affairs (Q. 11),
- *Lack of belief* that rulers fulfill their duties (Q. 8),
- *The belief* that Polish rulers pursue the interests of small, selected groups (Q. 9).

Innovators

- *High* acceptance of non-violent unconventional political participation acceptance (Q. 17–26),
- *Lack of agreement* with the thesis that democracy has an advantage over all other forms of government (Q. 6),
- *Dissatisfaction* with Polish democracy's functioning (Q. 7),
- *The belief* that rulers sometimes fulfill their duties (Q. 8),
- *The belief* that Polish rulers pursue the interests of small, selected groups (Q. 9).

Retreaters

- *Low* level of conventional political participation (Q. 1–16),
- *Low* acceptance of unconventional political participation (Q. 17–52),
- *Lack of decision concerning* whether democracy has an advantage over all other forms of government (Q. 6),
- *Lack of decision concerning* whether one can be satisfied with Polish democracy's functioning (Q. 7),
- *Lack of sense of influence* on their country's affairs (Q. 10),
- *Lack of sense of influence* on their city or commune's affairs (Q. 11),
- *The belief* that rulers *mainly pursue their own interests* or the interests of small, selected groups (Q. 9).

Rebels

- *High* acceptance of non-violent unconventional political participation (Q. 17–26),
- *Lack of agreements* with the thesis that democracy has an advantage over all other types of government (Q. 6),
- *Dissatisfaction* with Polish democracy's functioning (Q. 7),
- *The belief* that rulers never fulfill their duties (Q. 8),
- *The belief* that *rulers mainly pursue their own interests* or the interests of small, selected groups (Q. 9).

As I generalized the description of individual participation models and categories of reactions to structure, I was able to create the below table, which can help us orientate in the values of variables that I assigned to each model. I based the selection of values on two principles. First, I based the selection of values on a priori depictions concerning features that should distinguish a participation model and type of reaction to the structure. Second, I based the selection of values on the analysis of marginal distributions of variables, including correlations, qualified as sets of factors that characterize the individual models.

I selected variables and values that define them for each of the five attitudes. In the next step, in the whole set of results, I aggregated the respondents in terms of their answers to questions specified in Qualification 1. I assigned a proper attitude to each research participant if he or she provided set answers to every question that characterized the attitude.

And so, for example, in Qualification 1, in the case of *Innovators*, I decided that the following features and answers characterize the group: high acceptance of non-violent unconventional political participation, "I do not agree" in Q. 6, "dissatisfied" in Q. 7, "sometimes/most of the time" in Q. 8, "they pursue the interests of small, selected groups" in Q. 9. I qualified all the respondents that provided the above answers to the above questions to the group of *Innovators*.

I grouped the remaining attitudes in a similar fashion. I created a separate category for all respondents, whom I did not assign any attitude, which I called the "out of scale" category.

I included a respondent in a group of attitudes by means of the following algorithm:

$$\mathbf{P_i} = \prod_{\mathbf{j,k}} \mathbf{Q_j O_k}$$

In which:

$\mathbf{P_i}$ – means a particular attitude (i=1,...5)

$\mathbf{Q_j}$ – a question that qualifies somebody to an appropriate attitude

$\mathbf{O_k}$ – an answer that qualifies somebody to an appropriate attitude

It is worth to present the detailed record of characteristics, which illustrates what exactly it could include in each participation model.

Classification 1

	Conformists	Ritualists	Innovators	Retreaters	Rebels
Conventional political participation (involvement level) (1–16)	high	high		low	
Unconventional political participation (involvement level) (17–52)	low	low		low	

(*continued*)

Table 4.10. Continued

	Conformists	Ritualists	Innovators	Retreaters	Rebels
Non-violent unconventional political participation (acceptance level) (17–26)			high		high
Violent unconventional political participation (acceptance level) (27–52)					
Question 6. Do you agree or disagree with the statement that democracy has an advantage over all other forms of government (democracy is the best out of them)?	agrees	agrees	disagrees	finds it hard to tell	disagrees
Question 7. Please evaluate Polish democracy's functioning.	satisfied	finds it hard to tell	dissatisfied	finds it hard to tell	dissatisfied
Question 8. Do you think that it is possible to be convinced that Polish rulers fulfill their duties?	always	most of the time	sometimes / most of the time		never
Question 9. Do you think that Polish rulers are involved in important matters/ interests to achieve something solely for themselves, or do they try to act in the interest of the general population?	they act for the benefit of general social interests	they pursue the interests of small, selected social groups	they pursue the interests of small, selected social groups	they are primarily engaged in doing business for their own benefit / they pursue the interests of small, selected social groups	they are primarily engaged in doing business for their own benefit / they pursue the interests of small, selected social groups

Table 4.10. Continued

	Conformists	Ritualists	Innovators	Retreaters	Rebels
Question 10. Do you think that people like you have an influence on the country's affairs?	yes	no		no	
Question 11. Do you think that people like you have an influence on the affairs of their city or commune?		no		no	

Source: *Partycypacja polityczna Polaków – nowe wyzwania i formy aktywności* study, 2017, NCN grant 4884, N=603.

The analysis of data presented in the table lets us state that the assignment of specified features and values to the model involves numerous difficulties. I cannot describe some of the answers' categories as those that characterize a specified participation model or a type of reaction to structure, such as the level of violent unconventional political participation's acceptance. We can characterize these categories as, to some extent, marginal. The categories cannot form a basis for the description of different participation models when we refer to R. K. Merton's typology.

We can confirm the thesis after we conduct a statistical analysis which involves the aggregate attribution of values of variables' individual groups to earlier proposed models or types (Table 5.1).

Table 5.1 Participation models/types of reactions to the social and political structure

Classification		
	N	Percentage
Conformists		2.0
Ritualists		1.5
Innovators		1.2
Retreaters		0.7
Rebels		1.0
Out of scale		93.6
Total	603	100.0

Source: *Partycypacja polityczna Polaków – nowe wyzwania i formy aktywności* study, 2017, NCN grant 4884, N=603.

The analysis either informs that variables assigned to individual participation models in such a broad context, cannot properly define the nature of models, or categories do not reflect the actual attitudes of citizens. By categories, I mean *conformists*, *ritualists*, etc. If we select ranges this way, it becomes clear that only one to two percent of social and political modes of behavior correspond to the categories from the quoted typology. Therefore, we should characterize more than ninety percent of modes of behavior as "beyond the scale."

Therefore, I started the next stage of analyses. The next stage of analyses, on the one hand, involved the reduction of variables assigned to each participation model, whereas, on the other hand, the next stage of analyses involved a combination of some attitudes' categories.

First, I limited the groups of variables as well as variables for some models or types of reactions. I limited the number of the above from ten to, for example, eight because of their irrelevancy. Moreover, I limited the use of certain individual variables' values for some participation models. For example, in the case of *rebels* and *innovators*, I decided to abandon the following variables: "Do you think that people like you have an influence on the country's affairs?" and "Do you think that people like you have an influence on the affairs of their city or commune?"

Next, in the second classification, after the statistical analysis, I decided not to use some of the variables' values. In the case of the *conformists* model, I decided to delete the low acceptance of unconventional political participation at the involvement level because I observed that the category proved completely unknown. In general, even at the level of acceptance of any unconventional participation forms, such an approach was out of the question. Notably, the violent unconventional forms of participation were out of the question and meant another value from this group of variables that I had to abandon.

Classification 2

	Conformists	Ritualists	Innovators	Retreaters	Rebels
Conventional political participation (involvement level) (1–16)	high	high		low	
Unconventional political participation (involvement level) (17–26)		low		low	
Non-violent unconventional political participation (acceptance level) (17–26)			high		high
Violent unconventional political participation (acceptance level) (27–52)	low				
Question 6. Do you agree or disagree with the statement that democracy has an advantage over all other forms of government (democracy is the best out of them)?	agrees	agrees	disagrees	finds it hard to tell	disagrees

	Conformists	Ritualists	Innovators	Retreaters	Rebels
Question 7. Please evaluate Polish democracy's functioning.	satisfied	finds it hard to tell	dissatisfied	finds it hard to tell	dissatisfied
Question 8. Do you think that it is possible to be convinced that Polish rulers fulfill their duties?	always	most of the time	sometimes / most of the time		never
Question 9. Do you think that Polish rulers are involved in important matters/ interests to achieve something solely for themselves, or do they try to act in the interest of the general population?	they act for the benefit of general social interests	they pursue the interests of small, selected social groups	they pursue the interests of small, selected social groups	they are primarily engaged in doing business for their own benefit / they pursue the interests of small, selected social groups	they are primarily engaged in doing business for their own benefit / they pursue the interests of small, selected social groups
Question 10. Do you think that people like you have an influence on the country's affairs?	yes	no		no	
Question 11. Do you think that people like you have an influence on the affairs of their city or commune?		no		no	

Source: *Partycypacja polityczna Polaków – nowe wyzwania i formy aktywności* study, 2017, NCN grant 4884, N=603.

The advanced analyses changed the frequency of individual participation models. I combined the *Innovators* and *Rebels* types of reaction into one category of *System's Critics* to create a more accurate and advanced typology of participation models and types of reactions to the structure. I present the results of the analysis in the next stage in Table 5.2.

Table 5.2 Participation models/types of reaction to social and political structure (Classification 2)

Classification 2		
	N	Percentage
Conformists	22	3.6
Ritualists	9	1.5
Retreaters	126	20.9
Critics	111	18.4
Out of scale	335	55.6
Total	603	100.0

Source: *Partycypacja polityczna Polaków – nowe wyzwania i formy aktywności* study, 2017, NCN grant 4884, N=603.

The change of some variables' qualifications and the reduction of values assigned to them determined a distinct image of participation types' classification. I should now present a detailed record of features that illustrates what I could include in each participation model. In this typology, the *Conformists* group grew in number but did not exceed four percent of research participants. On the other hand, the *Retreaters* groups grew in number significantly and amount to over one-fifth of research participants. Moreover, I could observe a significant rise in the numbers of individuals who oppose the system and do not accept the means and instruments used to achieve goals. The above group, known as *Critics*, was able to amount to almost one-fifth of research participants. Nevertheless, I had to characterize more than half of the research participants as "out of scale."

To further determine exactly how the formation of system participants' attitudes to its structure proceeds, I reduced variables and their values once again. I abandoned the variable concerning whether the respondents agree with the statement that democracy has an advantage over all other forms of government (democracy is the best out of them). After the analysis, I observed the insignificance of differences and that the question does not generate statistically important differences, apart from an obvious differentiation. The differentiation dealt with the fact that *Conformists* and *Ritualists* mostly agree with the thesis, whereas other groups have a different opinion. In particular, the latter observation applies to *Critics*, i.e., *Innovators* and *Rebels* treated as one group. Moreover, I abandoned the variable concerning the issue of elites engagement in important affairs and interests, i.e., whether leaders want to achieve something solely for themselves or whether they try to act in the interest of the general population.

Classification 3

	Conformists	Ritualists	Innovators	Retreaters	Rebels
Conventional political participation (involvement level) (1–16)	high	high		low	
Unconventional political participation (involvement level) (17–52)		low		low	
Non-violent unconventional political participation (acceptance level) (17–26)			high	low	high
Violent unconventional political participation (acceptance level) (27–52)	low				

	Conformists	Ritualists	Innovators	Retreaters	Rebels
Question 7. Please evaluate Polish democracy's functioning.	satisfied	finds it hard to tell	dissatisfied		dissatisfied
Question 8. Do you think that it is possible to be convinced that Polish rulers fulfill their duties?	always / most of the time				never / sometimes
Question 10. Do you think that people like you have an influence on the country's affairs?	yes	no		no	

Source: *Partycypacja polityczna Polaków – nowe wyzwania i formy aktywności* study, 2017, NCN grant 4884, N=603.

After a series of statistical analyses, I attempted once more to define the involvement of participation models that I separated a priori. The definition let me describe the participation models more accurately but in a synthetical sense. I observed that, paradoxically, in the context of certain categories, *Innovators* and *Rebels* are not the only groups that we can classify as critics of the system's goals. Apart from *Innovators* and *Rebels*, we can also partially classify *Ritualists* and *Retreaters* as critics of the system's goals. Most *Retreaters* present attitudes similar to those of *Innovators* and *Rebels* concerning the negative evaluation of Polish democracy's functioning and the belief that rulers never or only sometimes fulfill their duties. Moreover, we can characterize the latter opinion as a link between *Ritualists* and *Innovators* and *Rebels*.

The integration of variables used to characterize the individual participation models as well as types of reactions to structure led to a clear rise in the number of citizens classified in individual categories. First, the percentage of "out of scale" respondents dropped. In the case of Classification 3, the percentage did not even reach fifty percent of respondents. Second, the percentage of individuals that we can include in every group rises. Especially, we can categorize more research participants as the broadly understood category of *Critics*. As a result, the *Critics* group will amount to almost one-fifth of research participants. Moreover, we can categorize more research participants as *Retreaters*. As a result, the model known as *Retreaters* will amount to almost a quarter of research participants. Interestingly, some of the discovered subgroups within the aggregated model of *Critics* mean quite strange and incoherent types of attitudes. The set of questions that qualified respondents to each group was separate in relation to attitudes. Therefore, for example, the level of conventional political participation (1–16) meant one of the elements that categorized a respondent as a *Ritualist,* but the element did not belong to the classification of *Innovators* and *Rebels*. As we compare these attitudes after we grouped them according to the level of participation forms' acceptance and research participants' opinions concerning the belief that rulers never or only sometimes fulfill their duties, we can observe similarities between the attitudes. For example, we can observe somewhat similar views and levels of participation forms' acceptance between *Innovators* and *Rebels* and a small group of *Ritualists*.[11] In turn, a small percentage of *Retreaters* identifies with the approach of *Critics*, i.e., *Innovators* and *Rebels*. I find it difficult to explain this phenomenon and comment on it in an unambiguous way. The above may prove that we deal with an extreme incoherence of views and the lack of decision in terms of self-definition in existing forms of participation.

11 The set of questions the included the respondents in each group was separate from attitudes. Therefore, for example, the level of conventional political participation (1–16) meant one of the elements that qualified a respondent to *Ritualists* attitude but did not mean an element of *Innovators* and *Rebels* classification. When we compare these attitudes after grouping in terms of the participation forms' acceptance level and respondents' opinions concerning the belief that rulers never/sometimes fulfill their duties, we can observe that the attitudes show consistency.

Table 5.3 Participation models/types of reaction to social and political structure (Classification 3)

Classification 3		
	N	Percentage
Conformists	40	6.6
Ritualists	39	6.5
Retreaters	148	24.5
Rebels/Innovators	76	12.6
Ritualists/Rebels/Innovators	14	2.3
Retreaters/Rebels/ Innovators	21	3.5
Out of scale	265	44
Total	603	100.0

Source: *Partycypacja polityczna Polaków – nowe wyzwania i formy aktywności* study, 2017, NCN grant 4884, N=603.

The next step in the series of analyses involved another "reduction of distance" between the indexes of participation models. I limited the sets of variables to six. The sets of variables included: the level of involvement in conventional political participation, the level of involvement in unconventional political participation, the level of non-violent and violent unconventional political participation acceptance, the assessment of democracy's actual functioning, and the issue concerning the perception of citizens' influence on country's affairs. In the context of each variable or set of variables, I assigned specified values to individual models. As I divided the population into five types of attitudes in each qualification, I gradually tried to group them and, at the same time, maintain the groups' initial names. On each stage, I could observe that they were not numerous, so I aggregated them into one attitude: *Critics*. As a result of that iteration of analysis, I obtained a classification which involves the following attitudes:

Conformists: conventional political participation at the involvement level – high value; violent unconventional political participation – low level of acceptance; satisfaction with Polish democracy's functioning; the sense of influence on the country's affairs.

Ritualists: conventional political participation at the involvement level – high value; violent unconventional political participation – low level of acceptance; lack of sense of influence on the country's affairs.
Retreaters: conventional political participation at the involvement level – low value; unconventional political participation at the level of acceptance – low value; lack of sense of influence on the country's affairs.
Critics: a broader category, which I obtained by means of this iteration. The category involves the following attitudes:
Innovators: non-violent unconventional political participation – high level of acceptance; dissatisfaction with democracy's functioning in Poland.
Rebels: non-violent unconventional political participation – high level of acceptance; dissatisfaction with democracy's functioning in Poland.

I present the described characteristics in the table below.

Classification 4

	Conformists	Ritualists	Innovators	Retreaters	Rebels
Conventional political participation (involvement level) (1–16)	high	high		low	
Unconventional political participation (involvement level) (17–26)		low		low	
Non-violent unconventional political participation (acceptance level) (17–26)			high		high

	Conformists	Ritualists	Innovators	Retreaters	Rebels
Violent unconventional political participation (acceptance level) (27–52)	low				
Question 7. Please evaluate Polish democracy's functioning.	satisfied		dissatisfied		dissatisfied
Question 10. Do you think that people like you have an influence on the country's affairs?	yes	no		no	

Source: *Partycypacja polityczna Polaków – nowe wyzwania i formy aktywności* study, 2017, NCN grant 4884, N=603.

As I developed the participation models according to Classification 4, I abandoned those *Ritualists* and *Retreaters* subgroups that presented similarities to *Critics* as the mentioned subgroups were erratic. Moreover, in total, those two submodels amounted to only 1.5 %.

Table 5.4 Participation models/types of reaction to social and political structure (Classification 4)

Classification 4		
	N	Percentage
Conformists	40	6.6
Ritualists	39	6.5
Retreaters	148	24.5
Critics	111	18.4
Out of scale	265	44.0
Total	603	100.0

As we summarize the cycle of conducted and presented analyses, we should ask ourselves at least three questions:

The first question deals with the issue of whether R. K. Merton's typology is adequate in the context of contemporary social and political reality in the twenty-first century. According to his postulate, one must bind the theoretical with the empirical. Perhaps, nowadays, we cannot empirically confirm the theoretical typology of citizens' reactions to structure and politics.

The second question deals with the issue of whether significant differences between Polish and American societies originate from Poland's or other country's characteristics, its experiences from the communist era. The above issue may also be the reason for the situation in which a lot of Poles remain outside the R. K. Merton's scale. By the experiences from the communist era, I mean the system of "real" socialism and traumatic experiences from the beginning of the post-1989 transformation.

The third question deals with the issue of whether used indexes present satisfactory accuracy. Maybe such an analytical approach was too in-depth. And the models' types are measured based on declarations, i.e., they are levels postulated in the realm of political participation.

The fact that the research participants declared at least an intermediate level of conventional political participation leads us to puzzling conclusions. These conventional forms of political participation involved, for example, voting in parliamentary and presidential elections, participation in local elections, discussions on politics, involvement in public consultations.[12] On the other hand, the above means declarative data, and the respondents did not regularly participate in politics, as their answers range from "often" to "sporadically." Nevertheless, we cannot state that Polish citizens participate in politics only to a small extent: some of them almost always participate, whereas others participate "rotationally," i.e., they vote from time to time. In turn, we should pay attention to the fact that recently we can observe a constant rise in voter turnout in Poland. Usually, we can observe the highest voter turnout during the presidential elections, but recently there

---

12 One can find detailed statistical data from the study in Chapter 3.

was a huge rise in voter turnout, especially during the municipal and parliamentary elections.

Table 5.5 Model of the rise of voter turnout in presidential elections

Voter turnout						
Presidential elections	2010[a]		2015[b]		2020[c]	
	Election	Runoff election	Election	Runoff election	Election	Runoff election
	54.94 %	55.31 %	48.96 %	55.34 %	64.51 %	68.18 %

Source: *Partycypacja polityczna Polaków – nowe wyzwania i formy aktywności* study, 2017, NCN grant 4884, N=1237.

a *Wybory Prezydenta Rzeczypospolitej Polskiej zarządzone na dzień 20 czerwca 2010* (Aug. 2020) <https://prezydent2010.pkw.gov.pl/PZT1/PL/WYN/W/index.htm>; *Wybory Prezydenta Rzeczypospolitej ponowne głosowanie w dniu 4 lipca 2010* (Aug. 2020) <https://prezydent2010.pkw.gov.pl/PZT/PL/WYN/W/index.htm>.
b *Obwieszczenie Państwowej Komisji Wyborczej z dnia 11 maja 2015 r. o wynikach głosowania i wyniku wyborów Prezydenta Rzeczypospolitej Polskiej, zarządzonych na dzień 10 maja 2015 r.* (Aug. 2020) <https://prezydent2015.pkw.gov.pl/pliki/1_Obwieszczenie.pdf>; *Obwieszczenie Państwowej Komisji Wyborczej z dnia 25 maja 2015 r. o wynikach ponownego głosowania i wyniku wyborów Prezydenta Rzeczypospolitej Polskiej* (Aug. 2020) <https://prezydent2015.pkw.gov.pl/pliki/1432571989_obwieszczenie.pdf>.
c *Wybory Prezydenta Rzeczypospolitej Polskiej z dnia 28 czerwca 2020* (Aug. 2020) <https://wybory.gov.pl/prezydent20200628/pl/frekwencja/1/Koniec/pl>; *Wybory Prezydenta Rzeczypospolitej z dnia 28 czerwca 2020* (Aug. 2020) <https://wybory.gov.pl/prezydent20200628/pl/frekwencja/2/Koniec/pl>.

Table 5.6 Model of the rise of voter turnout in parliamentary elections

Voter turnout 2			
Parliamentary elections	2011[a]	2015[b]	2019[c]
	48.92 %	50.91 %	61.74 %

Source: *Partycypacja polityczna Polaków – nowe wyzwania i formy aktywności* study, 2017, NCN grant 4884, N=1237.

a *Wybory do Sejmu i Senatu Rzeczypospolitej Polskiej 2011* (Aug. 2020) <https://wybory2011.pkw.gov.pl/att/pl/000000.html#tabs-1>.
b *Wybory do Sejmu i Senatu Rzeczypospolitej Polskiej 2015* (Aug. 2020) <https://parlament2015.pkw.gov.pl/Frekwencja/000000/4.html>.
c *Wybory do Sejmu i Senatu Rzeczypospolitej Polskiej 2019* (Aug. 2020) <https://sejmsenat2019.pkw.gov.pl/sejmsenat2019/pl/frekwencja/Koniec/sejm/pl/adm>.

In general, we can observe that there is a rise in local activism. The study shows that every tenth participant of the system works to solve local communities' problems. The communities include villages, cities, communes, districts, and regions. Over one-fourth of participants declare that they fulfill the above work occasionally. After I aggregated the data, I observed that thirty-six percent of Poles declare at least some involvement in their local community's affairs. The above thirty-six percent means a considerable part of the local community. I should add that the above numbers mean a significant rise in comparison to the data obtained a dozen or so years ago. In comparison to the results of the study conducted fifteen years ago, we can observe a rise in most forms of conventional participation. In such domains as voting in municipal elections and discussions on politics, the activity's rise amounts to between several to even ten percentage points. Moreover, we can observe that the activities for the benefit of the local community tripled, as in 2002 they amounted to 3.6 percent, whereas in 2017 they amounted to 10.3 percent.[13]

Another important issue does not originate from research but from observation and objective data. Namely, I mean the creation and activities of urban movements, which formed and started to act in many agglomerations and actively try to influence the local governments' politics. On the other hand, we can characterize the level of involvement in unconventional forms of political participation as relatively low. Therefore, we can presume that the above can become a plane of action for the type of reactions appropriate for *Critics*. Moreover, we can characterize the level of unconventional participation forms' acceptance as low too. If citizens decide to accept unconventional participation without reservation, the forms of participation must be relatively mild. By the above mild forms, I mean signing petitions, participation in a legally organized strike, or legally conducted demonstrations. The level of acceptance involved between one-fifth to one-third of the research participants.

In summary, we can observe that empirical data that directly refers to the participation issue shows that we cannot characterize citizens' activity as "that" small, and we can observe a rise in that activity. On the other hand,

13 Table 3.2 in Chapter 3.

we can characterize the willingness to accept and, even more so, to participate in unconventional forms of participation as quite low. Understandably, in some sense, the above happens at the postulated level.

In turn, when we use the R. K. Merton's typology, we can find more individuals on the system's fringes in comparison to what we could expect from directly collected empirical data. Most of these individuals would be *Retreaters* and *Critics*, whereas *Conformists* and *Ritualists* would form the minority. In other words, according to that typology, we could characterize the nature of Poles' approach to participation as semi-peripheral. One could explain the above with a wrong tradition that Poland inherited from the monocentric autocratic system. One could try to explain the above by references to the concept of political culture and suggest that in Poland, we deal with a type of political culture that Gabriel Almond would characterize as the subject-participant political culture.[14] However, the results of empirical studies confirm that the above type of political culture is widespread in Poland, but the above type is not dominant as we deal with the formation of civic culture for decades now.[15]

We can characterize the R. K. Merton's concept concerning the typology of citizens' reactions to structure and willingness to participate as undoubtedly appealing and theoretically interesting. Still, the empirical studies show that, in the contemporary social and political reality, Merton's concept does not describe the actual type of participatory behaviors in an adequate way, at least in the context of Polish reality.

---

14 G. A. Almond, G. B. Powell, *Comparative Politics. A Development Approach* (Boston, 1966), pp. 53–54.

15 The studies of Poles' political culture, conducted since 1985, present the above phenomenon. One can find the results of the studies in, for instance: J. Garlicki, A. Noga-Bogomilski, *Kultura polityczna w społeczeństwie demokratycznym* (Warszawa, 2004); J. Garlicki, *Demokracja i integracja europejska* (Toruń, 2005).

Chapter VI. Political participation models' typology: a posteriori approach

In some sense, it seems that, in political, social, cultural (although not consumption-related) senses, contemporary societies drift towards atomization, ideological anomy, apathy (including participatory apathy). One may also observe the phenomenon that we may call "electoral demoralization," manifested by voting for parties, which are populist, often extreme, and which sometimes declare promises, which are impossible to fulfill. One should also notice the frequent change in electoral preferences, known as electoral volatility. What happens is that party loyalty, and even ideological loyalty, disappear. However, on the other hand, strong, yet superficial political emotions are not foreign to society, as they bring participation in politics closer to tribal patterns, where *friend or foe* division was the central one. An important issue is to determine whether these anomic attitudes exist in Poland, and if so, on what scale. This process is always dynamic because the accumulation of a certain type of attitudes and activities increases at one moment to decrease at the other. One way or another, the process is subject to changes.

Faced with a research area that poses the previously mentioned problems, classical, a priori research patterns and methods may lose their (actual or assumed) exploratory power.

The concept of citizens' reaction to structure that R. K. Merton proposed[1] is not confirmed in studies and does not adequately describe actual types of participatory behavior in the contemporary world. Therefore, it is necessary to examine reality differently. The same variables may and should constitute the basis, given that one analyzes them not according to predetermined assumptions, but real measurement results.

At this point, it is worth referring to a classic of political marketing, B. Newman, who states that "a basic skill is ... to divide the whole country into regions and smaller social communities that showed differences in

1 Merton, "Social Structure...," p. 672.

demographic and socioeconomic profiles as well as in attitudes towards various issues raised in the campaign."[2]

In this sense, the scope of the analytical work conducted in this chapter corresponds to an a posteriori segmentation. Let me remind you that W. Cwalina and A. Falkowski[3] list two basic approaches to segmentation implementation. They refer to the classic approach as a priori. It consists in the division of some whole (economic, social, political) based on predetermined features (mainly demographic and psychographic). In turn, the second approach is explorative and lacks top-down assumptions. Cwalina and Falkowski refer to it as a posteriori and the approach is based on the analysis of empirical data collected during the application of different statistical techniques.[4]

An important element of the segmentation proposed below is that it is based not on sociodemographic features as it is commonly accepted, but on expressed attitudes and behavioral characteristics.

In the further course of analyses, I subjected the groups of research participants, formed as a result of the division with respect to the fourth classification, to statistical tests.[5] I considered each of the resulting factions individually in order to check its homogeneity and detect any discrepancies in the intensity of the traits present, and, in the next stage, I conducted a new division of the studied population.

In order to achieve maximum effect, I used classification codes created on the basis of the six previously constructed indexes, i.e., conventional and unconventional political participation, the level of acceptance of unconventional non-violent political participation (17–26), the level of acceptance of unconventional political participation (27–52), and the respondents' answers to questions 7 and 10. I generated an individual six-digit code for each research participant.

---

2 Quoted in: M. Mazur, *Marketing polityczny* (Warszawa: Wydawnictwo naukowe PWN, 2002), p. 66.

3 W. Cwalina, A. Fałkowski, *Marketing polityczny. Perspektywa psychologiczna* (Gdańsk: Gdańskie Wydawnictwo Psychologiczne, 2006).

4 M. Wedel, W. A. Kamakura, *Market Segmentation. Conceptual and Methodological Foundations* (Boston: Springer, 2000).

5 Described in the previous chapter.

Six questions or groups of questions, selected because of previous analyses as those that best define citizens' attitudes towards the political system, constituted the basis of the analysis. These were the variables used in the fourth qualification relating to R. K. Merton's typology. It is also worth noting that during the focus group interviews conducted, their participants indicated these issues as particularly important in determining citizens' attitudes towards the political system and their willingness to participate (or lack of such willingness).

The first question (Do you think that people like you have an influence on the country's affairs?) is, as one might say, a classic question about the belief (or lack of such belief) that citizens feel they may actively participate in politics. The second important variable is the question about the evaluation of Polish democracy's functioning. The next questions constitute a classification into four groups of participatory reactions. The first question involves a set of questions concerning participation in conventional forms of political participation. The second group deals with participation in various unconventional forms. The next two groups of variables address the level of citizens' acceptance of violent or non-violent (the fourth category) unconventional participation.

In all variables (after their recoding), I used a dichotomous division/scale: yes (1), no (0). In the case of a syndrome of data on participation or acceptance of different varieties of participation, it implies some degree of aggregation according to the rule of a low (or even "null") or high indicator. I created six-digit code syndromes (configurations) from these six groups of variables or the variables themselves and then calculated the number of each configuration's repetitions (Annex 6). Eleven configurations received more than fifteen indications (i.e., more than 2.5 % of the sample) which I considered a borderline number. The four configurations with between thirty-one and sixty-two indications proved the most numerous (i.e., between 5.2 and 10.3 %).

Table 6.1. Components of classification codes

Index number	Index description	Index value
1	Question 10. Do you think that people like you have an influence on the country's affairs?	1: no, 2: yes, 3: difficult to say
2	Question 7. Please evaluate Polish democracy's functioning. Are you satisfied with its functioning:	1: dissatisfied, 2: satisfied, 3: difficult to say
3	Conventional political participation (involvement level) (1–16)	0: low, 1: high
4	Unconventional political participation (level) (17–52)	0: low, 1: high
5	Unconventional non-violent political participation (acceptance level) (17–26)	0: low, 1: high
6	Unconventional political participation (acceptance level) (27–52)	0: low, 1: high

Source: *Partycypacja polityczna Polaków – nowe wyzwania i formy aktywności* study, 2017, NCN. grant 4884, N=603.

Table 6.2 Configurations of attitudes towards system and participation

Question 10. Do you think that people like you have an influence on the country's affairs? 1: no 2: yes 3: difficult to say	Question 7. Please evaluate Polish democracy's functioning. Are you satisfied with its functioning: 1: Dissatisfied 2: Satisfied 3: Difficult to say	Conventional political participation (involvement level) (1–16) 0: low 1: high	Unconventional political participation (acceptance level) (17–52) 0: low 1: high	Unconventional non-violent political participation (acceptance level) (17–26) 0: low 1: high	Unconventional political participation (acceptance level) (27–52) 0: low 1: high	Response codes (six-digit)	Number of configuration iterations	Percentage of repetitions	Percentage of all combinations
1	1	0	0	0	0	110000	62	20,13	10,3
1	2	0	0	0	0	120000	36	11,69	6,0
2	2	1	0	0	0	221000	35	11,36	5,8
2	2	0	0	0	0	220000	31	10,06	5,1
1	3	0	0	0	0	130000	26	8,44	4,3
2	1	1	1	0	0	211100	25	8,12	4,1
2	1	0	0	0	0	210000	22	7,14	3,6
1	1	0	0	1	1	110011	21	6,82	3,5
2	1	1	0	0	0	211000	17	5,52	2,8
2	2	0	0	1	1	220011	17	5,52	2,8
1	1	1	1	1	1	111111	16	5,19	2,7

Source: *Partycypacja polityczna Polaków – nowe wyzwania i formy aktywności* study, 2017, NCN grant 4884, N=603.

These codes involved:

- "110000," which meant individuals who believe that they have no influence on the affairs of the country, are dissatisfied with the functioning of democracy, participate neither in conventional nor unconventional forms, accept neither non-violent nor violent unconventional participation: we may describe them as *dissatisfied citizens with a sense of apathy* (10.3 %);
- "120000," which meant individuals who believe that they have no influence on the affairs of the country, but are satisfied with the functioning of democracy, similarly to the previous group participate neither in conventional nor unconventional forms, accept neither non-violent nor violent unconventional participation: these individuals are *satisfied with democracy*, who, on the other hand, are *apathetic political system participants* (6 %);
- "221000," which meant those who believe that they have an influence on the affairs of the country, are satisfied with the functioning of democracy, participate in conventional forms but do not participate in unconventional forms, accept neither non-violent nor violent unconventional participation: these individuals are *supporters of the system, who are conventionally active* (5.8 %);
- "220000," which meant those who believe that they have an influence on the affairs of the country, are satisfied with the functioning of democracy, participate neither in conventional nor unconventional forms, do not accept neither non-violent nor violent unconventional participation: these individuals constitute a group, which *supports the system*, but *does not participate* (5.2 %);
- "130000," which meant citizens who do not feel that they have an influence on the affairs of the country, have no opinion on the functioning of democracy in the country, and neither participate in nor support any forms of participation: these citizens constitute a decidedly *apathetic* group;
- "211100," which meant system's participants who believe they have an influence on the affairs of the country but are dissatisfied with the functioning of democracy, nevertheless participate both conventionally and unconventionally: we may describe this group as *critical activists*;

- "210000," which meant a group that believes it has an influence on the affairs of the country, but is not satisfied with the way democracy works in Poland in reality; the group is completely inactive, neither in an actual way nor in support of various forms of participation: these individuals are *inactive ritualists* (if we refer to R. K. Merton's terms);
- "110011," which meant radical citizens, who do not feel they have an influence on the affairs of the country, are dissatisfied with the functioning of democracy, accept (and, therefore, perhaps participate) in unconventional forms of participation, both non-violent and violent: these individuals constitute a group of *critical activists who have no problem with the use of violence*;
- "211000," which meant a social group that believes it has an influence on the affairs of the country but is not satisfied with the functioning of democracy, participates in conventional forms of participation, whereas it does not participate in or accept unconventional forms of participation: these are citizens whom we may describe as *conventional activists, who are dissatisfied with the functioning of the system*;
- "220011," which meant the category of system participants who believe that they are able to influence the affairs of the country, are satisfied with the way the democratic system in the country works, but, paradoxically, they are willing to accept non-violent or even violent participation: these individuals constitute a group of citizens who, despite believing that the system functions properly, are *activists who accept unconventional participation*;
- "111111," which meant a group that we may call extreme (in some respects), as they believe that they have no influence on the affairs of the country, are dissatisfied with the functioning of democracy, participate in both conventional and unconventional forms of political participation, accept both non-violent and violent unconventional participation: members of this group are *active critical participants of the system, who are ready to contest it in all available forms*.

The next step of the analyses involved a combination of syndromes from the entire sample that was included in the study due to a certain level of similarity, but not identity involving a similar orientation, the concept of political participation. This was a further, higher level of aggregation than that shown in Table 6.2.

We may identify four major segments that concern more than eighty percent of citizens: *Critical, Supporting Apathetic*, and *Active 1 plus 2*; e.g., the most numerous category *Critical* combines three subgroups. Most research participants believe that they have no influence on the affairs of the country and are not satisfied with the functioning of democracy. This critical attitude unites them (hence the name); on the other hand, they participate in different forms, from conventional participation through participation in all varieties of participation (the second subgroup) to those who accept violent unconventional participation and are active on the Internet. This broad group comprises one-third of society.

I assigned the group supporting the system (*conformists*, as R. K. Merton would have said), but with different levels of activity to the category *Supporting*. Thus, these individuals include both those who participate conventionally and those who use conventional and unconventional but non-violent forms, and even citizens who support the system but are inactive. In Polish society, this segment amounts to 26.5 percent.

The segment's designation *Apathetic* stems from the fact that it concerns citizens who are either dissatisfied with the functioning of democracy or those who feel that they have no influence on the affairs of the country or both of these groups.

They are united by their lack of political activity and lack of interest in and acceptance of practically all forms of participation. This segment amounts to nearly a quarter of Polish society. It is worth pointing out that within each of the more numerous segments there are subgroups, a kind of subclasses (gradable or dichotomously differentiated in terms of certain features). In the first part of this chapter, I characterized the few segments called *Active 1* and *Active 2*. The first segment involves proponents of active conventional participation who are not satisfied with the functioning of the system. The second segment involves system participants who believe they are able to influence national affairs, are satisfied with how democracy works in the country, but accept violent participation and are active on the Internet. Each group amounts to 2.8 %, therefore they are relatively small in number.

Only about ten percent amount to the amorphous segment, which I designated as *uncategorized*.

It was the algorithm of modeling and creating layers of data aggregation selection range.

I present the results of the aggregation analyses in Table 6.3.

Table. 6.3. Structure of attitudes towards the system and political participation (aggregate data)

Classification	Response codes*	Number of configuration iterations for a code	Number of combinations within the classification	Percentage (for codes)	Percentage (for classifications)
Critical	211100	25	210	4.1	34.8
	110011	21		3.5	
	111111	16		2.7	
	111011	14		2.3	
	111100	14		2.3	
	110111	13		2.2	
	111000	13		2.2	
	211111	13		2.2	
	110100	10		1.7	
	210111	10		1.7	
	210100	9		1.5	
	210011	8		1.3	
	211011	7		1.2	
	230000	7		1.2	
	111101	4		0.7	
	231000	4		0.7	
	210101	3		0.5	
	230100	3		0.5	
	231111	3		0.5	
	110101	2		0.3	
	111001	2		0.3	
	230111	2		0.3	
	231011	2		0.3	
	231100	2		0.3	
	110001	1		0.2	
	210001	1		0.2	
	211001	1		0.2	

(*continued*)

Table. 6.3. Continued

Classification	Response codes*	Number of configuration iterations for a code	Number of combinations within the classification	Percentage (for codes)	Percentage (for classifications)
Supporting	221000	35	160	5.8	26.5
	220000	31		5.1	
	210000	22		3.6	
	120011	13		2.2	
	121000	13		2.2	
	221111	11		1.8	
	220100	6		1.0	
	221011	5		0.8	
	221100	5		0.8	
	221101	3		0.5	
	320000	3		0.5	
	121011	2		0.3	
	220111	2		0.3	
	321000	2		0.3	
	321100	2		0.3	
	221001	1		0.2	
	320011	1		0.2	
	320100	1		0.2	
	321011	1		0.2	
	321111	1		0.2	
Apathetic	110000	62	140	10.3	23.3
	120000	36		6.0	
	130000	26		4.3	
	330000	7		1.2	
	330011	2		0.3	
	330111	2		0.3	
	330100	1		0.2	
	330101	1		0.2	
	331001	1		0.2	
	331100	1		0.2	
	331101	1		0.2	
Active 1	211000	17	17	2.8	2.8
Active 2	220011	17	17	2.8	2.8

Table. 6.3. Continued

Classification	Response codes*	Number of configuration iterations for a code	Number of combinations within the classification	Percentage (for codes)	Percentage (for classifications)
Uncategorized	130011	9	59	1.5	9.8
	131000	7		1.2	
	120100	6		1.0	
	310000	6		1.0	
	120111	4		0.7	
	121111	3		0.5	
	310111	3		0.5	
	311111	3		0.5	
	130100	2		0.3	
	130111	2		0.3	
	131011	2		0.3	
	131100	2		0.3	
	310011	2		0.3	
	121100	1		0.2	
	130001	1		0.2	
	130101	1		0.2	
	220001	1		0.2	
	310001	1		0.2	
	310101	1		0.2	
	311000	1		0.2	
	311011	1		0.2	

*I generated response codes based on responses to the following questions with regard to the established order:
Question 10. Do you think that people like you have an influence on the country's affairs? (1: no, 2: yes 3: difficult to say)
Question 7. Please evaluate Polish democracy's functioning. Are you satisfied with its functioning: (1: Dissatisfied, 2: Satisfied, 3: Difficult to say)
Conventional political participation (level) (1–16) (0: low, 1: high)
Unconventional political participation (level) (17–52) (0: low, 1: high)
Unconventional non-violent political participation (acceptance level) (17–26) (0: low, 1: high)
Unconventional political participation (acceptance level) (17–52) (0: low, 1: high)

Source: *Partycypacja polityczna Polaków – nowe wyzwania i formy aktywności* study, 2017, NCN grant 4884, N=603.

A cognitively interesting and important issue is to cognize what are the social, demographic, and geographic characteristics of individual social segments and their corresponding models of political participation. I analyzed all types which differed in attitude to the system and participation model, but the three basic and most numerous types (*Critical*, *Supporting*, and *Apathetic*) were worth describing in detail. Segments *Active 1* and *Active 2* proved to be too sparse to perform sociodemographic correlation analysis, and the group of the *uncategorized*, as the name suggests, proved to be too amorphous.

I present the results of the correlation analysis in Table 6.4.

Table 6.4. Classifications versus sociodemographic variables

Sociodemographic questions		Classification						
		Critical	Supporting	Apathetic	Active 1	Active 2	uncategorized	Total
		%	%	%	%	%	%	%
Education	primary	16.7	36.6	26.7	0.0	10.0	10.0	100.0
	vocational	24.7	31.8	25.9	1.2	3.5	12.9	100.0
	secondary	36.4	22.6	26.1	3.8	0.8	10.3	100.0
	higher	39.2	27.8	18.5	2.6	4.0	7.9	100.0
Age	18–34	38.5	28.0	21.7	1.9	3.1	6.8	100.0
	35–64	31.3	25.6	23.8	2.8	3.4	13.1	100.0
	65+	39.4	27.0	23.8	4.1	0.8	4.9	100.0
Size of locality (recoded)	village	32.8	30.5	23.3	1.8	3.1	8.5	100.0
	city	36.1	24.2	23.2	3.4	2.6	10.5	100.0
Sex	male	38.8	29.2	16.5	2.7	2.1	10.7	100.0
	female	31.1	24.0	29.5	2.9	3.5	9.0	100.0
Size of locality	village | colony	29.4	30.5	25.0	1.9	3.8	9.4	100.0
	village on the outskirts of a city	41.3	30.2	19.0	1.6	1.6	6.3	100.0
	city with less than 20,000 inhabitants	43.3	22.2	24.7	1.2	1.2	7.4	100.0
	city with between 20,000 and 100,000 inhabitants	26.5	24.5	28.7	3.2	4.3	12.8	100.0
	city with between 100,000 and 200,000 inhabitants	37.2	32.5	14.0	4.7	2.3	9.3	100.0
	city with more than 200,000 inhabitants	37.7	22.8	21.6	4.3	2.5	11.1	100.0

(continued)

Table 6.4. Continued

Sociodemographic questions		Classification						
		Critical	Supporting	Apathetic	Active 1	Active 2	uncategorized	Total
		%	%	%	%	%	%	%
Voivodeship	Lower Silesian	34.2	26.3	28.9	5.3	0.0	5.3	100.0
	Kuyavian-Pomeranian	27.3	27.3	31.8	4.5	4.5	4.5	100.0
	Lublin	23.5	11.8	47.1	0.0	0.0	17.6	100.0
	Lubusz	47.1	17.6	11.8	5.9	5.9	11.8	100.0
	Łódź	30.4	31.4	24.5	2.0	4.9	6.9	100.0
	Lesser Poland	31.1	35.6	26.7	2.2	0.0	4.4	100.0
	Masovian	36.2	26.2	17.7	2.3	4.6	13.1	100.0
	Opole	71.4	0.0	0.0	0.0	14.3	14.3	100.0
	Subcarpathian	38.1	38.1	9.5	0.0	0.0	14.3	100.0
	Podlaskie	31.6	26.3	31.6	0.0	0.0	10.5	100.0
	Pomeranian	33.3	9.5	14.3	9.5	4.8	28.6	100.0
	Silesian	28.9	31.6	27.6	5.3	0.0	6.6	100.0
	Holy Cross	46.2	7.7	30.8	7.7	0.0	7.7	100.0
	Warmian-Masurian	51.6	29.0	9.7	0.0	6.5	3.2	100.0
	Greater Poland	35.5	16.1	35.5	0.0	0.0	12.9	100.0
	West Pomeranian	46.2	23.1	15.4	0.0	0.0	15.4	100.0

Table 6.4a Correlations between variables (qualifications versus sociodemographic variables)

Variables	Sociodemographic questions					
	Education (recoded question)	(recoded question)	Size of locality (recoded question)	Sex	Size of locality	Voivodeship
Qualification	ns.	ns.	ns.	ρ= -0,099 (p≤0,05)	ns.	ns.

Source: *Partycypacja polityczna Polaków – nowe wyzwania i formy aktywności* study, 2017, NCN grant 4884, N=1237.

The model of political participation defined as *Critical* means a segment of society that exhibits very interesting characteristics. Citizens with higher or secondary education show a tendency to manifest this type of political participation. We may see age dependence as a so-called *curvilinear*. That is, it is the domain of younger voters aged between eighteen and thirty-four, and seniors who are over sixty-five years of age. Other motives and rationale likely lead them to critical attitudes towards the functioning of the system and the ruling elite. It is more common for men who live in cities, mainly in large cities (more than 200,000 inhabitants) and medium-sized cities (between 100,000 and 200,000 inhabitants) Inhabitants of small towns and villages on the outskirts of cities also express this stance. Such attitudes are more common in Opole, West Pomeranian, and Lubusz voivodeships (i.e., in the west of the country), but also Warmian-Masurian and Holy Cross voivodeships. The reasons for criticism are likely different in these regions.

The second-largest segment is *Supporting*, i.e., citizens who support the functioning of the system and probably the ruling camp, as I characterized them earlier. In the case of this model of attitudes towards political participation, we should notice a significant difference, compared to the previous collective. Individuals with primary education, who live in the countryside (villages and villages on the outskirts of cities) and those who live in medium-sized cities (between 100,000 and 200,000 inhabitants) are more likely to show such attitudes. This model of approach to participation is more common in the following voivodeships: Subcarpathian, Silesian, Lesser Poland. Therefore, it is the southeastern zone of Poland and Silesia. It is the education and region of the country, and partly the place of residence (village versus big city) that creates the biggest difference between the two segments.

The third model of political participation (or rather lack of the said participation), defined as *Apathetic*, is also a segment that more often includes individuals with primary education, not very diverse in terms of place of residence, who most often come from small towns (between 20,000 and 100,000 inhabitants). Women and citizens from Lublin and Podlaskie voivodeships (i.e., the so-called "eastern wall" of the country), but also those from Greater Poland and Kuyavian-Pomeranian voivodeships, tend to have such reactions to politics.

As we interpret the results of the analyses presented above, we may, on the one hand, state that the differences between the models of approach to participation are not statistically significant. However, on the other hand, we may observe certain trends. The differences between the segments are to some extent, though quite clearly, coincident with voter preferences and ideological orientations (or even ideology-related orientations). The social and geographical characteristics of the political participation model called *Supporting*, i.e., living in the countryside, having primary education, or even being located in Subcarpathian or Lesser Poland voivodeships, correlate clearly with the fact that in the last parliamentary (as well as presidential) elections, the right-wing, conservative party Law and Justice (PiS), which has been solely ruling in Poland since 2015, achieved a clear advantage in these regions. In contrast, the segment *Critical* to a greater extent includes citizens with higher (or at least secondary) education, who more frequently (though not exclusively) live in cities, especially those with populations amounting to over 200,000 inhabitants, and come mainly from the voivodeships in the west of the country (West Pomeranian, Lubusz). There, Civic Platform (PO) traditionally wins. Recently, Civic Coalition (formed by PO) also achieved victory there. Centrist-liberal and left-wing parties obtain better results there than anywhere else in Poland.

It is hard to speak of coincidence here. Politics in Poland and many other countries become heavily conditioned by social status, region of the country, tradition, and influence of religion, and attachment to religious values, or, on the contrary, deprecation of them. Consequently, the level of political participation, civic engagement, and its nature (eufunctional or dysfunctional towards political reality) depend largely on who is in power in a given term.

The analysis of the relationship between declarations concerning ideological orientation and the way of participating or not participating in public and political life provides evidence of the ideological influence on the formation of political participation models. In the study, I used a more detailed breakdown of its participants (on a scale from 1 "Far-left" to 7 "Far-right"),[6] but for the purpose of the analysis, I aggregated individuals

6 The full scale is: 1 – far-left, 2 – left, 3 – center-left, 4 – center, 5 – center-right, 6 – right, 7 – far-right (1 and 2 mean left, 3, 4, and 5 mean center, and 6 and 7 mean right); and the "I do not have explicit political views" attitude is not included in the scale.

declaring their beliefs into three groups: right – center – left. I present data concerning this correlation in Table 6.5.

Table 6.5 **Typology of the main political participation models and the declared ideological orientation of citizens**

Classification		Political views			
		left	center	right	no clear views or off the scale
	% of total respondents	%	%	%	%
Critical	34.8	53.6	46.6	23.0	30.8
Supporting	26.5	8.9	22.3	52.7	17.0
Apathetic	23.3	26.8	16.2	10.5	34.4

Source: *Partycypacja polityczna Polaków – nowe wyzwania i formy aktywności* study, 2017, NCN grant 4884, N=603.

The dependency study data show that supporters of the right are mainly political system's participants whom we may describe as *Supporting*.[7] Citizens who declare themselves to be the political center mainly belong to the *Critical* type or, to a much lesser extent, the *Supporting* type. In contrast, representatives who declare themselves to be left-wing are *Critical* or *Apathetic*. These correlations confirm previous findings that the political participation pattern is determined by values, ideological beliefs, and political views concerning not so much the political system, but its functioning and the evaluation of the ruling group.

Contrary to the opinions evaluating the activity of citizens in the European Union as well as in Poland, their activity does not decrease at all. It is quite the opposite. In Poland, the activity grows – conventional participation is no exception. Participation in elections increases. In Poland, participation

7 It is worth recalling the political situation during the period of the study (2017–2018): the right-wing United Right, which consisted of three entities that differed in the scale of their ideological face, was the solely ruling coalition from 2015 to 2019 (and retained power after the 2019 elections). The coalition included the absolutely dominant Law and Justice (PiS) party, the more rightward-shifting United Poland party, as well as the right-liberal Agreement party.

increases especially in parliamentary and presidential elections, but also in local government elections. On the other hand, forms of protest on the fringes between conventional and unconventional participation increase. The reasons for protests and the motivations of participating citizens vary. Nevertheless, one may see that the scale of protests in Poland increases, be it due to the interests of various professional groups, or due to the issue of justice reform, and, most recently, in opposition to the controversial verdict of the Constitutional Tribunal on the further tightening the abortion laws, which would ban it even in the case of an incurable birth defect.

One might think that the likely scenario would be the increase in the segment *Critical* and a decline in the model of the segment's participation, which this study calls *Supporting*. It is difficult to decide unequivocally what will happen to the model of participation, or rather the lack of participation referred to as *Apathetic*. Will there be an increase in the amorphousness of citizens' reactions and their participation in politics? Much depends on the situation on the political scene, the activities of the government, and the parliamentary and governmental majority. An important factor will be the nature of the political dispute between the strongest (so far) political groupings, i.e., the United Right (mainly Law and Justice) and Civic Coalition, the core of which is Civic Platform (PO). The question remains whether the dispute will escalate (and there is much evidence that it will happen) and whether these entities will end their struggle to delegitimize each other (both in Poland and abroad).

Summarizing the results of Polish citizens' participation models analysis, we cannot say that society is not active. Despite the anomic tendencies in the modern world, political participation in Poland grows. It is not clear whether that growth results from the current political situation, social and political conflicts, and contradictions of internalized values, or whether it is a more lasting effect of the society's activation, the increase in social and political awareness, and the creation of a civic network of independently-created ties, and sometimes against those in power.

Concluding remarks

The results of empirical research and the conducted analyses move us towards the identification of the following three contemporary trends in Poles' political participation.

First, as in other Western European societies, Poles' political participation is subject to transgression, taking diverse, fluid forms which go beyond electoral-type participation. Citizens increasingly more often and more willingly use the opportunity for unconventional political activity, e.g., demonstrations or strikes of various types. Second, the phenomenon of political participation in Poland is subject to globalization processes: both conventional and unconventional political participation becomes more similar to the patterns known from Western European democracies. Third, the Internet gains an important role as a platform for political activity, as well as a forum for shaping opinions and exchanging information. Contrary to analysts' expectations, online participation patterns are shaped from the bottom up.

The results of the study allow neither for unambiguous positive verification of the hypotheses posed at the outset nor their rejection. The actual situation, or rather the process, is quite complex. I verified some of the five stereotypical opinions negatively, some positively, and in some, I had to draw conclusions beyond the scope of the hypotheses.

The hypothesis created on the basis of popular opinions (including those disseminated by the media), which suggests that citizens are apolitical, not interested in politics, and have no knowledge of the political processes, procedures, and institutions, does not provide a clear answer in the process of empirical verification. On the one hand, Poles' knowledge of politics, facts, and legal regulations leaves a lot to be desired. On the political capital scale, the cognitive dimension (Index 6) does not give rise to the claim that there is a foundation of political participation capital in the form of knowledge on the structures and procedures of the democratic process.

On the other hand, the interest in politics is quite high and on a fairly upward trajectory. According to the survey, as many as 34.7 percent of citizens say they "try to know as much as possible not only about current events but also about the mechanisms of political life." One-third declare that "one must be fundamentally aware of what is happening in the country." Only 4.2 percent state they are not interested in politics at all. These are, of course, declarations and it is difficult to decide unambiguously to what extent the so-called pursued level is consistent with the postulated level. Nevertheless, in comparison with the results of studies conducted a few or a dozen or so years ago, the level of declarations concerning the interest in politics clearly increased.

However, I verified the hypothesis that Poles are politically inactive negatively. Political participation (especially in conventional forms) steadily increases in Poland. In particular, participation in parliamentary and local government elections increases. More often than in other countries, citizens of the Republic of Poland discuss politics or persuade their friends to behave politically in a particular way. Poles are less frequently involved in working to solve local community problems, although this involvement clearly grows. The model of direct participation in politics, i.e., active, continuous, support-oriented, and goal-oriented, is not very widespread in Poland. On the other hand, there is a growing involvement in the sphere of the so-called "third sector," i.e., activity in various types of non-governmental organizations, especially in the field of charity and education. One may formulate a thesis concerning the formation of the "involved dilettantes" category in Polish society, i.e., those who declare a superficial interest in politics, possess superficial knowledge of political phenomena and processes, and operate on the fringes between what is social and what is political.

During the research, I confirmed another hypothesis that the level of trust in political institutions is low in Poland. Three-quarters of research participants said they are not convinced that rulers do what they are supposed to do. Moreover, the research participants declared that elites pursue the interests of small, selected social groups, or even that they are primarily engaged in doing business for their own benefit. It is worth mentioning that the term "elites" has a bad connotation for the Poles and is not only a worn-out term but also a pejorative one; Poles identify it with pathologies of power, possession of financial means, and media influence.[1]

---

1 Study by *Polityka* weekly: M. Janicki, "Kto w Polsce należy do elity," *Polityka*, July 4, 2017.

Actually, there is no acceptance capital for politicians, politics, and political parties. Among other things, a survey by the CBOS Foundation shows that trust in both the legislative and executive branches is negligible and negative evaluations of their work outnumber positive ones.

During the research, I verified the hypothesis that Poles accept violence in the sphere of political participation negatively. Admittedly, there is public acquiescence of protests, but these are protests that rather do not involve violence.

To sum up the results of the analysis of the research concerning political participation, we should say that (contrary to popular opinion) Polish citizens prefer conventional participation over its other forms. One may observe an increase in activity in almost all types of activities in the political sphere. As I already described, elective participation dominates. In Poland, a kind of participation called socio-environmental, such as discussing politics with friends or convincing them to vote for a particular candidate, party, or issue is also widespread. To a much lesser extent, that participation involves direct involvement in politics, i. e., participating in the organization of an election campaign, running for election, or being a member of a party or other political organization.

Political participation's level is heavily determined socially: we might even say that it is "status-related." It means that the "upper" layer of the middle class, i.e., owners of small and medium enterprises, managers, in general individuals with academic education, citizens working in liberal professions, specialists, mean a group that participates in politics to a bigger extent than other groups, as research shows.

In terms of unconventional participation, we should state that Poles mostly choose forms, which we may call rather mild. What is dominant is participation in petition-signing events, ridiculing, and making fun of politicians, parties, and politics. Yet, to a lesser extent, it is also participation in legally organized strikes and participation in demonstrations. In the last few years, the social support and potential acceptance for non-violent social protests rose.

Research results allow us to state that the level of acceptance for violent protests is relatively high in Poland. Still, the accepted forms of violent protests do not belong to the group of the most extreme ones. For example, I mean the potential support for hunger strikes and government building occupation. We should underline that, according to research participants, acceptance of such actions is possible if conditions that prompt individuals to commit them are met. That support is not independent of the situation. Moreover, as we analyze the dynamics of changes in public mood, we should state that there was a decline in potential support for violent political participation (be it even in its slightly aggressive form) over the last years.

One might write a separate work on citizens' activity on the Internet. "New media" became significantly more important in social and political communication. In the 21st century, one must be aware that the instruments that the Internet established change the nature of both social and political interaction. First, it is the generativity of a kind of "social memory." Everything should be transparent. Intentions to hide certain facts will not become effective in new media. We should also mention the popular thesis that under conditions of dynamically developing electronic media (especially social media), the citizens' role radically changes. From his/her position as a receiver, the citizen may also become a sender of information. It is the process of journalists' role devolution, who lose the status of "Fourth Estate," especially among the younger generation. To an increasingly lesser extent, they set the so-called "agenda-setting" as they must reckon with that the social media will concentrate on other topics.

The study and the analysis of its results allowed me to isolate four main segments, which relate to over eighty percent of citizens: *Critical*, *Supporting Apathetic*, and *Active 1 plus 2*.

The *Critical* formed the most numerous group.

Most of them believe that they have no influence on the affairs of the country and are not satisfied with the functioning of democracy. They participate in different forms: from conventional forms, through the engagement in all varieties of participation, to those who accept violent unconventional participation and are active on the Internet. This broad group comprises one-third of society. Potentially, the group may constitute fodder for the development of a competitive authoritarianism model.[2] As a result of this large group's exploitation by populist and anti-democratic

2 S. Levitsky, L.A. Way, *Competitive Authoritarianism: Hybrid Regimes after the Cold War (Problems of International Politics)* (New York: Cambridge University Press, 2010).

forces, we may expect that democracy will be weakened by restrictions on the rule of law, opposition activity, and civil liberties. Such a scenario is not purely hypothetical, e.g., Venezuela under the rule of Hugo Chavez and Filip Maduro, Turkey under the rule of Recep Tayyip Erdoğan, as well as the Russian Federation in the 21st century. Currently, we may also observe that threat in the United States in the form of the QAnon movement, the members of which show features which are to a certain extent similar to those of the Polish *Critical* group, i.e., the acceptance for the use of violence in the political game and notable activity on the Internet.

I assigned the group supporting the system (*conformists*, as R. K. Merton would have said), but with different levels of activity to the category *Supporting*. Thus, these individuals include both those who participate conventionally and those who use conventional and unconventional but non-violent forms, and even citizens who support the system but are inactive. In Polish society, this segment amounts to 26.5 percent. We may see the numerosity of the compliant but also active citizens group as a chance for the Polish democracy. The authors of the European Commission's document, titled *The Future of Government 2030+* identified the scenario "Super Collaborative Government" as likely.[3] A group that lives according to the principles of respect to democratic values may become a factor that facilitates the creation of a sociopolitical construct that is beneficial for all and the main feature of which is the high level of participatory capital. In such a citizens model, there may be responsible participation in the creation of politics and shaping of society, in which the citizens live. However, the high presence of conflict-free, compliant, compromising, and tolerant citizens may also constitute a threat in the form of overregulation, implemented by the authorities in different spheres. The segment's designation *Apathetic* stems from the fact that it concerns either citizens who are dissatisfied with the functioning of democracy or citizens who feel that they have no influence on the affairs of the country or both of these groups.

What unites these citizens is their lack of political activity and their lack of interest in and acceptance of virtually all forms of participation. This

---

3 L. Vesnic-Alujevic, *The Future of Government 2030+: A Citizen-Centric Perspective on New Government Models* (Luxembourg: Publications Office of the European Union, 2019), p. 44.

segment amounts to nearly a quarter of Polish society. The *Apathetic* group's genesis remains inconclusive in the source literature: some researchers state that the said genesis in society means an expression of general well-being and satisfaction from the political system's operation; others, on the other hand, argue that the level of participation results from alienation, anomy, and lack of identification with the democratic system.[4] Independently from reasons, that group constitutes an important threat since the freedom of choice and democratic procedures do not have a relevant meaning in the situation when citizens lack interest in politics, government's actions, and lack the sense of affiliation with civil society.[5] Democracy without democrats (committed political life participants) appears impossible.[6]

The presence of individuals uninterested in politics decelerates the solving of important social problems and may also cause the decrease in authorities' responsibility, and, in the long run, cause fragmentation of collective life, social atomization, discord, and dispersal of the memory, meaning, and order community.

Based on the research results and presented values of each index, we may state that the "global," aggregate average for political participation capital amounts to 44.4. We should comment on the matter in the following words: in Poland, political participation capital surely is not on the "zero" level; it is in the intermediate state, a little below fifty on the scale from zero to hundred. The level may appear not to be high, but we should conclude that there are indexes that may boost that capital. As I presented, declared interest in politics, intergenerational capital, belief in the value of a democratic system, subjectivity expressed in the belief of influence in the local environment.

---

4 M. Kaase, "Perspektywy badań partycypacji politycznej" in: *Zachowania polityczne,* R.J. Dalton, H.-D. Klingemann (Wydawnictwo Naukowe PWN: Warszawa 2010), p. 359; M. Cześnik. *Partycypacja wyborcza w Polsce. Perspektywa porównawcza* (Warszawa: Scholar, 2007), p. 20; J. Raciborski. *Polskie wybory* (Warszawa: Scholar, 1997), p. 244.

5 A. Touraine, *What is Democracy?* (Oxford: Westview Press, 1997), pp. 26–27.

6 A.K. Koźmiński, P. Sztompka, *Rozmowa o wielkiej przemianie* (Warszawa: Wydawnictwo Wyższej Szkoły Przedsiębiorczości i Zarządzania im. Leona Koźmińskiego, 2004), p. 116.

In Poland, political participation capital is not insignificant and we may clearly observe the symptoms of its strengthening and development, e.g., in terms of a rise in activity in local communities. Meanwhile, numerous scholars working on the issue of political participation are convinced that the potentials for citizen involvement in public and then political affairs are created precisely at the level of cities, villages, and municipalities.

Annex 1. Research methods description and research sample characteristics

I empirically studied the issue of political participation in Polish society and the nature of the capital, which may constitute the foundation for the said issue. I conducted the study in 2017 and 2018 as part of *Partycypacja polityczna Polaków – nowe wyzwania i formy aktywności* (Political Participation of Poles – New Challenges and Forms of Activity) research grant, financed by the National Science Center of Poland (2014/13/B/HS5/00555), which was awarded to the University of Warsaw team of experts that I led. I conducted the studies using three methods; the studies involved three stages.

Stage one involved studies conducted with the use of quantitative methods in a strict sense; the said methods mean focus group interviews known as focuses in short. That phase mainly served the goal of learning how the citizens think about politics but also how they perceive the contemporary or possible engagement in political activity. What was also relevant was the issue of how citizens speak of politics and the need to determine which problems are important to the research participants. The results of qualitative research allowed me to create and calibrate a tool for quantitative research (interview questionnaire).

Stage two involved the principal and most important study, which I conducted using a quantitative method in a narrow sense, i.e., computer-assisted telephone interviewing (CATI) on a sample of 1237 respondents.

In relation to classic standardized interviews, computer-assisted telephone interviewing involves a set of methodological, psychological-interactive, and organizational-technical advantages, which make them especially attractive. In the methodological aspect, we observe a higher availability of research participants in comparison to other methods, e.g., classic questionary face-to-face studies. In the psychological-interactive aspect, we observe a much higher comfort of interaction between the interviewer and the respondent. In the organizational-technical aspect, the high degree of control over the research process means an important feature of telephone studies. Computer assistance and telephone contact also mean a factor that greatly reduces the financial and organizational expenditure required to conduct a study. As a result of computer-assisted telephone studies' advantages presented above, we acquire a higher percentage of those who agree to participate in a study in comparison to other research methods (higher response rate level). Moreover, the elements I mentioned result in much higher data quality, i.e., precision, accuracy, low error level, credibility, and relevance. Most importantly, computer-assisted telephone studies involve the ability to generalize sample results to higher populations in comparison to other available research methods. The ability to generalize study results from the sample to the population is possible thanks to sampling based on classic sampling in telephone studies, i.e., Random Digit Dialing that is modified and adapted to new phenomena, such as cellular telephony.[1]

The third stage means quantitative study to supplement the knowledge and obtain clarification on certain issues, conducted in 2018 using Individual In-depth Interviews (IDI) method.

Therefore, I used a full triangulation of research methods. After I conducted focused group interviews and obtained the results, I constructed indexes to conduct research based on Computer Assisted Telephone Interviewing.[2] It was the CATI method that allowed me to collect the data required to analyze participation capital in Polish society. In the end, I supported the data with individual group interviews.

Below, I present the basic sociodemographic characteristics of the sample for qualitative research that illustrate the nature of sample structure.

---

1 It is the work of Clyde Tucker, Robert Casady, and James Lepkowski, "Sample Allocation For Stratified Telephone Sample Designs" in: *Proceedings of the Survey Research Methods Sections* (Alexandria: American Statistical Association, 1992), pp. 566–571.

2 I conducted the study using the CATI method as part of *Partycypacja polityczna Polaków – nowe wyzwania i formy aktywności* (Political Participation of Poles – New Challenges and Forms of Activity) research grant, financed by the National Science Center of Poland (2014/13/B/HS5/00555). I conducted the study in 2017. The sample amounted to N=1237 participants. I conducted participation/module of questions concerning political participation capital based on the subsample that amounted to 603 respondents.

Table 1.1. Structure of the sample according to sex

Sex	N	%
Male	589	47.6
Female	648	52.4
Total	**1237**	**100.0**

Source: *Partycypacja polityczna Polaków – nowe wyzwania i formy aktywności* study, 2017, NCN grant 4884, N=1237.

Table 1.2. Sample's age structure after the intervals aggregation to three categories

Age	N	%
18–34	342	27.6
35–64	649	52.5
65+	246	19.9
Total	**1237**	**100.0**

Source: Partycypacja polityczna Polaków – nowe wyzwania i formy aktywności study, 2017, NCN grant 4884, N=1237.

Table 1.3. The division of the sample according to the voivodeship of residence (which reflects the population's quantity structure in individual voivodeships)

Voivodeship	N	%
Lower Silesian	83	6.7
Kuyavian-Pomeranian	77	6.2
Lublin	75	6.1
Lubusz	27	2.2
Łódź	80	6.5
Lesser Poland	103	8.3
Masovian	174	14.1
Opole	27	2.1
Subcarpathian	68	5.5
Podlaskie	38	3.1
Pomeranian	71	5.8
Silesian	145	11.7
Holy Cross	37	3.0
Warmian-Masurian	54	4.4
Greater Poland	91	7.3
West Pomeranian	87	7.0
Total	**1237**	**100.0**

Source: *Partycypacja polityczna Polaków – nowe wyzwania i formy aktywności* study, 2017, NCN grant 4884, N=1237.

Table 1.4. Structure of the sample according to education

Education	N	%
Incomplete primary and primary	192	15.5
Junior high school	29	2.3
Vocational/secondary	647	52.3
Post-secondary	38	3.1
Higher	313	25.4
Post-tertiary (post-graduate)	6	0.5
Higher than post-graduate	12	0.9
Total	**1237**	**100.0**

Source: *Partycypacja polityczna Polaków – nowe wyzwania i formy aktywności* study, 2017, NCN grant 4884, N=1237.

Table 1.5. Structure of the sample according to performed profession and/or post

Professional status	N	%
companies' directors, presidents, corporate executives, owners and co-owners	153	12.4
those employed in creative occupations and specialists with higher education	106	8.6
technicians and other mid-level personnel, administrative workers, workers of shops and service outlets	226	18.2
skilled workers who perform simple works, contract workers, and foremen	141	11.4
farmers	77	6.2
pupils, students	79	6.4
old age pensioners and pensioners	360	29.1
unemployed	95	7.7
Total	**1237**	**100.0**

Source: *Partycypacja polityczna Polaków – nowe wyzwania i formy aktywności* study, 2017, NCN grant 4884, N=1237.

Annex 2. Quantitative research tool[1]

Module 0. Screening

M1. Respondent's sex
[single-answer question]

1: Male
2: Female

M2. What is your year of birth?
[open-ended question]

1: Respondent's year of birth

M2a. Year of birth (in intervals):

1. 18–34
2. 35–64
3. 65+

M3. What is your level of education?
[single-answer question]

1: Incomplete primary and primary
2: Junior high school
3: Vocational
4: Secondary (high school, technical high school)
5: Post-secondary
6: Higher – BA/BSc (Eng.) degree
7: Higher – BSc (Eng.) degree
8: Higher – MA degree
9: Higher – MSc (Eng.) degree

1 The analyses presented in this book are based on data collected during the study of the first and second questionary modules as well as of the question concerning the interest in politics (question 29, included in the third module).

10: Post-tertiary (post-graduate)
11: Higher than post-graduate

M9. Does the locality in which you live is:
[single-answer question]

1: Village/colony
2: Village on the outskirts of a city
3: City with less than 20,000 inhabitants
4: City with between 20,000 and 100,000 inhabitants
5: City with between 100,000 and 200,000 inhabitants
6: City with more than 200,000 inhabitants

Module 1. Participation/acceptance of political participation forms

We would like to know how you participate in politics and which ways do you perceive as morally acceptable, and which you do not.

Table 2.1. Group 1. Conventional political participation

Please think and answer whether:	Name in the researcher's language/label	Often	Rarely / sporadically	Never
1. Discusses politics	Political discussions			
2. Persuades someone to vote for a candidate or an issue	Political agitation			
3. Expresses his/her beliefs through badges, pins, stickers, or political slogans	Symbolic political actions			
4. Votes in parliamentary or presidential elections	Elections and referenda			
5. Votes in local elections				
6. Votes in referenda				
7. Participates in public consultations	Public consultations			
8. Participates in political meetings and/or rallies	Public gatherings			

Table 2.1. Continued

Please think and answer whether:	Name in the researcher's language/label	Often	Rarely / sporadically	Never
9. Communicates with politicians to "get something done"	Lobbing			
10. Organizes providing financial support to a candidate, organization, or affair	Donations			
11. Acts for the cause of local communities (village/city/ commune/country/region) problem-solving	Local activism			
12. Participates in electoral campaign organization	Supporting political campaigns			
13. Is (was) a member of, acts/-ed in, or created a political party, social movement, or other political organization	Party and organizational activity			
14. Ran for political office (local government, assembly, parliament)	Use of passive voting rights			
15. Held or holds a political office as he/she was elected (e.g., councilor, village leader, commune head)	Activities as a politician in office			

Table 2.2. Group 2. Unconventional non-violent political participation

Please recall and answer whether:	Name in the researcher's language/label	Often	Rarely / sporadically	Never	I accept without reservation	I accept under certain conditions or in certain situations	I do not accept regardless of circumstances
1. Signs petitions	*Petition campaign I*						
2. You collect signatures under petitions	*Petition campaign II*						
3. Participates in or organizes political demonstration, march (legalized)	Demonstrations, marches, pickets						
4. Participates in or organizes political demonstration, march (non-legalized)							
5. Participates in a legally organized strike	Strikes						
6. Participates in a wildcat (illegal) strike							
7. Ridicules politicians and politics, and makes fun of them in the public sphere	Political practical jokes, Cacareco votes						

Please recall and answer whether:	Name in the researcher's language/label	Often	Rarely / sporadically	Never	I accept without reservation	I accept under certain conditions or in certain situations	I do not accept regardless of circumstances
8. Organizes a boycott or participates in it	Boycotts						
9. Violates the law during protests (civil disobedience)	Civil disobedience						
10. Creates alternative political institutions or supports the existing ones	Mirroring existing political institutions						

Table 2.3. Group 3. Unconventional violent political participation.

From the point of view of your morality, do you accept the following ways of influencing politics or not?	Name in the researcher's language/label	I accept without reservation	I accept under certain conditions or in certain situations	I do not accept regardless of circumstances
1. Undertaking a hunger strike	Self-destructive violence			
2. Destruction of one's own property (e.g., incinerating one's own home)	Self-destructive violence			
3. Self-harm, committing suicide (e.g., self-immolation)	Self-destructive violence			
4. Insulting (shouting, placing inscriptions insulting somebody's dignity)	Verbal and paraverbal violence (threats and intimidation)			
5. Use of threats of violence	Verbal and paraverbal violence (threats and intimidation)			
6. Blackmail	Verbal and paraverbal violence (threats and intimidation)			
7. Mild violation of bodily integrity, e.g., egging, throwing mud, spitting	Violation of bodily integrity/ physical abuse			
8. Severe violation of bodily integrity, e.g., throwing rocks, Molotov cocktails, battery	Violation of bodily integrity/ physical abuse			
9. Government office occupation	Riots			

From the point of view of your morality, do you accept the following ways of influencing politics or not?	Name in the researcher's language/label	I accept without reservation	I accept under certain conditions or in certain situations	I do not accept regardless of circumstances
10. (Passive) blocking of traffic routes	Riots			
11. Destruction of low-value public property (e.g., trash cans, road signs, signboards, and office signs) by a crowd or an organized group	Riots			
12. Destruction of higher-value public property (e.g., vandalizing of or stealing from government offices, setting company car on fire) by a crowd or an organized group (acceptance)	Riots			
13. Destruction of low-value public property (e.g., breaking windows) by a crowd or an organized group	Riots			
14. Destruction of higher-value public property (e.g., vandalizing company's headquarters or flat, setting a car on fire, stealing from or occupying shops, offices, and properties) by a crowd or an organized group	Riots			

(*continued*)

Table 2.3. Continued

From the point of view of your morality, do you accept the following ways of influencing politics or not?	Name in the researcher's language/label	I accept without reservation	I accept under certain conditions or in certain situations	I do not accept regardless of circumstances
15. Fighting with officials (police, military) by a crowd or an organized group	Riots			
16. Battery (lynches) of public officials	Riots			
17. Kidnapping a public official	Kidnapping/abduction			
18. Kidnapping another individual (public official's relative)/taking hostages	Kidnapping/abduction			
19. Planned assassination of a politician or public official	Assasination/Terrorism			
20. Planned assassination of public officials (direct terrorism)	Assasination/Terrorism			
21. Planned assassination of private individuals (indirect terrorism)	Assasination/Terrorism			
22. Planned destruction of high-value public or private property in terms of material and symbolic value (blasting a building, monument)	Assasination/Terrorism			

From the point of view of your morality, do you accept the following ways of influencing politics or not?	Name in the researcher's language/label	I accept without reservation	I accept under certain conditions or in certain situations	I do not accept regardless of circumstances
23. Planning and conducting the forced or violent deposition of officials	Coup d'état			
24. Irregular struggle of minor paramilitary or military groups, armed with guns	Guerilla warfare			
25. Total, fundamental, and quick change of existing political order (political system), combined with numerous, nationwide acts of violence: destroying and taking property without the owner's consent, battery, assassinations	Revolution			
26. Regular struggle of units organized into an army, armed with guns	Civil war			

Table 2.4. Group 4. Political participation on the Internet

Please think and answer whether:	Name in the researcher's language/ label	Often	Rarely / sporadically	Never	I accept without reservation	I accept under certain conditions or in certain situations	I do not accept regardless of circumstances
1. Do you browse the Internet in search of political content (Explain, if necessary, that you mean such information channels as newsrooms, citizen journalism websites, social media, encyclopedia websites, social media aggregators, traditional websites, blogs, microblogs, discussion forums, chats/ IRCs, Usenet newsgroups)	Interest in politics on the Internet				. . .	. . .	. . .
2. Likes/dislikes/subscribes/ upvotes/downvotes (Explain, if necessary: symbolically expresses acceptance or lack of acceptance for posted content or posts (like/dislike/ sub/upvote/downvote, etc.))	Commenting politics on the Internet						
3. Shares content on the Internet services, sends links, memes, articles, comments, presentations, and other content	Interest in politics on the Internet						

Please think and answer whether:	Name in the researcher's language/ label	Often	Rarely / sporadically	Never	I accept without reservation	I accept under certain conditions or in certain situations	I do not accept regardless of circumstances
4. Comments on Internet content	Commenting politics on the Internet						
5. Participates in discussion (forums and discussion groups, chats, exchange of emails)	Interest in politics on the Internet						
6. Collectively comments on or ridicules other users, politics, politicians	Commenting politics on the Internet						
7. Induces others to take action on the Internet or beyond it	Interest in politics on the Internet						
8. Sends Internet donations to movements, parties, and political undertakings	Sharing information on the Internet						
9. Creates memes							

(*continued*)

Table 2.4. Continued

Please think and answer whether:	Name in the researcher's language/ label	Often	Rarely / sporadically	Never	I accept without reservation	I accept under certain conditions or in certain situations	I do not accept regardless of circumstances
10. Creates films, recordings	Sharing information on the Internet						
11. Has a blog, microblog, profile on social media, website, YouTube channel, discussion forum, or discussion group	Sharing information on the Internet						
12. Writes and publishes articles	Sharing information on the Internet						
13. Participates in virtual sit-ins	Sharing information on the Internet						
14. Participates in stealing and leaking data, and acts of destroying content	Sharing information on the Internet						

Module 2. Participatory capital

Question 5. Are you interested in political matters and important events in your country?

[single-answer question]

1: I am not interested in political matters at all
2: Political matters interest me as long as my living conditions depend on political decisions
3: One must be fundamentally aware of what is happening in the country
4: I try to know as much as possible not only about current events but also about the mechanisms of political life

Question 6. Do you agree or disagree with the statement that democracy has an advantage over all other forms of government (democracy is the best out of them)?

[single-answer question]

1: I disagree
2: I agree
3: Difficult to say

Question 7. Please evaluate Polish democracy's functioning. Are you satisfied with its functioning:

[single-answer question]

1: Dissatisfied
2: Satisfied
3: Difficult to say

Question 8. What do you think: in Poland, is it possible to be convinced that the rulers do what they are supposed to do?

[single-answer question]

1: Never
2: Sometimes
3: Most of the time
4: Always

Question 9. Do you think that those in power in Poland are involved in important matters/interests to achieve something solely for themselves, or do they try to act in the interest of the general population?
[single-answer question]

1: They are primarily engaged in doing business for their own benefit
2: They pursue the interests of small, selected social groups
3: They act for the benefit of general social interests

Question 10. Do you think that people like you have an influence on the affairs of the country?
[single-answer question]

1: No
2: Yes
3: Difficult to say

Question 11. Do you think that people like you have an influence on the affairs of the country?
[single-answer question]

1: No
2: Yes
3: Difficult to say

Question 12. Do you think that most Poles trust politicians or rather ordinary citizens?
[single-answer question]

1: The majority trusts neither the former nor the latter
2: They rather trust politicians
3: They rather trust ordinary citizens
4: They trust both groups

Question 13. Do you think that most people in our country will try to use you for their own purposes if they can, or will they try to act fair?
[single-answer question]

1: They will try to use me
2: They will try to act fair

Question 14. Do people more often try to help others, or do they care only about themselves?
[single-answer question]

1: People try to help others
2: People care only about themselves

Question 15. In your opinion, can most people in Poland be trusted or one needs to be careful as he or she contacts them?
[single-answer question]

1: One may trust the majority of people
2: One needs to be careful as he/she contacts others

Question 16. When small groups with strong ties arise in our country, for whose benefit do they work?
[single-answer question]

1: For the benefit of their own narrowly defined (particularistic) interests
2: For the benefit of the broader community's interests (local, professional, community-based)
3: For the benefit of both their own interests and those of the wider community

Question 17. By means of referring to your knowledge of politics, please answer the following questions.

		Answer qualification	
Questions content	Respondent's answer [open-ended question]	Correct answer	Incorrect answer
Which opposition party has the most MPs in the Sejm (lower house of Polish parliament)?			
What type of majority is required to change the Constitution of Poland?			
Which party's politicians most often refer to Christian values in their statements?			
What is the position of Mateusz Morawiecki in the Polish government?			
Who decides whether laws passed by the Sejm are in accordance with the Constitution of Poland?			
In the context of parliamentary elections to the Sejm, which voting system is used in Poland: majoritarian or proportional?			

Question 18. Please answer whether you agree with the following statements:

[single-answer question]

1. **Poland should not accept refugees from Africa and Arab countries**
   1: I agree with that statement
   2: I disagree with that statement

2. Anarchists and nationalists should be forbidden from speaking out and demonstrating their views even if they are not breaking the law
1: I agree with that statement
2: I disagree with that statement

Question 19. Are you a member of a party, political faction, or a social movement, which takes a stance on political matters?
[single-answer question]

1: Yes
2: No

Question 20. Do you act in an NGO, association, or a labor union, which defends group or environmental interests, and by those means enters the political sphere?
[single-answer question]

1: Yes
2: No

Question 21. Has your family given you an attachment to certain values and/or political orientations (e.g., liberal, national, or left-wing)?
[single-answer question]

1: No
2: I was persuaded to choose a specific political option
3: I was given certain universal values

Question 22. Do you believe that the contemporary generation of 18–20-year-olds is more engaged in political matters than the previous generations or less?
[single-answer question]

1: They are less involved
2: I do not see any differences in the involvement
3: They are more involved

Question 23. In which way should the economy be organized, how should the economic order look like? Please answer the question following the 1–10 scale, where 1 means more companies in private hands and 10 – more companies owned by the state.

[single-answer question]

1: More companies in private hands
2:
3:
4:
5:
6:
7:
8:
9:
10: More companies owned by the state

Question 24. Do you believe that citizens should be more resourceful or that the state should help ordinary citizens more? Please answer the question following the 1–10 scale, where 1 means that citizens should care more about their needs themselves and 10 – the government should care about the citizens' needs.

[single-answer question]

1: Citizens should care more about their needs
2:
3:
4:
5:
6:
7:
8:
9:
10: The government should care more about the citizens' needs

Question 25. What is your opinion concerning competition?
[single-answer question]

1: Competition is a good thing
2: Competition is a harmful thing

Module 3. Democracy, media, interest in politics

Question 26. What positive associations do you get when you hear the word "democracy?"
[3 responses maximum, randomization]

1: Political freedom, e.g., freedom of movement
2: The citizens' right to participate in social and political life
3: Multi-party system
4: Freedom of speech
5: Independent media
6: Equal rights for men and women
7: Higher social equality
8: Regular and competitive elections
9: Respect for minorities
10: The rule of law
11: Equality before the law
12: Material living conditions improvement
13: More jobs, lower unemployment
14: Less corruption and abuse of political influence
15: Other (please specify which)

Question 27. What negative associations do you get when you hear the word "democracy?"
[3 responses maximum, randomization]

1: Fragmentation on the political scene
2: Elections that favor a particular party
3: Political correctness limiting the freedom of speech
4: Media in the hands of international corporations that have their own interests

5: Higher social inequality
6: Material living conditions deterioration
7: Fewer jobs, higher unemployment
8: More corruption and abuse of political influence
9: Codified law serves particularistic interests
10: Democracy means chaos and disorder
11: Other (please specify which)

Question 28. Please answer whether and how often do you get the news concerning our country's political problems from the following sources.

Singular	Source of information	Often	Rarely	Never
1	From television			
2	From radio			
3	From everyday press			
4	From family home			
5	From sociopolitical weeklies			
6	From colleagues or "well-informed friends"			
7	From books			
8	From the church			
9	From subjects taught at school or university			
10	From the Internet, from Internet newsrooms, websites, portals, discussion groups			
11	From the information I acquire during the meetings of social organizations, e.g., youth organizations, NGOs, parties			
12	From other sources (please specify which)			

Question 29. Are you interested in political matters and important events in your country?
[single-answer question]

1: I am not interested in political matters at all
2: Political matters interest me as long as my living conditions depend on political decisions
3: One must be fundamentally aware of what is happening in the country
4: I try to know as much as possible not only about current events but also about the mechanisms of political life

Question 30. What is more valuable to you?
[single-answer question]

1: Freedom of morality
2: Economic freedom
3: I do not know, it is hard to tell

Question 31. What is more valuable to you?
[single-answer question]

1: A strong state that takes care of as many aspects of citizens' life
2: Limited state that interferes with people's lives as rare as possible
3: Lack of state
4: I do not know, it is hard to tell

Module 4. Metrics

M4. What is your marital status?
[single-answer question]

1: Bachelor/miss
2: Married
3: Civil union
4: Divorced
5: Widower/widow

M5. What is your household's total monthly net income?
[open-ended question]

1: income amount

M5a. Please place your household's net income in one of the following ranges:
[single-answer question]

1: Less than PLN 1000
2: Between PLN 1000 and 1500
3: Between PLN 1501 and 2000
4: Between PLN 2001 and 3000
5: Between PLN 3001 and 5000
6: Between PLN 5001 and 10000
7: Over PLN 10000

M6. How many individuals live with you in your household?
[open-ended question]

1: enter the number of individuals

M7. Which of the following statements best characterize how the income is managed in your household?
[single-answer question]

1: We have enough to buy everything that we need, and we can save for the future
2: We have enough to buy everything that we need without any special reservations, but we do not save for the future
3: We live on a budget. Therefore, we have enough to buy everything that we need
4: We live on a budget so that we have enough to save for more important shopping
5: Money satisfies only our basic needs
6: We cannot even buy the cheapest food with our money

M8. How would you describe your attitude to religious faith? Which of the following statements characterizes you best now?
[single-answer question]

1: Atheist
2: I have doubts concerning the faith
3: I believe. but do not practice religion
4: I believe and practice religion
5: Difficult to say

M10. What are your political views?
[single-answer question]

1: Far-left
2: Left
3: Center-left
4: Center
5: Center-right
6: Right
7: Far-right
8: I do not have explicit political views
9: Beyond the above scale

M11. What is more valuable to you?
[single-answer question]

1: The state engaged in the economy, that regulates and limits the free market
2: The state unengaged in the economy that does not interfere with the free market
3: Lack of state
4: I do not know, it is hard to tell

M12. What is more valuable to you?
[single-answer question]

1: Ideologically or religiously committed state
2: Ideologically neutral state
3: Lack of state
4: I do not know, it is hard to tell

M13. What is more valuable to you?
[single-answer question]

1: The welfare of the individual
2: The general welfare
3: I do not know, it is hard to tell

M14. What is more valuable to you?
[single-answer question]

1: Personal freedom over security
2: Security over personal freedom
3: I do not know, it is hard to tell

M15. What socio-professional group do you belong to?
[single-answer question]

1. Companies' directors, presidents, and management of companies, institutions, and government and local government administration
2. Those employed in creative occupations and specialists with higher education, engineers, doctors, lawyers, teachers
3. Technicians and other mid-level personnel, nurses, NCOs, policemen
4. Office administration workers, secretaries, post office workers, receptionists, telephonists
5. Employees of stores, service points, personal services, security; conductors, babysitters, drivers
6. Skilled workers and foremen who work outside agriculture and forestry
7. Menial workers who conduct simple tasks outside agriculture and forestry, cleaners, janitors Support workers

8. Contract workers and foremen who work in agriculture or forestry, fishermen
9. Individual farmers and their relatives who help them
10. Owners and co-owners of companies, establishments, sales outlets, commission agents, and others conducting nonfarm business
11. Pupils, students
12. Pensioners
13. Old age pensioners
14. unemployed
15. Individuals who care for houses, housewives
16. Unemployed due to other reasons

M15a. What section does your current staff position belong to? *[multiple choice question]*

1. Agriculture, forestry, venery, and fishery
2. Mining and quarrying
3. Process manufacturing
4. Electricity, gas, steam, and hot water generation and supply
5. Water supply; sewerage, waste management, and remediation activities
6. Construction
7. Trade: repair of motor vehicles
8. Transport and storage
9. Accommodation and food service activities
10. Information and communication
11. Financial and insurance activities
12. Real estate activities
13. Professional, scientific, and technical activities
14. Administration and support service activities
15. Public administration and defense; compulsory social security
16. Education
17. Human health and social work activities
18. Arts, entertainment, and recreation
19. Other service activities

M16. For which political grouping did you vote in the last Sejm elections held on October 25, 2015?

[single-answer question]

1: Law and Justice [PiS]
2: Civic Platform [PO]
3: Kukiz'15
4: Modern [Nowoczesna]
5: Polish People's Party [PSL]
6: The United Left (Democratic Left Alliance [SLD], Your Movement [Twój Ruch], Polish Socialist Party [PPS], Labour Union [UP], and The Greens [Partia Zieloni])
7: KORWiN (Coalition for the Renewal of the Republic – Liberty and Hope)
8: Together [Partia Razem]
9: Other (please specify which)

M17. If the elections to the Sejm were held this Sunday, for which party would you vote?

[single-answer question]

1: Law and Justice [PiS]
2: Civic Platform [PO]
3: Kukiz'15
4: Modern [Nowoczesna]
5: Polish People's Party [PSL]
6: Democratic Left Alliance [SLD]
7: Together [Partia Razem]
8: Other (please specify which)

M18. In which voivodeship do you live?

[single-answer question]

1: Lower Silesian
2: Kuyavian-Pomeranian
3: Lublin
4: Lubusz

5: Łódź
6: Lesser Poland
7: Masovian
8: Opole
9: Subcarpathian
10: Podlaskie
11: Pomeranian
12: Silesian
13: Holy Cross
14: Warmian-Masurian
15: Greater Poland
16: West Pomeranian

Annex 3.

Table 3.1. Partial and sum components of the participatory capital index.

Index number	Questions content	Statistics for each component of the index				Aggregate statistics for the index*		
		N	$\bar{X}$	SD	d^2	$\bar{X}$	SD	d^2
1	Question 5. Are you interested in political matters and important events in your country?	603	0.687	0.464	0.215	0.687	0.464	0.215
2.1	Question 6. Do you agree or disagree with the statement that democracy has an advantage over all other forms of government (democracy is the best out of them)?	477	0.755	0.431	0.186	0.510	0.337	0.113
2.2.	Question 7. Please evaluate Polish democracy's functioning. Are you satisfied with its functioning:	502	0.414	0.493	0.243			
3.1	Question 8. What do you think: in Poland, is it possible to be convinced that the rulers do what they are supposed to do?	603	0.229	0.420	0.176	0.267	0.388	0.150
3.2	Question 9. Do you think that those in power in Poland are involved in important matters/interests to achieve something solely for themselves, or do they try to act in the interest of the general population?	603	0.305	0.461	0.212			

Table 3.1. Continued

Index number	Questions content	Statistics for each component of the index				Aggregate statistics for the index*		
		N	$\bar{X}$	SD	d^2	$\bar{X}$	SD	d^2
4.1	Question 10. Do you think that people like you have an influence on the affairs of the country?	566	0.396	0.490	0.240	0.528	0.408	0.166
4.2	Question 11. Do you think that people like you have an influence on the affairs of the country?	564	0.702	0.458	0.210			
5.1	Question 12. Do you think that most Poles trust politicians?	301	0.467	0.500	0.250	0.443	0.274	0.075
5.2	Question 13. Do you think that most people in our country will try to use you for their own purposes if they can, or will they try to act fair?	603	0.574	0.495	0.245			
5.3	Question 14. Do people more often try to help others, or do they care only about themselves?	603	0.438	0.497	0.247			
5.4	Question 15. In your opinion, can most people in Poland be trusted or one needs to be careful as he or she contacts them?	603	0.180	0.385	0.148			
5.5	Question 16. When small groups with strong ties arise in our country, for whose benefit do they work?	603	0.558	0.497	0.247			

Index number	Questions content	Statistics for each component of the index				Aggregate statistics for the index*		
		N	$\bar{X}$	SD	d^2	$\bar{X}$	SD	d^2
6.1	Question 17. Which opposition party has the most MPs in the Sejm (lower house of Polish parliament)?	603	0.671	0.470	0.221	0.470	0.294	0.087
6.2	Question 17. What type of majority is required to change the Constitution of Poland?	603	0.250	0.433	0.188			
6.3	Question 17. Which party's politicians most often refer to Christian values in their statements?	603	0.819	0.385	0.148			
6.4	Question 17. What is the position of Mateusz Morawiecki in the Polish government?	603	0.285	0.452	0.204			
6.5	Question 17. Who decides whether laws passed by the Sejm are in accordance with the Constitution of Poland?	603	0.486	0.500	0.250			
6.6	Question 17. In the context of parliamentary elections to the Sejm, which voting system is used in Poland: majoritarian or proportional?	603	0.308	0.462	0.213			
7.1	Question 18a. Poland should not accept refugees from Africa and Arab countries	603	0.383	0.486	0.237	0.498	0.336	0.113
7.2	Question 18b. Anarchists and nationalists should be forbidden from speaking out and demonstrating their views even if they are not breaking the law	603	0.613	0.488	0.238			

(continued)

Table 3.1. Continued

Index number	Questions content	Statistics for each component of the index				Aggregate statistics for the index*		
		N	$\bar{X}$	SD	d^2	$\bar{X}$	SD	d^2
8.1	Question 19. Are you a member of a party, political faction, or a social movement, which takes a stance on political matters?	603	0.040	0.196	0.038	0.062	0.192	0.037
8.2	Question 20. Do you act in an NGO, association, or a labor union, which defends group or environmental interests, and by those means enters the political sphere?	603	0.083	0.276	0.076			
9	Question 21. Has your family given you an attachment to certain values and/or political orientations (e.g., liberal, national, or left-wing)?	603	0.700	0.459	0.210	0.700	0.459	0.210

*all variables, regardless of the number of components, were recoded to the interval (0; 1)

Source: *Partycypacja polityczna Polaków – nowe wyzwania i formy aktywności* study, 2017, NCN grant 4884, N=603.

Annex 4.

Table 4.1. Participatory index. Synthetic indexes.

Index	Index intensity level
Index 1. Interest in politics	68.7
Index 2. Attitude to democracy	51.0
Index 3. Political trust	26.7
Index 4. Sense of influence on decision	52.8
Index 5. Social trust	44.3
Index 6. Knowledge on politics	47.0
Index 7. Political tolerance	49.8
Index 8. Direct political involvement	6.2
Index 9. Intergenerational capital	70.0

Source: *Partycypacja polityczna Polaków – nowe wyzwania i formy aktywności* study. 2017. NCN grant 4884. N=603.

Annex 5.

Table 5.1. Participatory capital index (standardized on a scale from zero to a hundred percent). Data weighted according to PESEL.

Categories	Variable values	mean $\bar{x}$	standard deviation SD	variance D^2	Pearson correlation coefficient	multiple correlation coefficient R^2	correlation ratio (eta) η	the measure of effect's force η^2
Participatory capital index for all research participants		44.4	16.2	263.5	-	-	-	-
Sex	Female	45.8	16.1	258.4			0.08	0.01
	Male	43.0	16.3	265.4				
Age	Between 18 and 35 years	45.1	17.2	295.7	-0.02	0.000	0.03	0.00
	Between 35 and 65 years	43.9	16.7	278.4				
	Over 65 years	44.5	13.7	187.4				
Education	Primary	43.6	16.5	272.6	0.19	0.04	0.26	0.07
	Vocational	39.2	15.4	235.9				
	Secondary	43.1	16.3	264.5				
	Higher	50.7	14.8	219.2				
Size of locality	Village/colony	41.8	15.8	251.0			0.122	0.015
	Village on the outskirts of a city	45.9	16.3	265.5				

(*continued*)

Table 5.1. Continued

Categories	Variable values	mean $\bar{x}$	standard deviation SD	variance D^2	Pearson correlation coefficient	multiple correlation coefficient R^2	correlation ratio (eta) η	the measure of effect's force η^2
Size of locality	Village/colony	40.1	16.1	257.6	0.16	0.03	0.19	0.04
	Village on the outskirts of a city	47.0	14.1	199.9				
	City with less than 20,000 inhabitants	44.4	14.6	212.4				
	City with between 20,000 and 100,000 inhabitants	44.5	18.3	335.5				
	City with between 100,000 and 200,000 inhabitants	46.1	12.4	152.7				
	City with more than 200,000 inhabitants	48.1	16.7	279.3				
Attitude to religious faith	Atheist	47.7	15.8	250.1	-0.02	0.00	0.10	0.01
	Having doubts concerning faith	45.1	12.1	146.6				
	Believing but not practicing religion	42.7	15.7	245.7				
	Believing and practicing religion	44.3	16.4	269.5				
	Difficult to say	50.4	24.3	589.1				

Categories	Variable values	mean $\bar{x}$	standard deviation SD	variance D^2	Pearson correlation coefficient	multiple correlation coefficient R^2	correlation ratio (eta) η	the measure of effect's force η^2
Political views	Far-left	31.2	10.9	118.9	-0.23	0.05	0.45	0.20
	Left	43.3	13.4	178.6				
	Center-left	53.2	11.7	136.6				
	Center	49.7	13.1	170.7				
	Center-right	50.5	17.8	317.0				
	Right	53.0	15.5	240.9				
	Far-right	30.0	11.6	133.7				
	I do not have explicit political views	37.4	14.2	201.4				
	Beyond the above scale	46.8	19.3	373.4				
Attitudes to the state (economy)	The state engaged in the economy that regulates and limits the free market	44.3	16.2	261.9	-0.06	0.00	0.11	0.01
	The state unengaged in the economy that does not interfere with the free market	45.9	16.5	273.1				
	Lack of state	43.8	14.3	203.2				
	I do not know, it is hard to tell	39.8	15.3	233.0				

Table 5.1. Continued

Categories	Variable values	mean $\bar{x}$	standard deviation SD	variance D^2	Pearson correlation coefficient	multiple correlation coefficient R^2	correlation ratio (eta) η	the measure of effect's force η^2
Attitudes to the state	Ideologically or religiously committed state	46.6	17.4	304.0	-0.12	0.01	0.12	0.01
	Ideologically neutral state	44.1	15.7	246.2				
	Lack of state	38.1	0.0	0.0				
	I do not know, it is hard to tell	38.4	16.1	258.0				
Values evaluation (security)	Personal freedom over security	43.3	16.0	256.5	0.01	0.00	0.09	0.01
	Security over personal freedom	46.2	16.3	265.8				
	I do not know, it is hard to tell	42.7	16.4	270.1				
Voter preferences in 2015	Law and Justice [PiS]	46.5	16.7	277.6	-0.16	0.03	0.26	0.07
	Civic Platform [PO]	44.4	14.4	207.9				
	Kukiz'15	45.6	19.0	362.8				
	Modern [Nowoczesna]	51.2	11.4	130.9				
	Polish People's Party [PSL]	43.4	7.7	59.6				
	The United Left [Zjednoczona Lewica]	49.2	11.7	136.3				
	KORWiN	48.8	17.8	291.6				
	Together [Partia Razem]	52.7	13.4	179.7				
	I did not participate in voting	37.0	15.9	252.8				
	Other (please specify which)	66.7	0.0	0.0				
	I refuse to answer	41.5	19.8	393.2				
	I do not remember	39.6	17.6	308.4				

Categories	Variable values	mean $\bar{x}$	standard deviation SD	variance D^2	Pearson correlation coefficient	multiple correlation coefficient R^2	correlation ratio (eta) η	the measure of effect's force η^2
Income–self-assessment	We have enough to buy everything what we need, and we can save for the future	48.3	14.7	216.6	-0.27	0.07	0.30	0.09
	We have enough to buy everything that we need without any special reservations, but we do not save for the future	48.7	14.8	218.3				
	We live on a budget. Therefore, we have enough to buy everything that we need	46.5	16.0	255.7				
	We live on a budget so that we have enough to save for more important shopping	38.5	16.7	278.1				
	Money satisfies only our basic needs	38.0	16.1	260.6				
	We cannot even buy the cheapest food with our money	33.0	12.7	160.7				

(*continued*)

Table 5.1. Continued

Categories	Variable values	mean $\bar{x}$	standard deviation SD	variance D^2	Pearson correlation coefficient	multiple correlation coefficient R^2	correlation ratio (eta) η	the measure of effect's force η^2
Social and professional group	Companies' directors, presidents, and corporate executives…	56.5	12.6	159.6	-0.12	0.01	0.38	0.14
	Those employed in creative occupations and specialists with higher education…	52.0	17.2	296.7				
	Technicians and other mid-level personnel…	45.8	15.5	239.6				
	Office administration workers…	47.5	14.6	213.3				
	Employees of stores, service points…	39.7	16.4	267.4				
	Skilled workers who work outside agriculture and forestry	33.4	18.0	325.4				
	Menial workers who work outside agriculture and forestry	38.8	12.7	160.2				
	Contract workers and foremen who work in agriculture or forestry	55.4	12.9	167.2				
	Individual farmers and their relatives who help them	38.6	14.1	197.4				
	Companies' owners and co-owners…	42.8	14.8	219.2				
	Pupils, students	53.3	17.6	309.9				
	Pensioners	42.5	13.6	185.1				
	Old age pensioners	45.2	14.3	205.0				
	Unemployed	39.3	15.7	247.8				
	Individuals who care for houses, housewives	34.9	14.3	205.5				
	Unemployed due to other reasons	50.0	15.7	246.6				

Categories	Variable values	mean $\bar{x}$	standard deviation SD	variance D^2	Pearson correlation coefficient	multiple correlation coefficient R^2	correlation ratio (eta) η	the measure of effect's force η^2
Interest in political matters	I am not interested in political matters at all	28.1	.	-1744.6	0.15	0.02	0.25	0.06
	Political matters interest me as long as my living conditions depend on political decisions	42.7	15.1	227.1				
	One must be fundamentally aware of what is happening in the country	50.5	14.5	210.0				
	I try to know as much as possible not only about current events but also about the mechanisms of political life	47.9	12.1	146.1				
Attitudes to the state	A strong state that takes care of as many aspects of…	43.8	16.0	257.2	-0.04	0.00	0.14	0.02
	Limited state that interferes with people's lives as rare as possible	47.3	15.8	249.1				
	Lack of state	36.0	15.3	234.5				
	I do not know, it is hard to tell	39.0	18.0	323.1				

Source: *Partycypacja polityczna Polaków – nowe wyzwania i formy aktywności* study, 2017, NCN grant 4884, N=603.

Annex 6.

Table 6.1. Statistics for each component of the index and aggregate statistics for the indexes.

Index number	Questions content	Statistics for each component of the index				Statistics for the index*		
		N	Mean	Standard deviation	Variance	Mean	Standard deviation	Variance
1	Question 5. Are you interested in political matters and important events in your country?	603	0.687	0.464	0.215	0.687	0.464	0.215
2.1	Question 6. Do you agree or disagree with the statement that democracy has an advantage over all other forms of government (democracy is the best out of them)?	477	0.755	0.431	0.186	0.510	0.337	0.113
2.2.	Question 7. Please evaluate Polish democracy's functioning. Are you satisfied with its functioning:	502	0.414	0.493	0.243			
3.1	Question 8. What do you think: in Poland, is it possible to be convinced that the rulers do what they are supposed to do?	603	0.229	0.420	0.176	0.267	0.388	0.150
3.2	Question 9. Do you think that those in power in Poland are involved in important matters/interests to achieve something solely for themselves, or do they try to act in the interest of the general population?	603	0.305	0.461	0.212			

(*continued*)

Table 6.1. Continued

Index number	Questions content	Statistics for each component of the index				Statistics for the index*		
		N	Mean	Standard deviation	Variance	Mean	Standard deviation	Variance
4.1	Question 10. Do you think that people like you have an influence on the affairs of the country?	566	0.396	0.490	0.240	0.528	0.408	0.166
4.2	Question 11. Do you think that people like you have an influence on the affairs of the country?	564	0.702	0.458	0.210			
5.1a	Question 12. Do you think that most Poles trust politicians?	301	0.467	0.500	0.250	0.616	0.274	0.075
5.1b	Question 12. Do you think that most Poles trust ordinary citizens?	553	0.710	0.454	0.206			
5.2	Question 13. Do you think that most people in our country will try to use you for their own purposes if they can, or will they try to act fair?	603	0.574	0.495	0.245			
5.3	Question 14. Do people more often try to help others, or do they care only about themselves?	603	0.438	0.497	0.247			
5.4	Question 15. In your opinion, can most people in Poland be trusted or one needs to be careful as he or she contacts them?	603	0.180	0.385	0.148			
5.5	Question 16. When small groups with strong ties arise in our country, for whose benefit do they work?	603	0.558	0.497	0.247			

Index number	Questions content	Statistics for each component of the index				Statistics for the index*		
		N	Mean	Standard deviation	Variance	Mean	Standard deviation	Variance
6.1	Question 17. Which opposition party has the most MPs in the Sejm (lower house of Polish parliament)?	603	0.671	0.470	0.221	0.643	0.294	0.087
6.2	Question 17. What type of majority is required to change the Constitution of Poland?	603	0.250	0.433	0.188			
6.3	Question 17. Which party's politicians most often refer to Christian values in their statements?	603	0.819	0.385	0.148			
6.4	Question 17. What is the position of Mateusz Morawiecki in the Polish government?	603	0.285	0.452	0.204			
6.5	Question 17. Who decides whether laws passed by the Sejm are in accordance with the Constitution of Poland?	603	0.486	0.500	0.250			
6.6	Question 17. In the context of parliamentary elections to the Sejm, which voting system is used in Poland: majoritarian or proportional?	603	0.308	0.462	0.213			
7.1	Question 18a. Poland should not accept refugees from Africa and Arab countries	603	0.383	0.486	0.237	0.498	0.336	0.113
7.2	Question 18b. Anarchists and nationalists should be forbidden from speaking out and demonstrating their views even if they are not breaking the law	603	0.613	0.488	0.238			

(*continued*)

Table 6.1. Continued

Index number	Questions content	Statistics for each component of the index				Statistics for the index*		
		N	Mean	Standard deviation	Variance	Mean	Standard deviation	Variance
8.1	Question 19. Are you a member of a party, political faction, or a social movement, which takes a stance on political matters?	603	0.040	0.196	0.038	0.062	0.192	0.037
8.2	Question 20. Do you act in an NGO, association, or a labor union, which defends group or environmental interests, and by those means enters the political sphere?	603	0.083	0.276	0.076			
9.1	Question 21. Has your family given you an attachment to certain values and/or political orientations (e.g., liberal, national, or left-wing)?	603	0.700	0.459	0.210	0.501	0.329	0.108
9.2	Question 22. Do you believe that the contemporary generation of 18–20-year-olds is more engaged in political matters than the previous generations or less?	603	0.302	0.460	0.211			

*all variables, regardless of the number of components, were recoded to the interval (0; 1)
Source: *Partycypacja polityczna Polaków – nowe wyzwania i formy aktywności* study, 2017, NCN grant 4884, N=603.

Annex 7. Correlations between variables (qualifications versus sociodemographic variables)

Variables	Sociodemographic questions						
	Education (recoded question)	(recoded question)	Size of locality (recoded question)	Sex	Voivodeship	Size of locality	Political party
1. Are you interested in politics?	R= 0.155 (p≤0.05)	R= 0.113 (p≤0.05)	ns.	ns.	ns.	ns.	ns.
2. Discusses politics	R= 0.091 (p≤0.05)	R= 0.165 (p≤0.05)	P= 0.074 (p≤0.1)	R= -0.130 (p≤0.05)	ns.	R= 0.165 (p≤0.05)	ρ= 0.080 (p≤0.01)
3. Persuades someone to vote for a candidate or an issue	ns.	ns.	ns.	R= 0.115 (p≤0.05)	ns.	ns.	ns.
4. Expresses his/her beliefs through badges. pins. stickers. or political slogans	ns.	R= -0.130 (p≤0.05)	ns.	ns.	ns.	ns.	ns.
5. Votes in parliamentary or presidential elections	R= 0.145 (p≤0.05)	R= 0.137 (p≤0.05)	ns.	ns.	ns.	ns.	ns.
6. Votes in local elections	R= 0.133 (p≤0.05)	R= 0.162 (p≤0.05)	ns.	ns.	ns.	ns.	ns.
7. Votes in referenda	R= 0.213 (p≤0.05)	R= 0.096 (p≤0.05)	R= 0.106 (p≤0.05)	P= -0.079 (p≤0.1)	ns.	R= 0.134 (p≤0.05)	ns.
8. Participates in public consultations	R= 0.083 (p≤0.05)	ns.	ns.	R= -0.095 (p≤0.05)	ρ= 0.074 (p≤0.1)	ns.	ns.
9. Participates in political meetings and/or rallies	R= 0.102 (p≤0.05)	ns.	ns.	ns.	ns.	R= 0.086 (p≤0.05)	ns.

Variables	Sociodemographic questions						
	Education (recoded question)	(recoded question)	Size of locality (recoded question)	Sex	Voivodeship	Size of locality	Political party
10. Communscates with politicians to "get something done"	R= 0.078 (p≤0.1)	R= -0.100 (p≤0.05)	ns.	ns.	ns.	ns.	ns.
11. Organszes providing financial support to a candidate. organszation. or affair	R= 0.101 (p≤0.05)	ns.	ns.	ns.	ns.	ns.	ns.
12. Acts for the cause of local communsties (village/city/commune/country/region) problem-solving	R= 0.099 (p≤0.05)	ns.	R= -0.103 (p≤0.05)	R= -0.160 (p≤0.05)	ns.	R= -0.086 (p≤0.05)	ρ= 0.083 (p≤0.01)
13. Participates in electoral campaign organszation	R= 0.115 (p≤0.05)	ns.	R= -0.094 (p≤0.05)	ns.	ρ= 0.081 (p≤0.05)	ns.	ns.
14. Is (was) a member of. acts/-ed in. or created a political party. social movement. or other political organszation	R= 0.078 (p≤0.1)	R= 0.105 (p≤0.05)	ns.	ns.	ns.	R= 0.086 (p≤0.05)	ns.
15. Ran for political office (local government. assembly. parliament)	ns.	R= 0.132 (p≤0.05)	R= -0.109 (p≤0.05)	P= -0.069 (p≤0.1)	ns.	R= -0.101 (p≤0.05)	ns.
16. Held or holds a political office as he/she was elected (e.g.. councilor. village leader. commune head)	R=-0.083 (p≤0.05)	R= 0.091 (p≤0.05)	R= -0.230 (p≤0.05)	R= -0.102 (p≤0.05)	ns.	R= -0.208 (p≤0.05)	ns.
17a. Signs petitions	R=-0.266 (p≤0.05)	R= -0.102 (p≤0.05)	R= 0.083 (p≤0.05)	ns.	ns.	R= 0.117 (p≤0.05)	ρ= 0.142 (p≤0.05)
17b. Signs petitions (acceptance)	R= 0.154 (p≤0.05)	R= -0.076 (p≤0.1)	ns.	ns.	ns.	ns.	ns.

Variables	Sociodemographic questions						
	Education (recoded question)	(recoded question)	Size of locality (recoded question)	Sex	Voivodeship	Size of locality	Political party
18a. You collect signatures under petitions	ns.	ns.	ns.	ns.	ρ= 0.091 (p≤0.05)	ns.	ns.
18b. You collect signatures under petitions (acceptance)	R= 0.129 (p≤0.05)	R= -0.089 (p≤0.05)	ns.	ns.	ns.	ns.	ρ= 0.117 (p≤0.05)
19a. Participates in or organszes political demonstration. march (legalized)	R= 0.111 (p≤0.05)	R= -0.083 (p≤0.05)	R= 0.088 (p≤0.05)	ns.	ns.	R= 0.138 (p≤0.05)	ρ= 0.144 (p≤0.05)
19b. Participates in or organszes political demonstration. (nonlegalized) march (acceptance)	R= 0.146 (p≤0.05)	R= -0.108 (p≤0.05)	R= 0.155 (p≤0.05)	R= -0.072 (p≤0.1)	ns.	R= 0.145 (p≤0.05)	ρ= 0.239 (p≤0.05)
20a. Participates in or organszes political demonstration. march (non-legalized)	ns.	ns.	ns.	ns.	ns.	ns.	ρ= 0.100 (p≤0.05)
20b. Participates in or organszes political demonstration. (nonlegalized) march (acceptance)	R= 0.131 (p≤0.05)	R= -0.201 (p≤0.05)	R= 0.115 (p≤0.05)	ns.	ns.	R= 0.128 (p≤0.05)	ρ= 0.318 (p≤0.05)
21a. Participates in legally organszed strike	ns.	ns.	ns.	ns.	ρ= 0.077 (p≤0.1)	ns.	ns.
21b. Participates in legally organszed strike (acceptance)	R= 0.108 (p≤0.05)	ns.	R= 0.108 (p≤0.05)	R= -0.109 (p≤0.05)	ρ= 0.084 (p≤0.05)	R= 0.133 (p≤0.05)	ρ= 0.116 (p≤0.05)
22a. Participates in wildcat (illegal) strike	ns.	ns.	ns.	ns.	ns.	R= 0.069 (p≤0.1)	ρ= 0.126 (p≤0.05)
22b. Participates in wildcat (illegal) strike (acceptance)	R= 0.094 (p≤0.05)	R= -0.214 (p≤0.05)	R= 0.098 (p≤0.05)	ns.	ρ= 0.097 (p≤0.05)	R= 0.126 (p≤0.05)	ρ= 0.233 (p≤0.05)

(continued)

Variables	Sociodemographic questions						
	Education (recoded question)	(recoded question)	Size of locality (recoded question)	Sex	Voivodeship	Size of locality	Political party
23a. Ridicules politicians and politics. and makes fun of them in public sphere	R= 0.095 (p≤0.05)	R= -0.093 (p≤0.05)	ns.	R= -0.217 (p≤0.05)	ns.	ns.	ρ= 0.167 (p≤0.05)
23b. Ridicules politicians and politics and makes fun of them in public sphere (acceptance)	R= 0.126 (p≤0.05)	R= -0.172 (p≤0.05)	R= 0.079 (p≤0.1)	R= -0.258 (p≤0.05)	ρ= 0.099 (p≤0.05)	R= 0.098 (p≤0.05)	ρ= 0.304 (p≤0.05)
24a. Organszes a boycott or participates in it	R= 0.073 (p≤0.1)	ns.	R= 0.077 (p≤0.1)	ns.	ns.	R= 0.133 (p≤0.05)	ns.
24b. Organszes a boycott or participates in it (acceptance)	R= 0.151 (p≤0.05)	R= -0.089 (p≤0.05)	R= 0.130 (p≤0.05)	R= -0.130 (p≤0.05)	ns.	R= 0.162 (p≤0.05)	ρ= 0.305 (p≤0.05)
25a. Violates the law during protests (civil disobedience)	ns.	ns.	R= 0.077 (p≤0.1)	ns.	ns.	R= 0.096 (p≤0.05)	ρ= 0.155 (p≤0.05)
25b. Violates the law during a protests (civil disobedience) (acceptance)	R= 0.120 (p≤0.05)	ns.	R= 0.098 (p≤0.05)	R= -0.130 (p≤0.05)	ns.	R= 0.096 (p≤0.05)	ρ= 0.295 (p≤0.05)
26a. Creates alternative political institutions or supports the existing ones	ns.	ns.	ns.	ns.	ns.	ns.	ns.
26b. Creates alternative political institutions or supports the existing ones (acceptance)	R= 0.114 (p≤0.05)	R= -0.148 (p≤0.05)	ns.	ns.	ns.	ns.	ρ= 0.119 (p≤0.05)
27. Undertaking a hunger strike (acceptance)	R= 0.131 (p≤0.05)	ns.	R= 0.093 (p≤0.05)	ns.	ns.	R= 0.113 (p≤0.05)	ρ= 0.166 (p≤0.05)
28. Destruction of one's own property (e.g.. destruction of one's own home) (acceptance)	R= 0.118 (p≤0.05)	R= -0.167 (p≤0.05)	ns.	ns.	ns.	R= 0.089 (p≤0.05)	ρ= 0.178 (p≤0.05)
29. Self-harm. committing suicide (e.g.. self-immolation) (acceptance)	R= 0.073 (p≤0.1)	R= -0.082 (p≤0.05)	ns.	R= -0.083 (p≤0.05)	ns.	R= 0.077 (p≤0.1)	ρ= 0.128 (p≤0.05)

Variables	Sociodemographic questions						
	Education (recoded question)	(recoded question)	Size of locality (recoded question)	Sex	Voivodeship	Size of locality	Political party
30. Insulting (shouting. placing inscriptions insulting somebody's dignsty) (acceptance)	ns.	R= -0.126 (p≤0.05)	R= 0.068 (p≤0.1)	R= -0.108 (p≤0.05)	ns.	R= 0.111 (p≤0.05)	ρ= 0.180 (p≤0.05)
31. Use of threats of violence (acceptance)	ns.	R= -0.080 (p≤0.05)	ns.	R= -0.071 (p≤0.1)	ns.	ns.	ns.
32. Blackmail (acceptance)	ns.	ns.	R= 0.083 (p≤0.05)	ns.	ns.	R= 0.084 (p≤0.05)	ns.
33. Mild violation of bodily integrity. e.g.. egging. throwing mud. spitting (acceptance)	ns.	ns.	ns.	ns.	ns.	ns.	ρ= 0.109 (p≤0.05)
34. Severe violation of bodily integrity. e.g.. throwing rocks. Molotov cocktails. battery (acceptance)	ns.	ns.	ns.	ns.	ns.	R= 0.075 (p≤0.1)	ns.
35. Government office occupation (acceptance)	R= 0.134 (p≤0.05)	R= -0.073 (p≤0.1)	R= 0.124 (p≤0.05)	ns.	ns.	R= 0.156 (p≤0.05)	ρ= 0.229 (p≤0.05)
36. (Passive) blocking of traffic routes (acceptance)	R= 0.087 (p≤0.05)	ns.	R= 0.069 (p≤0.1)	ns.	ns.	R= 0.092 (p≤0.05)	ρ= 0.109 (p≤0.05)
37. Destruction of low-value public property (e.g.. trash cans. road signs. signboards. and office signs) by a crowd or an organszed group (acceptance)	ns.	R= -0.071 (p≤0.1)	ns.	ns.	ns.	ns.	ρ= 0.102 (p≤0.05)
38. Destruction of higher-value public property (e.g.. vandalizing of or stealing from government offices. setting company car on fire) by a crowd or an organszed group (acceptance)	ns.	ns.	ns.	ns.	ns.	P= 0.074 (p≤0.1)	ns.

(continued)

Variables	Sociodemographic questions						
	Education (recoded question)	(recoded question)	Size of locality (recoded question)	Sex	Voivodeship	Size of locality	Political party
39. Destruction of low-value public property (e.g.. breaking windows) by a crowd or an organszed group (acceptance)	ns.	ns.	ns.	ns.	ns.	R= 0.068 ($p \leq 0.1$)	ns.
40. Destruction of higher-value public property (e.g.. vandalizing company's headquarters or flat. setting a car on fire. stealing from or occupying shops. offices. and properties) by a crowd or an organszed group (acceptance)	ns.	ns.	ns.	ns.	ns.	R= 0.068 ($p \leq 0.1$)	ns.
41. Fighting with officials (police. military) by a crowd or an organszed group (acceptance)	ns.	ns.	R= 0.129 ($p \leq 0.05$)	ns.	ns.	R= 0.134 ($p \leq 0.05$)	ρ= 0.184 ($p \leq 0.05$)
42. Battery (lynches) of public officials (acceptance)	ns.	ns.	ns.	ns.	ns.	ns.	ns.
43. Kidnapping a public official (acceptance)	ns.	ns.	R= 0.076 ($p \leq 0.1$)	ns.	ns.	R= 0.088 ($p \leq 0.05$)	ns.
44. Kidnapping another individual (public official's relative)/taking hostages (acceptance)	ns.	ns.	R= 0.072 ($p \leq 0.1$)	ns.	ns.	R= 0.092 ($p \leq 0.05$)	ns.
45. Planned assassination of a politician or public official (acceptance)	ns.	ns.	R= 0.094 ($p \leq 0.05$)	ns.	ns.	R= 0.077 ($p \leq 0.1$)	ns.
46. Planned assassination of public officials (direct terrorism) (acceptance)	ns.	ns.	R= 0.078 ($p \leq 0.1$)	ns.	ns.	R= 0.080 ($p \leq 0.05$)	ns.
47. Planned assassination of private individuals (indirect terrorism) (acceptance)	ns.	ns.	ns.	ns.	ns.	R= 0.067 ($p \leq 0.1$)	ns.

Variables	Sociodemographic questions						
	Education (recoded question)	(recoded question)	Size of locality (recoded question)	Sex	Voivodeship	Size of locality	Political party
48. Planned destruction of high-value public or private property in terms of material and symbolic value (blasting a building. monument) (acceptance)	ns.	ns.	ns.	ns.	ns.	R= 0.090 ($p \leq 0.05$)	ns.
49. Plannsng and conducting forced or violent deposition of officials (acceptance)	ns.	R= -0.123 ($p \leq 0.05$)	ns.	ns.	ns.	R= 0.102 ($p \leq 0.05$)	ρ= 0.134 ($p \leq 0.05$)
50. Irregular struggle of minor paramilitary or military groups. armed with guns (acceptance)	R= 0.109 ($p \leq 0.05$)	R= -0.162 ($p \leq 0.05$)	R= 0.068 ($p \leq 0.1$)	ns.	ns.	R= 0.082 ($p \leq 0.05$)	ρ= 0.110 ($p \leq 0.05$)
51. Total. fundamental. and quick change of existing political order (political system). combined with numerous. nationwide acts of violence: destroying and taking property without the owner's consent. battery. assassinations (acceptance)	R= 0.087 ($p \leq 0.05$)	R= -0.177 ($p \leq 0.05$)	ns.	ns.	ns.	R= 0.075 ($p \leq 0.1$)	ρ= 0.113 ($p \leq 0.05$)
52. Regular struggle of unsts organszed into an army. armed with guns (acceptance)	ns.	R= -0.081 ($p \leq 0.05$)	ns.	ns.	ns.	ns.	ns.
53. Do you browse the Internet in search of political content	R= 0.351 ($p \leq 0.05$)	R= -0.241 ($p \leq 0.05$)	R= 0.147 ($p \leq 0.05$)	R= -0.121 ($p \leq 0.05$)	ns.	R= 0.170 ($p \leq 0.05$)	ρ= 0.195 ($p \leq 0.05$)
54. Likes/dislikes/subscribes/upvotes/downvotes	R= 0.215 ($p \leq 0.05$)	R= -0.256 ($p \leq 0.05$)	R= 0.094 ($p \leq 0.05$)	ns.	ρ= 0.069 ($p \leq 0.1$)	R= 0.134 ($p \leq 0.05$)	ρ= 0.185 ($p \leq 0.05$)
55. Shares content on the Internet services. sends links. memes. articles. comments. presentations. and other content	R= 0.218 ($p \leq 0.05$)	R= -0.267 ($p \leq 0.05$)	R= 0.098 ($p \leq 0.05$)	ns.	ns.	R= 0.153 ($p \leq 0.05$)	ρ= 0.181 ($p \leq 0.05$)

(continued)

Variables	Sociodemographic questions						
	Education (recoded question)	(recoded question)	Size of locality (recoded question)	Sex	Voivodeship	Size of locality	Political party
56. Comments on Internet content	R= 0.171 ($p \leq 0.05$)	R= -0.236 ($p \leq 0.05$)	R= 0.121 ($p \leq 0.05$)	ns.	ns.	R= 0.165 ($p \leq 0.05$)	ρ= 0.181 ($p \leq 0.05$)
57. Participates in discussion (forums and discussion groups. chats. exchange of emails)	R= 0.178 ($p \leq 0.05$)	R= -0.219 ($p \leq 0.05$)	R= 0.108 ($p \leq 0.05$)	R= -0.108 ($p \leq 0.05$)	ns.	R= 0.143 ($p \leq 0.05$)	ρ= 0.124 ($p \leq 0.05$)
58a. Collectively comments on or ridicules other users. politics. politicians	ns.	R= -0.123 ($p \leq 0.05$)	ns.	R= -0.078 ($p \leq 0.1$)	ns.	R= 0.069 ($p \leq 0.1$)	ρ= 0.151 ($p \leq 0.05$)
58b. Collectively comments on or ridicules other users. politics. politicians (acceptance)	R= 0.151 ($p \leq 0.05$)	R= -0.134 ($p \leq 0.05$)	R= 0.100 ($p \leq 0.05$)	R= -0.153 ($p \leq 0.05$)	ns.	R= 0.088 ($p \leq 0.05$)	ρ= 0.223 ($p \leq 0.05$)
59. Induces others to take action on the Internet or beyond it	R= 0.156 ($p \leq 0.05$)	R= -0.148 ($p \leq 0.05$)	ns.	ns.	ns.	ns.	ns.
60. Sends Internet donations to movements. parties. and political undertakings	R= 0.091 ($p \leq 0.05$)	ns.	ns.	ns.	ns.	R= 0.081 ($p \leq 0.05$)	ns.
61. Creates memes	ns.	ns.	ns.	ns.	ns.	ns.	ns.
62. Creates films. recordings	ns.	R= -0.084 ($p \leq 0.05$)	ns.	ns.	ns.	ns.	ρ= 0.078 ($p \leq 0.1$)
63. Has a blog. microblog. profile on social media. website. YouTube channel. discussion forum. or discussion group	R= 0.091 ($p \leq 0.05$)	R= -0.112 ($p \leq 0.05$)	ns.	ns.	ns.	ns.	ns.
64. Writes and publishes articles	ns.	R= -0.094 ($p \leq 0.05$)	ns.	ns.	ns.	ns.	ρ= 0.088 ($p \leq 0.1$)

Variables	Sociodemographic questions						
	Education (recoded question)	(recoded question)	Size of locality (recoded question)	Sex	Voivodeship	Size of locality	Political party
65a. Participates in virtual sit-ins	R= 0.086 (p≤0.05)	R= -0.092 (p≤0.05)	ns.	ns.	ρ= 0.096 (p≤0.05)	R= 0.092 (p≤0.05)	ρ= 0.110 (p≤0.05)
65b. Participates in virtual sit-ins (acceptance)	R= -0.260 (p≤0.05)	R= -0.210 (p≤0.05)	R= 0.158 (p≤0.05)	R= -0.125 (p≤0.05)	ρ= 0.089 (p≤0.05)	R= 0.195 (p≤0.05)	ρ= 0.315 (p≤0.05)
66a. Participates in stealing and leaking data. and acts of destroying content	ns.	ns.	ns.	ns.	ns.	ns.	ns.
66b. Participates in stealing and leaking data. and acts of destroying content (acceptance)	ns.	R= -0.160 (p≤0.05)	ns.	R= -0.092 (p≤0.05)	ns.	R= 0.069 (p≤0.01)	ρ= 0.083 (p≤0.1)
Question 5. Are you interested in political matters and important events in your country?	ρ= 0.109 (p≤0.05)	ρ= 0.128 (p≤0.05)	ns.	ρ= -0.141 (p≤0.05)	ns.	ns.	ns.
Question 6. Do you agree or disagree with the statement that democracy has an advantage over all other forms of government (democracy is the best out of them)?	R= 0.099 (p≤0.05)	R= 0.138 (p≤0.05)	ns.	ns.	ns.	ns.	ns.
Question 7. Please evaluate Polish democracy's functionsng. Are you satisfied with its functionsng:	R= -0.100 (p≤0.05)	ns.	ns.	ns.	ns.	ns.	ρ= -0.467 (p≤0.05)
Question 8. What do you think: in Poland. is it possible to be convinced that the rulers do what they are supposed to do?	R= -0.082 (p≤0.05)	ns.	R=-0.074 (p≤0.1)	ns.	ns.	R= -0.084 (p≤0.05)	ρ= -0.462 (p≤0.05)

(continued)

Variables	Sociodemographic questions						
	Education (recoded question)	(recoded question)	Size of locality (recoded question)	Sex	Voivodeship	Size of locality	Political party
Question 9. Do you think that those in power in Poland are involved in important matters/interests to achieve something solely for themselves. or do they try to act in the interest of the general population?	ns.	ns.	ns.	ns.	$\rho = -0.094$ ($p \leq 0.05$)	ns.	$\rho = -0.463$ ($p \leq 0.05$)
Question 10. Do you think that people like you have an influence on the affairs of the country?	R= 0.113 ($p \leq 0.05$)	ns.	ns.	R= -0.076 ($p \leq 0.1$)	ns.	ns.	ns.
Question 11. In your opinson. do people like you have an influence on the affairs of your city or commune?	R= 0.132 ($p \leq 0.05$)	R= -0.129 ($p \leq 0.05$)	ns.	R= -0.072 ($p \leq 0.1$)	ns.	ns.	ns.
Question 12. Do you think that most Poles trust politicians or rather ordinary citizens?	ns.	ns.	ns.	ns.	ns.	$\rho = -0.067$ ($p \leq 0.05$)	ns.
Question 13. Do you think that most people in our country will try to use you for their own purposes if they can. or will they try to act fair?	ns.	$\rho = 0.102$ ($p \leq 0.05$)	ns.	ns.	ns.	ns.	$\rho = -0.129$ ($p \leq 0.05$)
Question 14. Do people more often try to help others. or do they care only about themselves?	ns.	$\rho = 0.117$ ($p \leq 0.05$)	ns.	$\rho = 0.105$ ($p \leq 0.05$)	ns.	$\rho = 0.086$ ($p \leq 0.05$)	ns.

Variables	Sociodemographic questions						
	Education (recoded question)	(recoded question)	Size of locality (recoded question)	Sex	Voivodeship	Size of locality	Political party
Question 15. In your opinson. can most people in Poland be trusted or one needs to be careful as he or she contacts them?	ρ= -0.142 ($p \leq 0.05$)	ns.	ρ= -0.086 ($p \leq 0.05$)	ns.	ns.	ρ= -0.117 ($p \leq 0.05$)	ns.
Question 16. When small groups with strong ties arise in our country. for whose benefit do they work?	ρ= 0.130 ($p \leq 0.05$)	ρ= -0.120 ($p \leq 0.05$)	ns.	ρ= 0.102 ($p \leq 0.05$)	ns.	ρ= 0.077 ($p \leq 0.1$)	ns.
Question 18. Do you agree with the following statements: Poland should not accept refugees from Africa and Arab countries	R= -0.070 ($p \leq 0.1$)	R= -0.099 ($p \leq 0.05$)	R= -0.123 ($p \leq 0.05$)	R= -0.117 ($p \leq 0.05$)	ns.	R= -0.135 ($p \leq 0.05$)	ρ= -0.379 ($p \leq 0.05$)
Question 18. Do you agree with the following statements: anarchists and nationalists should be forbidden from speaking out and demonstrating their views even if they are not breaking the law	R= -0.208 ($p \leq 0.05$)	R= 0.273 ($p \leq 0.05$)	R= -0.089 ($p \leq 0.05$)	ns.	ns.	R= -0.120 ($p \leq 0.05$)	ρ= 0.085 ($p \leq 0.1$)
Question 19. Are you a member of a party. political faction. or a social movement. which takes a stance on political matters?	ns.	ns.	ns.	ns.	ns.	ns.	ns.
Question 20. Do you act in an NGO. association. or a labor unson. which defends group or environmental interests. and by those means enters the political sphere?	ns.	ns.	ns.	ns.	ns.	ns.	ns.

(continued)

Variables	Sociodemographic questions						
	Education (recoded question)	(recoded question)	Size of locality (recoded question)	Sex	Voivodeship	Size of locality	Political party
Question 21. Has your family given you an attachment to certain values and/ or political orientations (e.g.. liberal. national. or left-wing)?	R= 0.183 ($p \leq 0.05$)	ns.	ns.	ns.	ns.	ns.	ns.
Question 22. Do you believe that the contemporary generation of 18–20-year-olds is more engaged in political matters than the previous generations or less?	ns.	ns.	ns.	ns.	ns.	ρ= 0.076 ($p \leq 0.1$)	ns.

Source: *Partycypacja polityczna Polaków – nowe wyzwania i formy aktywności* study, 2017, NCN grant 4884, N=603.

Annex 8. Correlations between variables (questionary variables versus variables, according to which I qualified the attitudes)

Variables	Questions qualifying the attitudes					
	Question 6. Do you agree or disagree with the statement that democracy has an advantage over all other forms of government (democracy is the best out of them)? 1: I disagree 2: I agree	Question 7. Please evaluate Polish democracy's functioning. Are you satisfied with its functioning: 1: Dissatisfied 2: Satisfied	Question 8. What do you think: in Poland. is it possible to be convinced that the rulers do what they are supposed to do? 1: Never 2: Sometimes 3: Most of the time 4: Always	Question 9. Do you think that those in power in Poland are involved in important matters/ interests to achieve something solely for themselves. or do they try to act in the interest of the general population? 1: They are primarily engaged in doing business for their own benefit 2: They pursue the interests of small. selected social groups 3: They act for the benefit of general social interests	Question 10. Do you think that people like you have an influence on the affairs of the country? 1: No 2: Yes	Question 11. Do you think that people like you have an influence on the affairs of the country? 1: No 2: Yes
1. Are you interested in politics?						R= 0.160 ($p \leq 0.05$)
2. Discusses politics					R= 0.192 ($p \leq 0.05$)	

(continued)

Variables	Questions qualifying the attitudes					
	Question 6. Do you agree or disagree with the statement that democracy has an advantage over all other forms of government (democracy is the best out of them)? 1: I disagree 2: I agree	Question 7. Please evaluate Polish democracy's functioning. Are you satisfied with its functioning: 1: Dissatisfied 2: Satisfied	Question 8. What do you think: in Poland. is it possible to be convinced that the rulers do what they are supposed to do? 1: Never 2: Sometimes 3: Most of the time 4: Always	Question 9. Do you think that those in power in Poland are involved in important matters/ interests to achieve something solely for themselves. or do they try to act in the interest of the general population? 1: They are primarily engaged in doing business for their own benefit 2: They pursue the interests of small. selected social groups 3: They act for the benefit of general social interests	Question 10. Do you think that people like you have an influence on the affairs of the country? 1: No 2: Yes	Question 11. Do you think that people like you have an influence on the affairs of the country? 1: No 2: Yes
3. Persuades someone to vote for a candidate or an issue	R= -0.081 ($p \leq 0.05$)				R= 0.243 ($p \leq 0.05$)	
17a. Signs petitions					R= 0.188 ($p \leq 0.05$)	
17b. Signs petitions (acceptance)					R= 0.163 ($p \leq 0.05$)	

Variables	Questions qualifying the attitudes					
	Question 6. Do you agree or disagree with the statement that democracy has an advantage over all other forms of government (democracy is the best out of them)? 1: I disagree 2: I agree	Question 7. Please evaluate Polish democracy's functioning. Are you satisfied with its functioning: 1: Dissatisfied 2: Satisfied	Question 8. What do you think: in Poland. is it possible to be convinced that the rulers do what they are supposed to do? 1: Never 2: Sometimes 3: Most of the time 4: Always	Question 9. Do you think that those in power in Poland are involved in important matters/ interests to achieve something solely for themselves. or do they try to act in the interest of the general population? 1: They are primarily engaged in doing business for their own benefit 2: They pursue the interests of small. selected social groups 3: They act for the benefit of general social interests	Question 10. Do you think that people like you have an influence on the affairs of the country? 1: No 2: Yes	Question 11. Do you think that people like you have an influence on the affairs of the country? 1: No 2: Yes
20b. Participates in or organizes political demonstration. (nonlegalized) march (acceptance)			R= -0.190 ($p \leq 0.05$)			
23a. Ridicules politicians and politics. and makes fun of them in the public sphere	R= -0.082 ($p \leq 0.05$)	R= -0.227 ($p \leq 0.05$)	R= -0.157 ($p \leq 0.05$)			

(continued)

Variables	Questions qualifying the attitudes					
	Question 6. Do you agree or disagree with the statement that democracy has an advantage over all other forms of government (democracy is the best out of them)? 1: I disagree 2: I agree	Question 7. Please evaluate Polish democracy's functioning. Are you satisfied with its functioning: 1: Dissatisfied 2: Satisfied	Question 8. What do you think: in Poland. is it possible to be convinced that the rulers do what they are supposed to do? 1: Never 2: Sometimes 3: Most of the time 4: Always	Question 9. Do you think that those in power in Poland are involved in important matters/ interests to achieve something solely for themselves. or do they try to act in the interest of the general population? 1: They are primarily engaged in doing business for their own benefit 2: They pursue the interests of small. selected social groups 3: They act for the benefit of general social interests	Question 10. Do you think that people like you have an influence on the affairs of the country? 1: No 2: Yes	Question 11. Do you think that people like you have an influence on the affairs of the country? 1: No 2: Yes
23b. Ridicules politicians and politics and makes fun of them in the public sphere (acceptance)	R= -0.081 ($p \leq 0.05$)	R= -0.219 ($p \leq 0.05$)	R= -0.175 ($p \leq 0.05$)			
24b. Organizes a boycott or participates in it (acceptance)	R= -0.093 ($p \leq 0.05$)	R= -0.176 ($p \leq 0.05$)	R= -0.158 ($p \leq 0.05$)			
25b. Violates the law during protests (civil disobedience) (acceptance)	R= -0.103 ($p \leq 0.05$)	R= -0.182 ($p \leq 0.05$)	R= -0.156 ($p \leq 0.05$)			

Variables	Questions qualifying the attitudes					
	Question 6. Do you agree or disagree with the statement that democracy has an advantage over all other forms of government (democracy is the best out of them)? 1: I disagree 2: I agree	Question 7. Please evaluate Polish democracy's functioning. Are you satisfied with its functioning: 1: Dissatisfied 2: Satisfied	Question 8. What do you think: in Poland. is it possible to be convinced that the rulers do what they are supposed to do? 1: Never 2: Sometimes 3: Most of the time 4: Always	Question 9. Do you think that those in power in Poland are involved in important matters/ interests to achieve something solely for themselves. or do they try to act in the interest of the general population? 1: They are primarily engaged in doing business for their own benefit 2: They pursue the interests of small. selected social groups 3: They act for the benefit of general social interests	Question 10. Do you think that people like you have an influence on the affairs of the country? 1: No 2: Yes	Question 11. Do you think that people like you have an influence on the affairs of the country? 1: No 2: Yes
35. Government office occupation (acceptance)	R= -0.076 ($p \leq 0.1$)	R= -0.182 ($p \leq 0.05$)				
53. Do you browse the Internet in search of political content		R= -0.162 ($p \leq 0.05$)			R= 0.244 ($p \leq 0.05$)	R= 0.165 ($p \leq 0.05$)
55. Shares content on the Internet services. sends links. memes. articles. comments. presentations. and other content					R= 0.161 ($p \leq 0.05$)	

(continued)

Variables	Questions qualifying the attitudes					
	Question 6. Do you agree or disagree with the statement that democracy has an advantage over all other forms of government (democracy is the best out of them)? 1: I disagree 2: I agree	Question 7. Please evaluate Polish democracy's functioning. Are you satisfied with its functioning: 1: Dissatisfied 2: Satisfied	Question 8. What do you think: in Poland. is it possible to be convinced that the rulers do what they are supposed to do? 1: Never 2: Sometimes 3: Most of the time 4: Always	Question 9. Do you think that those in power in Poland are involved in important matters/ interests to achieve something solely for themselves. or do they try to act in the interest of the general population? 1: They are primarily engaged in doing business for their own benefit 2: They pursue the interests of small. selected social groups 3: They act for the benefit of general social interests	Question 10. Do you think that people like you have an influence on the affairs of the country? 1: No 2: Yes	Question 11. Do you think that people like you have an influence on the affairs of the country? 1: No 2: Yes
58b. Collectively comments on or ridicules other users. politics. politicians (acceptance)	R= -0.080 ($p \leq 0.05$)	R= -0.151 ($p \leq 0.05$)	R= -0.184 ($p \leq 0.05$)			
65b. Participates in virtual sit-ins (acceptance)	R= -0.115 ($p \leq 0.05$)	R= -0.191 ($p \leq 0.05$)	R= -0.207 ($p \leq 0.05$)	R= -0.168 ($p \leq 0.05$)		
Question 5. Are you interested in political matters and important events in your country?					ρ= 0.262 ($p \leq 0.05$)	

Variables	Questions qualifying the attitudes					
	Question 6. Do you agree or disagree with the statement that democracy has an advantage over all other forms of government (democracy is the best out of them)? 1: I disagree 2: I agree	Question 7. Please evaluate Polish democracy's functioning. Are you satisfied with its functioning: 1: Dissatisfied 2: Satisfied	Question 8. What do you think: in Poland. is it possible to be convinced that the rulers do what they are supposed to do? 1: Never 2: Sometimes 3: Most of the time 4: Always	Question 9. Do you think that those in power in Poland are involved in important matters/ interests to achieve something solely for themselves. or do they try to act in the interest of the general population? 1: They are primarily engaged in doing business for their own benefit 2: They pursue the interests of small. selected social groups 3: They act for the benefit of general social interests	Question 10. Do you think that people like you have an influence on the affairs of the country? 1: No 2: Yes	Question 11. Do you think that people like you have an influence on the affairs of the country? 1: No 2: Yes
Question 7. Please evaluate Polish democracy's functioning. Are you satisfied with its functioning:	ρ= 0.130 (p≤0.05)		ρ= 0.554 (p≤0.05)			
Question 8. What do you think: in Poland. is it possible to be convinced that the rulers do what they are supposed to do?		R=0.546 (p≤0.05)		R= 0.559 (p≤0.05)	R= 0.227 (p≤0.05)	

(continued)

Variables	Questions qualifying the attitudes					
	Question 6. Do you agree or disagree with the statement that democracy has an advantage over all other forms of government (democracy is the best out of them)? 1: I disagree 2: I agree	Question 7. Please evaluate Polish democracy's functioning. Are you satisfied with its functioning: 1: Dissatisfied 2: Satisfied	Question 8. What do you think: in Poland. is it possible to be convinced that the rulers do what they are supposed to do? 1: Never 2: Sometimes 3: Most of the time 4: Always	Question 9. Do you think that those in power in Poland are involved in important matters/ interests to achieve something solely for themselves. or do they try to act in the interest of the general population? 1: They are primarily engaged in doing business for their own benefit 2: They pursue the interests of small. selected social groups 3: They act for the benefit of general social interests	Question 10. Do you think that people like you have an influence on the affairs of the country? 1: No 2: Yes	Question 11. Do you think that people like you have an influence on the affairs of the country? 1: No 2: Yes
Question 9. Do you think that those in power in Poland are involved in important matters/ interests to achieve something solely for themselves. or do they try to act in the interest of the general population?	$\rho = 0.083$ ($p \leq 0.05$)	$\rho = 0.520$ ($p \leq 0.05$)	$\rho = 0.564$ ($p \leq 0.05$)			
Question 10. Do you think that people like you have an influence on the affairs of the country?			$R = 0.227$ ($p \leq 0.05$)	$R = 0.271$ ($p \leq 0.05$)		

Variables	Questions qualifying the attitudes					
	Question 6. Do you agree or disagree with the statement that democracy has an advantage over all other forms of government (democracy is the best out of them)? 1: I disagree 2: I agree	Question 7. Please evaluate Polish democracy's functioning. Are you satisfied with its functioning: 1: Dissatisfied 2: Satisfied	Question 8. What do you think: in Poland. is it possible to be convinced that the rulers do what they are supposed to do? 1: Never 2: Sometimes 3: Most of the time 4: Always	Question 9. Do you think that those in power in Poland are involved in important matters/ interests to achieve something solely for themselves. or do they try to act in the interest of the general population? 1: They are primarily engaged in doing business for their own benefit 2: They pursue the interests of small. selected social groups 3: They act for the benefit of general social interests	Question 10. Do you think that people like you have an influence on the affairs of the country? 1: No 2: Yes	Question 11. Do you think that people like you have an influence on the affairs of the country? 1: No 2: Yes
Question 11. Do you think that people like you have an influence on the affairs of the country?					R= 0.503 ($p \leq 0.05$)	
Question 16. When small groups with strong ties arise in our country. for whose benefit do they work?					ρ= 0.198 ($p \leq 0.05$)	ρ= 0.211 ($p \leq 0.05$)

(continued)

Variables	Questions qualifying the attitudes					
	Question 6. Do you agree or disagree with the statement that democracy has an advantage over all other forms of government (democracy is the best out of them)? 1: I disagree 2: I agree	Question 7. Please evaluate Polish democracy's functioning. Are you satisfied with its functioning: 1: Dissatisfied 2: Satisfied	Question 8. What do you think: in Poland. is it possible to be convinced that the rulers do what they are supposed to do? 1: Never 2: Sometimes 3: Most of the time 4: Always	Question 9. Do you think that those in power in Poland are involved in important matters/ interests to achieve something solely for themselves. or do they try to act in the interest of the general population? 1: They are primarily engaged in doing business for their own benefit 2: They pursue the interests of small. selected social groups 3: They act for the benefit of general social interests	Question 10. Do you think that people like you have an influence on the affairs of the country? 1: No 2: Yes	Question 11. Do you think that people like you have an influence on the affairs of the country? 1: No 2: Yes
Question 18. Do you agree with the following statements: Poland should not accept refugees from Africa and Arab countries		R= 0.278 ($p \leq 0.05$)	R= 0.231 ($p \leq 0.05$)	R= 0.180 ($p \leq 0.05$)		
Question 18. Do you agree with the following statements: anarchists and nationalists should be forbidden from speaking out and demonstrating their views even if they are not breaking the law			R= -0.196 ($p \leq 0.05$)	R= -0.203 ($p \leq 0.05$)		

Variables	Questions qualifying the attitudes					
	Question 6. Do you agree or disagree with the statement that democracy has an advantage over all other forms of government (democracy is the best out of them)? 1: I disagree 2: I agree	Question 7. Please evaluate Polish democracy's functioning. Are you satisfied with its functioning: 1: Dissatisfied 2: Satisfied	Question 8. What do you think: in Poland. is it possible to be convinced that the rulers do what they are supposed to do? 1: Never 2: Sometimes 3: Most of the time 4: Always	Question 9. Do you think that those in power in Poland are involved in important matters/ interests to achieve something solely for themselves. or do they try to act in the interest of the general population? 1: They are primarily engaged in doing business for their own benefit 2: They pursue the interests of small. selected social groups 3: They act for the benefit of general social interests	Question 10. Do you think that people like you have an influence on the affairs of the country? 1: No 2: Yes	Question 11. Do you think that people like you have an influence on the affairs of the country? 1: No 2: Yes
Question 31. What is more valuable to you: strong state/ limited state/lack of state	$\rho = 0.088$ ($p \leq 0.05$)		$\rho = 0.171$ ($p \leq 0.05$)			
M8. How would you describe your attitude to religious faith?		$\rho = 0.286$ ($p \leq 0.05$)	$\rho = 0.272$ ($p \leq 0.05$)	$\rho = 0.220$ ($p \leq 0.05$)		
M12. What is more valuable to you: ideologically or religiously committed state/ideologically neutral state/lack of state	$\rho = 0.069$ ($p \leq 0.1$)		$\rho = -0.296$ ($p \leq 0.05$)	$\rho = 0.269$ ($p \leq 0.05$)		

Source: *Partycypacja polityczna Polaków – nowe wyzwania i formy aktywności* study, 2017, NCN grant 4884, N=603.

Bibliography

Almond, A.G., Bingham Powell, G. (1966). *Comparative Politics: A Development Approach*. Boston: Little Brown.

Arrow, K.J. (1999). 'Observations on social capital,' in: P. Dasgupta, I. Serageldin (eds.), *Social Capital: A multifaceted perspective*. Washington, D.C.: The Word Bank.

Bahry, D., Silver, B.D. (1990). 'Soviet Citizen Participation on the Eve of Democratization,' *The American Political Science Review* 3.

Barnes, S., Kasse, M. (1979). *Political Action: Mass Participation in Five Western Democracies*. London: Sage Publications.

Becker, G., (1964). *Human Capital*. New York: Columbia University Press.

Becla, A., Czaja, S. (2019). 'Kapitał i "antykapitał" społeczny jako czynniki wpływające na rozwój cywilizacyjny – próba identyfikacji teoretyczno-empirycznej na przykładzie Dolnego Śląska,' in: M. Adamczyk, A. Chmiel (eds.), *Społeczności lokalne. Przestrzeń dla współpracy i rozwoju*. Wrocław: Wydawnictwo Uniwersytetu Ekonomicznego we Wrocławiu.

Blomkvist, H. (2003). *Social Capital, Political Participation, And the Quality of democracy in India*. Paper prepared for the annual meeting of the American Political Science Association, Philadelphia.

Bourdieu, P. (1977). 'Outline of a Theory of Practice,' *Cambridge Studies in Social and Cultural Anthropology* 16.

Bourdieu, P. (1986). 'The Forms of Capital,' in: J. C. Richardson (ed.), *Handbook of Theory and Research of Sociology of Education*. New York: Greenwood Press.

Brady, H.E. (1999). 'Political Participation,' in: J.P. Robinson, P.R. Shaver, L.S. Wrightsman (eds.), *Measures of Social Psychological Attitudes*. San Diego: Academic Press.

Coleman, J. (1988). 'Social Capital in the Creation of Human Capital,' *American Journal of Sociology*, 95–120.

Coleman, J. S., (1988). 'Social capital in the creation of human capital,' *American Journal of Sociology*, 94, 95–120.

Crozier, M.J., Huntington S.P., Watanuki, J. (1975). *The Crisis of Democracy. Report on the Governability of Democracies to the Trilateral Commission*. New York: New York University Press, 1975.

Cwalina, W., Fałkowski, A., (2006). *Marketing polityczny. Perspektywa psychologiczna*. Gdańsk: Gdańskie Wydawnictwo Psychologiczne.

Cześnik, M. (2007). *Partycypacja wyborcza w Polsce. Perspektywa porównawcza*. Scholar: Warsaw.

Dahl, R.A. (1998). *O demokracji*. Kraków: Społeczny Instytut Wydawniczy "Znak".

Dalton, R.J., Klingemann, H.D. (2007). *The Oxford Handbook of Political Behavior*. Oxford: Oxford University Press.

Dalton, R.J., Klingemann, H.D. (2010). *Zachowania polityczne*. Warsaw: Wydawnictwo Naukowe PWN.

Dobek-Ostrowska, B., Garlicki, J. (2013). *Political Communication in the Era of New Technologies*. Warsaw: Peter Lang.

Durkheim, E. (1999). *The Division of Labor in Society*. New York: Free Press.

Etzioni, A. (1977). *Demonstration Democracy*. New York: Gordon and Breach.

Fine, B. (2002). 'They F**k You Up Those Social Capitalists,' *Antipode*, 34(4), 796–799.

Fischer, C. (2005). 'Bowling Alone: What's the Score?,' *Social Networks*, 27(2), 155–167.

Fukuyama, F.(1995). 'Social Capital and the global economy,' *Foreign Affairs*, 74(5), 89–103.

Garlicki, J. (2005). *Demokracja i integracja europejska. Studium osobistych i politycznych orientacji dwóch pokoleń Polaków*. Toruń: Wydawnictwo Adam Marszałek.

Garlicki, J. (2011). 'Kultura polityczna Polskich internautów,' *Studia Politologiczne* 21.

Garlicki, J. (2012). 'Dynamika kultury politycznej i partycypacji politycznej internautów w Polsce,' *Studia Politologiczne* 26.

Garlicki, J., Noga-Bogomilski, A. (2004). *Kultura polityczna w społeczeństwie demokratycznym*, Warsaw: Oficyna Wydawnicza Aspra.

Global Protest Tracker, https://carnegieendowment.org/publications/interactive/protest-tracker [accessed: January 2021].

Habermas, J. (1996). *Between Facts and Norms: Contribution to a Discourse Theory of Law and Democracy*. Cambridge: Cambridge University Press.

Haynes, P. (2009). *Before Going Any Further With Social Capital: Eight Key Criticisms to Address*, https://core.ac.uk/download/pdf/36025661.pdf [accessed: February 2020].

Hofstede, G., Hofstede G.J., Minkov M. (2010). *Cultures and Organizations: Software of the Mind*. New York: McGraw Hill Professional.

Huntington, S.P, Nelson J.M. (1976). *No Easy Choice. Political Participation in Developing Countries*. Cambridge, Massachusetts, London: Harvard University Press.

Inglehart, R. (1977). *The Silent Revolution. Changing Values and Political Styles among Western Publics*. Princeton: Princeton University Press.

Jackson, M.O. (2019). *A Typology of Social Capital and Associated Network Measures*. SSRN 2019 https://papers.ssrn.com/sol3/papers.cfm?abstract_id=3073496 [accessed: August 2020].

Jacobs, L.R., Cook, F.L., Delli Carpini M.X. (2009). *Talking together. Public Deliberation and Political Participation in America*. Chicago: University of Chicago Press.

Janicki, M. (2017). 'Kto w Polsce należy do elity,' *Polityka*, July 4th.

Kaase, M., Marsh, A. (1979). 'Political Action. A Theoretical Perspective,' in: S. H. Barnes, M. Kaase (eds.), *Political Action. Mass Participation in Five Western Democracies*. London: Sage Publications.

Kłoskowska, A. (1959). 'Modele społeczne i kultura masowa,' *Przegląd Socjologiczny*, 13(2), 49–50.

Koźmiński, A.K., Sztompka, P. (2004). *Rozmowa o wielkiej przemianie*. Warsaw: Wydawnictwo Wyższej Szkoły Przedsiębiorczości i Zarządzania im. Leona Koźmińskiego.

Lane, R. E. (1969). *Political Life. How and Why People Get Involved in Politics*. New York: Free Press.

Łętowska, E. (1994). *Po co ludziom konstytucja?*. Helsinki Foundation for Human Rights.

Levitsky, S., Way L.A. (2010). *Competitive Authoritarianism: Hybrid Regimes after the Cold War (Problems of International Politics)*. New York: Cambridge University Press.

Lin, N. (2001). *Social Capital*. Cambridge: Cambridge University Press.

Lin, N., Bonnie H., Erickson B.H. (2010). *Social Capital. An International Research Program*. Oxford: Oxford University Press.

Mazur, M. (2002). *Marketing polityczny*. Warsaw: Wydawnictwo naukowe PWN.

Merton, R.K. (1938). 'Social Structure and Anomie,' *American Sociological Review*, 3(5), 672–682.

Merton, R.K. (1968). *Social Theory and Social Structure*. New York: The Free Press.

Meyer, G., Ryszka, F. (1991). *Political Participation and Democracy in Poland and West Germany*. Warsaw: Ośrodek Badań Społecznych.

Mider, D. (2008). *Partycypacja polityczna w Internecie. Studium politologiczne*. Warsaw: Dom Wydawniczy Elipsa.

Mider, D. (2010). 'Partycypacja polityczna a legitymizacja systemu politycznego,' *Studia Politologiczne* 18.

Mider, D. (2014). 'Political Participation of Poles – Structure and Trends,' *Studia Politologiczne* 31.

Mider, D. (2017). *Polacy wobec przemocy politycznej: studium typów postaw i ocen moralnych*. Warsaw: Dom Wydawniczy Elipsa.

Mider, D., Błuszkowski, J. (2012). *Demokracja późnej nowoczesności*. Warsaw: Dom Wydawniczy Elipsa.

Milbrath, L.W. (1971). *Political Participation. How and Why Do People Get Involved in Politics?* Chicago: Rand McNally & Company.

Milbrath, L.W., Goel, M.L. (1977). *Political Participation. How and Why Do People Get Involved in Politics?* Chicago: Rand McNally College Publishing Company.

Misztal, B. (1977). *Zagadnienia społecznego uczestnictwa i współdziałania. Analiza w świetle teorii i badań socjologicznych*. Wrocław: Wydawnictwo Polskiej Akademii Nauk.

Neudert, L. M. (2018). 'Future Elections May Be Swayed by Intelligent, Weaponized Chatbots,' *MIT Technology Review* 2018, https://www.technologyreview.com/s/611832/future-electionsmay-be-swayed-by-intelligent-weaponized-chatbots/ [accessed: August 2020].

Nowak, S. (1979). 'System wartości społeczeństwa polskiego,' *Studia Socjologiczne* 4.

Parsons, T. (1951). *The Social System*. Glencoe. Illinois: The Free Press.

Poder, T.G. (2011). 'What is Really Social Capital? A Critical Review,' *The American Sociologist*, 42(4), 341–367.

Powell, G.B. (1982). *Contemporary Democracies*. Massachusetts: Harvard University Press.

Pross, H. (1992). *Protestgessellschaft*. Munich: Artemis and Winkler.

Putnam, R. (2000). *Bowling Alone. Collapse and Revival of American Community*. New York: Simon & Schuster.

Putnam, R. (2001). *Bowling Alone: The Collapse and Revival of American Community*. New York: Simon & Schuster.

Raciborski, J. (1997). *Polskie wybory*. Warsaw: Scholar.

Rawls, J. (1999). *A Theory of Justice. Revised Edition*. Cambridge: The Belknap Press of Harvard University Press.

Rose, A.M. (1950). 'A Deductive Ideal-Type Method,' *The American Journal of Sociology*, 56(1), 9, 35.

Sartori, G. (1987). *The Theory of Democracy Revisited*. Chatham: Chatham House Publishers, Inc.

Scheuerman, W.E. (2015). 'Recent Theories of Civil Disobedience: An Anti-Legal Turn?,' *Political Philosophy*, 23(4), 427–449.

Shahin, M. (2016). 'The Relationship between Social Capital and Political Participation,' *Mediterranean Journal of Social Sciences* 7, 136–142.

Stivers, R. (1994). *The Culture of Cynicism*. Oxford: Blackwell.

Teorell, J. (2003). 'Linking Social Capital to Political Participation: Voluntary Associations and Networks of Recruitment in Sweden,' *Scandinavian Political Studies*, 26(1), 49–66.

Teorell, J., Torcal M., Montero, J.R. (2007). 'Political Participation. Second Draft of Chapter 12 of Volume B: Population Studies. European Science Foundation, Science-Network on Citizenship,

Involvement and Democracy.' Unpublished. http://www.upf.edu/pdi/dcpis/mariano.torcal/en/publicaciones.html [accessed: September 2020].

Tittenbrun, J. (2016). *Anti-capital: Human, Social, and Cultural. The Mesmerising Misnomers*. London: Routledge.

Tönnies, F. (2002). *Community and Society*, Mineola, New York: Dover Publications.

Touraine, A. (1997). *What is Democracy?* Oxford: Westview Press.

Trompenaars, F., Hampden-Turner, C. (1999). *Riding the Waves of Culture. Understanding Cultural Diversity in Business.* London: Nicholas Brealley Publishing.

Tucker, C., Casady R., Lepkowski, J. (1992). *Sample Allocation For Stratified Telephone Sample Designs, Proceedings of the Survey Research Methods Sections*. Alexandria: American Statistical Association.

Van Deth, J.W. (2001). *Studying Political Participation: Towards Theory of Everything?*. Conference paper for the European Consortium for Political Research, "Electronic Democracy: Mobilisation, Organisation and Participation via new ICTs". Grenoble, April 2001.

Verba, S., Nie, N.H. (1987). *Participation in America. Political Democracy and Social Equality*. Chicago: The University of Chicago Press.

Verba, S., Scholzman, K. L., Brady, H.E. (1998). *Voice and Equality. Civic Voluntarism in American Politics.* Cambridge, Massachusetts, London: Harvard University Press.

Verba, S., Nie, N.H. and Kim, J. (1978). *Participation and Political Equality. A Seven Nation Comparison*. Cambridge, London, New York, Melbourne: Cambridge University Press.

Vesnic-Alujevic, L. et al. (2019). *The Future of Government 2030+ : A Citizen-Centric Perspective on New Government Models*. Luxembourg: Publications Office of the European Union.

Wardle, C., Derakshan, H. (2017). *Information Disorder Toward an interdisciplinary framework for research and policymaking*. Council of Europe report DGI. Downloaded from: https://rm.coe.int/information-disorder-toward-an-interdisciplinary-framework-for-researc/168076277 [accessed: August 2020].

Wedel, M., Kamakura, W.A. (2000). *Market Segmentation. Conceptual and Methodological Foundations*, Boston: Springer.

Zinn, H. (1968). *Disobedience and Democracy: Nine Fallacies on Law and Order*. New York: Random House Trade Paperbacks.

Index of Names

A
Almond Gabriel A. 100, 151
Arrow Kenneth J. 97

B
Barnes Simon H. 18
Becla Agnieszka 100
Berry M. 18, 21, 46, 67
Błuszkowski Jan 43
Bourdieu Pierre 8, 95, 96
Brady Henry E. 19, 20, 35

C
Carpini Michael X.D. 99, 102
Casady Robert 180
Coleman James S. 8, 95
Cook Fay L. 99, 102
Crozier Michel J. 44
Cwalina Wojciech 154
Czaja Stanisław 100
Cześnik Mikołaj 176

D
Dahl Robert A. 17
Dalton Russell J. 176
Derakshan Hossein 93
Dobek-Ostrowska Bogusława 92
Durkheim Émile 43, 128, 131

E
Erickson Bonnie 99
Etzioni Amitai 65

F
Falkowski Andrzej 154
Fischer Claude S. 96
Fukuyama Francis 8, 95

G
Goel Madan L. 18
Goldman Jerry 18, 21, 46, 67

H
Habermas Jürgen 17
Huntington Samuel P. 18, 23, 28, 29, 44, 127

I
Inglehart Ronald 65

J
Jackson Mathew O. 97, 98
Jacobs Lawrence R. 99, 102
Janda Kenneth 18, 21, 46, 67

K
Kaase Max 18, 74, 176
Kamakura Wagner A. 154
Karwat Mirosław 29, 30
Klingemann Hans-Dieter 176
Kłoskowska Antonina 11
Koźmiński Andrzej 176

L
Lane Robert E. 22
Lepkowski James 180
Łętowska Ewa 25
Lin Nan 8, 99

M
Marsh Alan 18, 74
Mazur Marek 154
Merton Robert K. 12, 101, 127–131, 137, 148, 151, 153, 155, 159, 160, 175

Meyer Gerd 18, 19
Mider Daniel 15, 20, 23, 36, 43, 73, 74, 85, 93, 99
Milbrath Lester W. 18, 28, 29, 31
Misztal Bronisław 27, 28, 46, 49–51
Montero Jose R. 27

M
Nelson Joan M. 18, 23, 29, 127
Neudert Lisa-Maria 93
Nie Norman H. 17, 22
Noga-Bogomilski Artur 100, 151
Nowak Stefan 44

P
Parsons Talcott 128
Powell George B. 21, 22, 67, 84, 100, 151
Pross Harry 65
Putnam Robert 8, 95, 98

R
Rawls John 26, 66
Rose Arnold M. 128
Ryszka Franciszek 19

S
Sartori Giovanni 17
Scheuerman William E. 66
Scholzman Kay L. 19
Sztompka 176

T
Teorell Jan 9, 2
Tittenburn Jacek 100
Tönnies Ferdinand 43
Torcal Mariano 27
Touraine Alain 176
Tucker Clyde 180

V
Van Deth Jan W. 19, 22, 23, 27, 94
Verba Sidney 17, 19, 22

W
Wardle Claire 93
Watanuki Jōji 44
Wedel Michel 154

Z
Zinn Howard 26, 66

Studies in Politics, Security and Society

Edited by Stanisław Sulowski

Vol. 1 Robert Wiszniowski (ed.): Challenges to Representative Democracy. A European Perspective. 2015.

Vol. 2 Jarosław Szymanek: Theory of Political Representation. 2015.

Vol. 3 Alojzy Z. Nowak (ed.): Global Financial Turbulence in the Euro Area. Polish Perspective. 2015.

Vol. 4 Jolanta Itrich-Drabarek: The Civil Service in Poland. Theory and Experience. 2015.

Vol. 5 Agnieszka Rothert: Power of Imagination. Education, Innovations and Democracy. 2016.

Vol. 6 Zbysław Dobrowolski: Combating Corruption and Other Organizational Pathologies. 2017.

Vol. 7 Vito Breda: The Objectivity of Judicial Decisions. A Comparative Analysis of Nine Jurisdictions. 2017.

Vol. 8 Anna Sroka: Accountability and democracy in Poland and Spain. 2017.

Vol. 9 Anna Sroka / Fanny Castro-Rial Garrone / Rubén Darío Torres Kumbrián (eds.): Radicalism and Terrorism in the 21st Century. Implications for Security. 2017.

Vol. 10 Filip Pierzchalski: Political Leadership in Morphogenetic Perspective. 2017.

Vol. 11 Alina Petra Marinescu: The Discursive Dimension of Employee Engagement and Disengagement. Accounts of keeping and leaving jobs in present-day Bucharest organizations. 2017.

Vol. 12 Jacek Giedrojć: Competition, Coordination, Social Order. Responsible Business, Civil Society, and Government in an Open Society. 2017.

Vol. 13 Filip Ilkowski: Capitalist Imperialism in Contemporary Theoretical Frameworks. 2017.

Vol. 14 Leszek Leszczyński / Adam Szot (eds.): Discretionary Power of Public Administration. Its Scope and Control. 2017.

Vol. 15 Tadeusz Klementewicz: Understanding Politics. Theory, Procedures, Narratives. 2017.

Vol. 16 Tomasz Bichta: Political Systems of the Former Yugoslavia. 2018

Vol. 17 Miroslav Palárik / Alena Mikulášová / Martin Hetényi / Róbert Arpáš: The City and Region Against the Backdrop of Totalitarianism. 2018

Vol. 18 Jolanta Itrich-Drabarek / Stanisław Mazur / Justyna Wiśniewska-Grzelak (eds.): The Transformations of the Civil Service in Poland in Comparison with International Experience. 2018..

Vol. 19 Jerzy Juchnowski / R. Jan Sielezin / Ewa Maj: The Image of “White” and “Red” Russia in the Polish Political Thought of the 19th and 20th Century. Analogies and Parallels. 2018.

Vol. 20 Roman Kuźniar: Europe in the International Order. 2018.

Vol. 21 Piotr Jaroszyński: Europe - the Clash of Civilisations. 2018.

Vol. 22 Stanisław Filipowicz: Truth and the Will to Illusion. 2018.

Vol. 23 Andrzej Szeptycki: Contemporary Relations between Poland and Ukraine. The “Strategic Partnership” and the Limits Thereof. 2019.

Vol. 24 Sylwester Gardocki / Rafał Ożarowski / Rafał Ulatowski (eds.): The Islamic World in International Relations. 2019.

Vol. 25 Jacek Zaleśny (ed.): Constitutional Courts in Post-Soviet States. Between the Model of a State of Law and Its Local Application. 2019.

Vol. 26 Andrzej Antoszewski / Przemysław Żukiewicz / Mateusz Zieliński / Katarzyna. Domagała: Formation of Government Coalition in Westminster Democracies. Towards a Network Approach. 2020.

Vol. 27 Joanna Osiejewicz: Global Governance of Oil and Gas Resources in the International Legal Perspective. 2020.

Vol. 28 Anita Oberda-Monkiewicz: Poland-Mexico towards a Strategic Partnership. 2020.

Vol. 29 Bartosz Czepil / Wojciech Opioła: Ethnic diversity and local governance quality. The case of Opole Province in Poland. 2020.

Vol. 30 Adam Szymański / Jakub Wódka / Wojciech Ufel / Amanda Dziubińska: Between Fair and Rigged. Elections as a Key Determinant of the 'Borderline Political Regime' - Turkey in Comparative Perspective. 2020.

Vol. 31 Tomasz Grzegorz Grosse (ed.): Fuel for Dominance. On the Economic Bases of Geopolitical Supremacy. 2020.

Vol. 32 Dariusz Jarosz / Maria Pasztor: From Subjection to Independence. Post-World War II Polish-Italian Relations. 2020.

Vol. 33 Paweł Sekuła: Chernobyl Liquidators. The Unknown Story. With the Testimony of the President of Latvia. 2020.

Vol. 34 Kamil Glinka (ed.): Urban Policy System in Strategic Perspective: From V4 to Ukraine. 2020.

Vol. 35 Paweł Lesiński: At the Origins of German Liberalism: the State in the Thought of Robert von Mohl. 2020.

Vol. 36 Jana Popovicsová (ed.): Reflexions about a Cultural and Social Phenomenon: Identity. 2020.

Vol. 37 Agnes Bernek: Geopolitics of Central and Eastern Europe in the 21st Century. From the Buffer Zone to the Gateway Zone. 2021.

Vol. 38 Marek Antoni Musioł: The European Union as a Post-Lisbon Regional Security Complex. 2021.

Vol. 39 Alina Petra Marinescu: Manipulation in the Disclosure of the *Securitate* Files. The Case of Mona Muscă. 2021

Vol. 40 Jiří Zákravský: Cycling Diplomacy. Undemocratic Regimes and Professional-Road Cycling Teams Sponsorship. 2021.

Vol. 41 Mirosław Karwat / Filip Pierzchalski / Marcin Tobiasz (eds.): Constituents of Political Theory. Selected Articles of the Warsaw School of Political Theory. 2021.

Vol. 42 Angieszka Bieńczyk-Missala: Preventing Mass Human-Rights Violations and Atrocity Crimes. 2021.

Vol. 43 Jan Ryszard Garlicki: Political Participation Capital. 2021.

www.peterlang.com

www.ingramcontent.com/pod-product-compliance
Ingram Content Group UK Ltd.
Pitfield, Milton Keynes, MK11 3LW, UK
UKHW021829100926
8556IPUK00004B/240

9 783631 866825